The Book of Mormon: It Begins with a Family

Arthur R. Bassett

John W. Welch

Marshall R. Craig

Allen E. Bergin

C. Terry Warner

Eugene England

Orson Scott Card

Robert A. Rees

Jeffrey R. Holland

Francine Bennion

Lenet H. Read

Chauncey C. Riddle

James R. Moss

Brian Best

Marilyn Arnold

W. Cole Durham, Jr.

Henry B. Eyring

Marjorie Meads Spencer

The Book of Mormon: It Begins with a Family

Deseret Book Company
Salt Lake City, Utah

The chapters in this book were first printed in the *Ensign,* a monthly magazine published by The Church of Jesus Christ of Latter-day Saints, between September 1976 and July 1978.

Printed in the United States of America
ISBN 0-87747-987-9
Library of Congress Catalog Card Number 83-73118

First printing November 1983

Contents

It Begins with a Family

Arthur R. Bassett

President Brigham Young once made an intriguing statement that has continued to fascinate me. He said: "Do you read the scriptures, my brethren and sisters, as though you were writing them a thousand, two thousand, or five thousand years ago? Do you read them as though you stood in the place of the men who wrote them? If you do not feel thus, it is your privilege to do so, that you may be as familiar with the spirit and meaning of the written word of God as you are with your daily walk and conversation, or as you are with your workmen or with your households."

He then continued with the promise, "You may understand what the Prophets understood and thought—what they designed and planned to bring forth to their brethren for their good. When you can thus feel, then you may begin to think that you can find out something about God, and begin to learn who he is." (*Journal of Discourses* 7:333.)

Too often many of us approach the scriptures as dispassionate observers. We want to receive instruction with no effort on our part. Ours is an age of spectators, an age that provides entertainment requiring little effort from us. However, the scriptures will not yield the excitement within them without effort on our part. President Young has suggested that we need to read them with a creative stance, to put ourselves into them. This may not be easy to do at first, but once it is accomplished the scriptures begin to take on a life of their own.

Parts of the Book of Mormon are as old as the tower of Babel; yet its themes are as current as tomorrow. Historical settings may change; people may dress differently and alter their surroundings; but mankind remains much the same. The problems of mankind are born anew in each generation. This is what makes the Book of Mormon such an intriguing venture, if one is truly interested in life.

The first half of the Book of Mormon provides an excellent opportunity for families to analyze some of the eternal problems of man and to share in the insights of others who lived at other times and in other places. The Prophet Joseph Smith said that through a study of the Book of Mormon and abiding by its precepts one can get closer to God than through a study of any other book. (See *History of the Church* 4:461.) That is an exciting promise, one worthy of our attention.

The Book of Mormon is rich with theological truths, but it is much more than a theological handbook. Its doctrines are couched in the vibrant setting of life at many levels. In its pages one walks the back streets of Jerusalem; trudges the arid stretches of the wilderness; sails the turbulent storms of the ocean; basks in the lush, vegetated regions of nature; visits in the palaces of kings and the hovels of the poor. And although the focus of the book is on the national level, one sees much of family life and relationships. The Book of Mormon is the most family-oriented book we have in the standard works. Only the early part of the Old Testament comes close to providing such vital insights into the problems and joys of families.

Lehi is not only a great prophet, he is also a concerned father who wrestles with many of the same problems as fathers today. We need to remember this facet of Lehi's life and to compare his insights and problems with our own. Too often we try to read the scriptures in an imaginative void, to make them speak without any effort on our own part. They become much richer as we blend our own experiences with those presented and as we make this venture a type of dialogue with the scriptures. We can take a vital lead from Nephi's suggestion: "I did liken all scriptures unto us, that it might be for our profit and learning." (1 Nephi 19:23.)

For example, parents will probably see things in the Book of Mormon that escape those who have not had the experience of parenthood. They should understand more easily why Lehi, in his vision of the Tree of Life, did not notice the filthiness of the water as Nephi did, though both prophets were shown the same vision. Nephi records, "So much was his mind swallowed up in other things that he beheld not the filthiness of the water" in the vision. (1 Nephi 15:27.)

As a father, Lehi had concerns that Nephi did not share, namely, his responsibility as head of the family. At the point in the vision when Lehi was shown the river, he began to be concerned about his family. He saw his wife and two of his sons and beckoned to them to join him. Further, he became worried when he found that Laman and Lemuel were not with them, and he directed his full attention to a search for the two wayward brothers, neglecting the particulars of the vision.

On the other hand, Nephi had not yet had the experience of fatherhood, and he therefore approached the vision from a different viewpoint. He was more interested in the particulars of the vision and focused on such details as the filthiness of the stream, which his father had also seen but had not observed closely because of his concern for his family.

Mothers should understand the heavy burdens placed upon Sariah as she left her home, her belongings, and her attachments to her friends and journeyed into the uncertainties of life in the wilderness, simply because of her faith in her husband, whom others called a visionary man. It should be remembered that she had not received the visions herself. A mother should be able to empathize with Sariah when she reached her extremity in the wilderness and murmured, fearing that she had lost not only her home and belongings, but her four sons as well. (See 1 Nephi 5:1-7.)

Fathers should understand the equally heavy burdens that Lehi bore, having his own faith undermined and tried by the doubts and legitimate concerns of his wife. Knowing that the Lord had directed him and that things would probably culminate in a positive manner did not alleviate the frustrations and perplexities of the moment. Lehi's faith as a prophet was forced to wrestle continually with his concerns as a father. His role was a complex one, and recognizing this complexity adds to our understanding of the total dimensions of life. Those who see Lehi only in his role as a prophet miss much of what the Book of Mormon reveals about fatherhood.

Brothers and sisters in a family will find interesting aspects of their own lives illuminated by the frictions that developed among the children of Lehi and Sariah. Some will be able to empathize with Nephi's frustration in not being able to understand fully his wayward brothers who would not support their father, the prophet of the Lord. Others will empathize with Laman and Lemuel and their frustrations with their younger brother and his seemingly "holier-than-thou" attitude. Still others will find themselves in Jacob's position, wanting to love and respect his elder brothers and to look to them for examples, only to find discord among them.

Those who read the writings of Jacob and forget the trauma of his early life will miss much of the pathos in his sermons on the family. Having been a witness to family conflict, having experienced the terrifying journey across the ocean—with the added turmoil of fighting between his brothers, with the sickness of Lehi and with Sariah brought near to death, with the prayers and pleadings of Nephi's wife and children—having seen the splitting of the family after Lehi's death, Jacob brings to his sermons profound insight into family life. His later sermons reflect the sensitivity born of his early beginnings.

As the child is father of the man, so the family is father of the nation in the Book of Mormon. As one moves forward in his reading, these family relationships should never be forgotten. They add much interest and greater dimensions to the account. When the split occurs between the brothers, and when battles begin between Nephite and Lamanite, one should remember that these initial battles were not between strangers, but between cousins and people who knew each other well.

We should remember that when Sherem came to oppose Jacob (see Jacob 7), Jacob probably knew his parents, or at least his grandparents. Who among us, when he finds the son or grandson of a friend, fails to see that person in the light of the parent he knew? And how much more intense is our concern for that son or daughter if he or she is rebellious? Or how much greater our happiness if that person has become a credit to the parent—or friend or acquaintance? Recognizing this relationship between Jacob and Sherem adds greater impact to the account.

How interesting it is to watch the children of our brothers and sisters, the children of cousins, or the children of close friends, and see them mature and take on responsibilities themselves. The Book of Mormon enables us to do something akin to that. These people had concerns like our own, and we need to remind ourselves of this constantly. They also were, to a degree, a product of their family setting. The Book of Mormon allows us to follow these families through several generations and to witness the problems that can occur within the family setting over long periods of time. Very few records in history do this more effectively.

Youth who have fathers and mothers in responsible positions in the Church should find a special interest in the account of Enos. They should sense something of the burden of mind he carried into the forest, being the son of a prophet, the nephew of another prophet, and the grandson of a third. As a person comes to maturity he must find out some things for himself; he must establish his own value system; he must make his own way. Those today who find themselves in this same situation will sense something of the urgency of the prayer of Enos.

Sometimes this burden becomes too much for some to carry. Erroneously, they decide that to become individuals in their own right they must leave the path of the parent. Unfortunately, the story of a rebellious child of a Church leader is an oft-repeated one. In an attempt to prove their freedom to their peers, they launch out in an attack on the life-style of their parents. Such young men and women should understand and learn from the experience of Alma the Younger and the sons of Mosiah. Sons of a king and of a prophet of God, they found that rebellion is not the path to happiness, nor to true self-fulfillment.

On the other hand, some parents will find themselves in the same predicament as Alma the Elder, having been rebellious youths themselves, having repented and brought their lives into conformity with the gospel, and then finding their own children falling into the same foolish mistakes. What had Alma the Younger known of the early life of Alma the Elder as one of the wicked priests of King Noah? Was he possibly justifying his own unrighteous actions on the basis of his father's early experiences? And how does a father who has had problems in his own youth counsel a wayward son, knowing intimately the problems and desires that stimulate the rebellion? Alma the Younger's counsel to his son Corianton in Alma 39-42 provides some important insights. Who among us who has had this problem can read the account of Alma without a personal interest in the narrative?

Sometimes grandparents have greater influence on grandchildren than do parents. Although I would not wish to imply that this was fully the case with the sons of Mosiah, I can never read the account of their missionary efforts without remembering the last speech of their grandfather, King Benjamin, to his people. (See Mosiah 1-4.) I have often wondered if the sons of Mosiah had a record of that speech. Certainly their grandfather would have had much cause for pride in the way his grandsons eventually adopted his values and put his principles into action.

The Book of Mormon is filled with such familial relationships, many of them only implied. For example, who was the wife of Alma the Elder? Who was this woman who came through the wilderness experience with Alma and struggled with him through the rebellion of their son? Or had she died and left Alma to carry this heavy burden himself? And what are we to say concerning the wife of Alma the Younger, who reared three sons (at least) while he was gone so much of the time, serving as a missionary for the Lord. She has to be one of the great souls of the scriptures.

Some of the most interesting aspects of the Book of Mormon are these unwritten parts, the parts we must fill in with our imagination if we are to read the scriptures as President Young suggested we read them. It becomes necessary for us to fill in the gaps and to attempt to reconstruct those relationships that are not mentioned specifically, but that are part of the family history of these people.

The major concerns of these families of the Book of Mormon are extremely relevant to our own age, because they are eternal concerns. They focus on facets of life that never change, those issues that are vital to self-fulfillment—that elusive goal that all of us seek but few of us find. These concerns are locked into three major problems we all face.

First, we look for guides in our pursuit of happiness. In constructing a value system we ask ourselves, almost from the time we first become aware of life, "What brings me greatest satisfaction?" "In what or in whom shall I place my faith in my pursuit of personal satisfaction?"

Second, as we become older and more aware of ourselves as being separate and distinct from others, we begin to wrestle with our self-image. As we have greater opportunities to compare ourselves with others, we also begin to ask ourselves, "What is my potential?" "Am I able to achieve the goals I set for myself?" Ultimately, the question becomes "Is there hope in life for me?"

Third, through all of this we attempt to decide what will be our relationship with others. We ask, either consciously or otherwise, "What do they have to do with me?" "Should I be of assistance to them in their frustrations, or do they exist to serve me in the pursuit of my own selfish ends?" "Do I serve, or do I exploit?"

Interestingly, these are the three major issues on which the Book of Mormon prophets placed their emphasis. All that they taught comes back to three major principles of faith, hope, and charity. Though we usually associate this triad with Mormon in the latter part of the Book of Mormon and with Paul in the New Testament, it was introduced into the Nephite scriptures by the first Nephi (see 2 Nephi 31:19-20) and continues to be used as a focal point by all the prophets of the book. As you read through the Book of Mormon, watch for this triad and use it as the major focal point of your own studies. It can be vital for those who are grasping for an understanding of the gospel.

The first point of the triad, faith, is vital. All of us have to choose some individuals or principles to follow. None of us can escape this decision. Our model may be a parent; it may be a teacher; it may be a friend or someone we admire as our hero; it may even be an abstract principle (although I suggest that principles do not really live in our lives until we see them embodied in the life of another person). Whom we trust or what we trust determines the course our lives will follow, and ultimately it determines what we will become. The choice of models is perhaps the single most important type of choice we make.

In our age, the age of the antihero, we have much to learn from the Nephites. For their prophets, the focal point was Christ. For them, faith in Christ was not only the first principle of the gospel, it was also the last. Christ was all that the Christian needed to know. He was the model. He was the Truth. He was the Light. He was the Way. Nephi recorded that his people talked often of the Master. They rejoiced in Christ; they taught about him; they prophesied concerning him; and they wrote about him so that their children might have a model to observe. (See 2 Nephi 25:26.) And Nephi concluded his own writing by commenting, as he addressed himself to all the world, "Hearken unto these words and believe in Christ; and if ye believe not in these words believe in Christ." (2 Nephi 33:10.)

Following the Master leads one to embrace the ordinances within His church. Through these ordinances, such as baptism, one makes covenants to follow the life-style of the Master and to rely wholly on him for help and strength in accomplishing this end. The disciple of Christ seeks to become more knowledgeable; he adds to his character such Christlike qualities as virtue, temperance, patience, brotherly kindness, humility, and diligence. All of these qualities are embodied in the Master and his life-style, and our acquiring them flows out of our faith in him.

Nephi came to this realization early in life in his experience with the vision of the Tree of Life. It led him to attempt seemingly impossible tasks. His motto became "I will go and do the things which the Lord hath commanded, for I know that the Lord giveth no commandments unto the children of men, save he shall prepare a way for them that they may accomplish the thing which he commandeth them." (1 Nephi 3:7.)

This is the same spirit that launches young men and women into the mission field, that allows them to face difficult tasks, and that enables the programs of the Church to succeed. In our day we ought to make certain that our focus is not diverted from the person of the Master. It is well to stress his teachings; it is well to build up his kingdom; but unless we keep him, *as a person,* central in our meetings and other activities, unless we remember *him* as we covenant to do when we partake of the sacrament, it becomes easier to lose our way. The structure of the gospel rests firmly embedded in the cement of a personal relationship with him.

Alma the Younger found this out the hard way. Often as a younger man he had heard his father speak of the Master; but he, like Laman and Lemuel, was past feeling, and he grew to be worldly and rebellious. He was responsible for leading many of the Nephite people to spiritual destruction. Finally, the Lord brought him through a chastening experience to help him realize the error of his way. For three days and nights his soul was "racked, even with the pains of a damned soul." (Alma 36:16.) He longed for extinction—not just for death, but for extinction.

Finally, in the depths of his anguish and torment, he remembered his father's teachings about Christ. His mind cried out for help, and help came. Through the aid of Christ his past was forgiven, and he wrote, "My soul was filled with joy as exceeding as was my pain! . . . There could be nothing so exquisite and so bitter as were my pains. . . . There can be nothing so exquisite and sweet as was my joy." (Alma 36:20-21.)

This brings us to the second point of the triad, hope. The key words of our day are the terms spoken of in existential philosophy: despair, anguish, and alienation—all of which are directly opposed to the principle of hope. The Book of Mormon responds that the end of man's existence is happiness. "Men are, that they might have joy" is the message of Lehi to his son Jacob. (2 Nephi 2:25.)

However, in our own day, most of our literary and dramatic arts focus on tragedy; our newspapers are filled with accounts of deception, perversion, and man's inhumanity to man. Disillusionment, cynicism, and lack of trust abound on all sides as a result. Helplessness and hopelessness are easy to understand.

The Book of Mormon prophets recognized this possibility in man. After a period of war and strife that Benjamin had known all of his life, the aged king recorded: "The natural man is an enemy to God, and has been from the fall of Adam, and will be, forever and ever, unless he yields to the enticings of the Holy Spirit, and putteth off the natural man." (Mosiah 3:19.)

However, anyone who puts this forth as the Book of Mormon concept of man has failed to see the teachings of the Book of Mormon prophets in their full perspective. Benjamin's son Mosiah, in turning over the government to a system of judges, wrote: "Now it is not common that the voice of the people desireth anything contrary to that which is right; but it is common for the lesser part of the people to desire that which is not right; therefore this shall ye observe and make it your law—to do your business by the voice of the people." (Mosiah 29:26.)

Few statements from political science have been more optimistic. The Book of Mormon recognizes man as a child of God and holds out the possibility of joy, even to those who have made grievous errors—this on the condition of a change in their lives, on the condition of coming to Christ with a broken heart and a contrite spirit. Some of the greatest people in the Book of Mormon had been wayward souls, men who recognized the error of their ways and made amends through the love and help of Christ. The Tree of Life is always within reach. The Book of Mormon is perhaps the greatest witness in literature to the power of repentance.

Alma the Elder, prophet of God and leader of the Church, was once counted among the corrupt priests of Noah, until Abinadi came with the message of Christ. His son, Alma the Younger—accompanied by his friends, the sons of Mosiah—devoted his entire energies to the destruction of the kingdom of God and the undermining of his father's work, until the Lord in his infinite love took a more direct hand in the matter and helped him to find his way back. These men, along with Amulek—who characterized his early life with these words: "I did harden my heart, for I was called many times and I would not hear; . . . I went on rebelling against God, in the wickedness of my heart" (Alma 10:6)—and Zeezrom, who had earlier been a corrupt and argumentative lawyer, became some of the most powerful missionaries in Nephite history. Alma and his son both became prophets of the Lord. Anyone who forgets the earlier experiences of these missionaries to the Zoramites misses much of the intensity of the drama of that mission.

These missionaries are a good example of the third point of the triad, the principle of charity, which the Book of Mormon defines as "the pure love of Christ." (Moroni 7:47.)

Once a person focuses steadfastly on the Master and gains the confidence in himself that is born of hope, these qualities then find an outlet in service and love extended to others. The Book of Mormon is a book of love; it is a book of service.

Nephi spoke of being "encircled about eternally in the arms of his [God's] love." (2 Nephi 1:15.) One would have to search long to find a more beautiful and descriptive metaphor in literature. Jacob, the child of the barren wilderness, spoke of feasting upon the love of God. (See Jacob 3:2.)

The love of the Master was not just an abstraction, an attribute of God's perfection in the eyes of the Nephites; it was a love born of common experience with mankind. Alma recorded of the Master: "He shall go forth, suffering pains and afflictions and temptations of every kind;... he will take upon him the pains and the sicknesses of his people. And he will take upon him death,... and he will take upon him their infirmities, that his bowels may be filled with mercy, according to the flesh, that he may know... how to succor his people according to their infirmities." (Alma 7:11-12.) Those who felt the impact of this love of Christ extended it to those they knew.

Much as I admire the young and idealistic Nephi, whose faith led him to be obedient to every command of God, I must admit that I am attracted more to the mature Nephi, who, as a father and a prophet of God, records: "O the pain, and the anguish of my soul for the loss of the slain of my people!... it well nigh consumeth me before the presence of the Lord" (2 Nephi 26:7), and "I pray continually for them [his people] by day, and mine eyes water my pillow by night, because of them; and I cry unto my God in faith, and I know that he will hear my cry" (2 Nephi 33:3). These are statements born of anguish and love on the part of a father recognizing more fully the worth of a soul.

These feelings are representative of all the prophets who follow Nephi. They are not eager to call down the wrath of God upon the sinner; they are trying in a compassionate fashion to do all possible to bring their people to a condition of joy. One of the most beautiful examples of this is the last speech of Benjamin, in which he counsels his people to serve each other, to render to every man according to his due, to teach their children to love and serve each other. For, he records, "when ye are in the service of your fellow beings ye are only in the service of your God." (Mosiah 2:17.)

True Christians, according to Benjamin, will not suffer that beggars ask in vain. They will impart of their substance to the poor; they will feed the hungry, clothe the naked, visit the sick, and administer to their relief, both spiritually and temporally. (See Mosiah 4:12-26.)

Faith, hope, and charity—these were the attributes of character that the Nephite prophets constantly brought before their people and before their families. They are attributes that we should seek in our own lives. They are three qualities that will guarantee us life with our Father in heaven throughout eternity.

Truly, the Book of Mormon is a text for our times; it is a text for all times. However, to get the most from it, we must learn to read it creatively. We must, as President Young suggests, read it as if we wrote it. Then we can begin to understand what the prophets understood, and begin to find out something about God.

Arthur R. Bassett is an associate professor of humanities at Brigham Young University.

They Came from Jerusalem

John W. Welch

Understanding the Book of Mormon—or any other ancient religious record—is not always easy. Even though the meaning of certain messages may be unmistakably clear, other scriptural passages are difficult to put into perspective and to comprehend fully. One of the reasons for this is the distance between us and the ancient world. We don't always know exactly why the prophets said what they said, to whom they said it, and what cultural practices or religious precepts colored the manner in which they acted or delivered their passage.

Even though our situation handicaps us in comprehending every detail of our ancient sacred writings, we can enhance our understanding by striving, among other things, to understand each text in its original context. This can be hard. It means that we must set to one side our purely modern concepts before we can appreciate and understand many Old World perspectives. It also means that we must accumulate a great deal of information. What did the ancients think about man, about God, about history, revelation, literature, languages, political institutions, economics, social life, philosophical attitudes, religious practices, theological precepts, and general human needs? That may sound overwhelming, but exploring such things is actually exciting and rewarding, for all these factors, to one extent or another, influenced the way in which the ancient prophets wrote and the messages that they propounded.

Developing a capacity for appreciating these kinds of ancient perspectives is often vital in understanding the Book of Mormon. Nephi understood this same truth when he saw the difference that even a few years made to his people, isolated from their native Hebrew culture and struggling to understand its sacred scriptural writings. He explained their difficulty: "For behold, Isaiah spake many things which were hard for many of my people to understand; for they know not concerning *the manner of prophesying* among the Jews. . . . [But] my soul delighteth in the words of Isaiah, for I came out from Jerusalem, and mine eyes hath beheld the things of the Jews, and I know that the Jews do understand the things of the prophets, and there is *none other people that understand* the things which were spoken unto the Jews like unto them, *save it be that they are taught after the manner of the things of the Jews.*" (2 Nephi 25:1, 5; italics added.)

What Nephi says here is significant. One cannot fully understand much of the scriptures without understanding the world in which they were written. To understand the ancient Nephite prophets, it follows that we must consider both "the manner of prophesying" and "the manner of the things" of their basic culture. We do this through a detailed process. Sometimes we must give attention to fragmentary bits of cultural evidence. Other times we may have to ponder that which seems foreign to our way of thinking. But the rewards of gaining a perspective on old world concerns can be substantial.

Sometimes these perspectives help us focus on the specific meaning or importance of a particular passage. Other times they spare us an erroneous interpretation. Generally, they help us appreciate the authenticity and historical integrity of the scriptures, especially of the Book of Mormon.

Always they remind us that there is more to inspired writing than first meets the eye.

Consider an example: King Mosiah established a form of government among the Nephites, saying, "Therefore, choose you by the voice of this people, judges, that ye may be judged according to the laws which have been given you by our fathers." (Mosiah 29:25.)

From a modern perspective we might think this verse tells of the establishment of a democratic or representative government very much like the one we now have in the United States. But on reflection we observe that Nephite politics were different from ours in many significant ways: the Nephites had no constitution, no bill of rights, no separate branches of government, and no parliamentary system of government. Their elected officers served for life, and apparently political parties and campaigning for election were discouraged.

Seen without modern influences, then, Nephite democracy assumes an ancient character all its own. On the one hand, the use of popular consent among the Nephites resembles very closely the rite of royal anointing such as David experienced in ancient Israel. (2 Samuel 5:1-3.) This popular allegiance supplied a special bond of legitimacy between the ruler and his people. In Zarahemla, moreover, the popular voice of allegiance also included a covenant that placed a primary moral responsibility of sustaining the law upon the people themselves. (Mosiah 29:30.)

Other discussions of ways in which ancient backgrounds set the stage for the Book of Mormon can be found in books like those by Hugh Nibley, who has explored at length many ancient Near Eastern backgrounds of the names, practices, and literature we find in the Book of Mormon.[1]

For the present, however, let us turn our attention to a few of "the things of the Jews" and to something of the "manner of prophesying" that relate to the early part of the Book of Mormon.

Because of the importance of culture, as we begin studying the early chapters of First Nephi we need to understand the religious history of Jerusalem in the seventh century B.C. Such an understanding will shed much light on Lehi and his heritage.

From what we know, Lehi must have been born around 650 B.C.[2] Thus, the era he knew in the prime of his life was the turbulent closing quarter of the seventh century B.C. During these few years great empires fell and others rose; allegiances were tested and tormented; religious zeal rose to some of its greatest heights and sank to some of its deepest despair. Out of this era emerged a few men with a profound sense of righteousness and with durable attitudes toward the meaning and purpose of human existence. Lehi was such a man.

We are not told where Lehi was born and reared, but we do know that he was not a member of the tribe of Judah. Lehi's tribe was Manasseh (Alma 10:3), one of the tribes of the northern kingdom of Israel, whose population had been deeply humiliated and partially taken into captivity by the Assyrians in 722 B.C. (see Psalm 79; 2 Kings 15:16-20, 29).[3]

Like Israel, the southern kingdom of Judah also came under the political control of Assyria, in 701 B.C. At the time of Lehi's birth some fifty years later, the kingdom of Judah was still paying a heavy tribute, and Judah's king, Manasseh (whose long reign lasted from 687 to 642 B.C.), was merely a puppet of the powerful Assyrian king, Ashurbanipal (699-633 B.C.). The influence of Assyrian manners, customs, dress, philosophy, and religion was deeply felt in Jerusalem during this period of subjugation; the worship of Jehovah was stifled and perverted as the little kingdom of Judah danced to the tune of its foreign lords.

Reform was badly needed, but obviously Judah could not move until Assyria had lost its grip. Remarkably, this happened with dramatic suddenness. By 635 B.C., Ashurbanipal had grown quite old, and his Assyrian supremacy was seriously threatened on many fronts. The Persians and Scythians were freely attacking the empire's borders, and by 626 B.C.

the Chaldeans had seized control following a bloody civil war. Only fourteen years later, Assyria's proud capital, Nineveh, fell to the Babylonians, and by 609 B.C. the last remnant of Assyrian resistance was wholly destroyed. The momentous turmoil caused by external power struggles worked first to stimulate Judah's incredible resurgence and then just as swiftly to cause its catastrophic destruction. Lehi personally witnessed it all.

Judah's upward cycle began in 640 B.C. when young, progressive King Josiah assumed the throne. Sensing the fresh winds of independence as Assyria declined, Josiah introduced over the next twenty years the most profound reforms Israel had ever known. In a bold move defying Assyria, he supported nationalist zeal and independence in Judah and Israel. He advocated the reunification of all Israel under a monarchy modeled after the Davidic kingdom. He purged the religion of pagan practices, eradicated magic and divination, advocated deep religious devotion, and, perhaps most dramatically, closed down all local shrines and centralized the worship of Jehovah at the temple in Jerusalem. Most of these reforms, it can be seen, remain alive in the attitudes strongly held by Book of Mormon prophets concerning a belief in central temple worship, the abhorrence of priestcrafts, the future hope for the reunification of all Israel, and the establishment of righteousness and devotion.[4]

Many of Josiah's reforms were motivated and strengthened by the rediscovery of the "book of the law" in 622 B.C., during a renovation of the temple. (See 2 Kings 22:3 to 23:25.) This book is thought to have been Deuteronomy, which, like the Book of Mormon, profoundly emphasizes the spirit rather than the letter of the law. The rediscovery of this lost book had profound impact on Lehi's generation. It showed among other things that the word of God would be preserved and would endure, even though it might be hidden from the world for a time.

The discovery of this book emphatically showed the Jews the importance of keeping careful religious records, a concern that is evident in Nephi's history. (See 1 Nephi 5:18-22; 9:3-6.) Josiah's people, like the Mulekites, had degenerated into waywardness at least partially because their record of the Sinai covenant was incomplete.

As the political scene in Jerusalem grew even more tense and as whole civilizations during this period faced the prospect of extinction, a great urge to recapture and preserve the records of past cultures swept the ancient Near Eastern world. Whether one looks to the attempt made in this period by the pharaohs of the Twenty-sixth Dynasty to recapture the glories of the past Pyramid Age, or to the effort in Assyria to copy and preserve royal libraries, or to Laban's jealous possession of the brass plates (see 1 Nephi 3:13), the phenomenon is the same: an intense awareness of civilization's frailty and a grasp in desperation to preserve it, accompanied by a premonition of impending doom. Lehi perceived this precisely.

Although Josiah's reforms were profound, they apparently did not become permanent. High hopes soon soured, and those with true religious desires were bitterly disappointed with Judah's woeful lack of spiritual progress. (See Jeremiah 6:16-21; 7:1-15.) When Josiah was killed in 609 B.C. by Egyptian troops marching belatedly to oppose Babylon's rise, many in Jerusalem saw his death as a sign of divine disapproval of his reforms. Local cult priests were pleased to see them pass.

From 609 to 599 B.C., Judah itself was torn from within by political and spiritual uncertainties, as the fortunes of Egypt and Babylon seesawed in the surrounding areas. Judah vacillated between peacefully supporting one or the other of these two powers, and threatening open warfare. Finally, in a maneuver of blatant arrogance, Jehoiakim, king of Judah, declared war on Babylon. Jeremiah had opposed such a move, but Judah, convinced of its own invincibility, could not be quelled by prophecy of the futility of war.

These became treacherous times for those like Lehi who spoke against Jerusalem or the pompous king of Judah. Consider the fate of Uriah ben Shemaiah, who like Jeremiah prophesied against Jerusalem during the reign of Jehoiakim (609-598 B.C.). Learning that the king sought his life, Uriah fled into Egypt—but he was pursued, captured, and brought back to Jerusalem, where he was executed and dishonorably buried. (Jeremiah 26:20-23.)[5] The same fate might have been Jeremiah's but for the special intervention of certain powerful elders and princes. (Jeremiah 26:16-19, 24.) Such a death could truly have been Lehi's fate as well. (See 1 Nephi 1:20.)

In December of 598 B.C., the Babylonians struck back, besieging Jerusalem. On March 16, 597 B.C.,[6] Nebuchadnezzar took the city and captured the king, who was apparently soon assassinated. Jehoiakim's family, including his many wives, along with court officials, leading citizens, seven thousand soldiers, and one thousand craftsmen, were deported to Babylon. (See 2 Kings 24:16; Jeremiah 24:1.)[7] This represented a tremendous drain on Jerusalem's leading and upper class, as well as a loss of about five percent of its total population. In addition, the Babylonians demanded a heavy tribute and placed Zedekiah, the third son of Josiah, on the throne at the age of twenty-one. But Zedekiah did not inspire much confidence, and his staff was inexperienced. In Jerusalem the people blindly preferred Jehoiachin, the exiled son of the recently assassinated king, while throughout the world the shadow of Nebuchadnezzar became ever more foreboding.

It was in 597 B.C.,[8] the first year of the reign of Zedekiah, that Lehi heard further prophecies of destruction, perhaps from Jeremiah (see 1 Nephi 1:4), and witnessed continued agitations for war in Judah. The people of Judah again became arrogant, and false messianic hopes were high. Looking back over the thirty-five years just past, Lehi, like others, may have then wondered what use Josiah's reforms had served, whether the fate of his northern homeland in 722 B.C. would overtake the south, whether the true Davidic messiah would ever emerge, whether righteousness would ever reign over a united house of Israel, whether a pure center for worship could ever be maintained in Israel as a whole, and whether the sacred law of the covenant could survive where even the law of Assyria had not.

In a setting such as this, with his world perilously close to destruction, Lehi went forth and "prayed unto the Lord, yea, even with all his heart, in behalf of his people." (1 Nephi 1:5.) The vision that came led him out from Jerusalem to prepare a nation in a promised land where a righteous people could be prepared for Christ's coming. (See 1 Nephi 2:20, 23-24; 12:4-12.) The Book of Mormon, as a record of Lehi's people awaiting and receiving Christ, reflects and fulfills many of the hopes that had been of utmost concern to the world in which Lehi had lived.

These things show but a few of the attitudes and concerns of the world out of which the Book of Mormon grew. While many other observations could be made with respect to the ancient world and the Book of Mormon, these few ideas at least give us a starting point from which to approach the things of the Jews and the manner of prophecy that we encounter in the early chapters of the Book of Mormon.

To the modern mind, some of these things may seem strange, and so may many other features of ancient writing.[9] But such strangeness emphasizes the importance of reading these texts from an Old World perspective. When we understand more about the world in which the scriptures were written, we will also understand more about the significance and meaning of the scriptures themselves. We will understand what was said and why. This understanding will in turn help us to see how the scriptures can be used as guides in our own lives.

John W. Welch is an associate professor of law at the J. Reuben Clark Law School at Brigham Young University.

Notes

1. See especially *Lehi in the Desert and the World of the Jaredites* (Bookcraft, 1952); *An Approach to the Book of Mormon* (Deseret Book, 1964); *Since Cumorah: The Book of Mormon in the Modern World* (Deseret Book, 1967).

2. He had four mature sons by 600 B.C. and died an old man ca. 580 B.C. (2 Nephi 4:12.)

Being born approximately 650 B.C., Lehi would have been precisely contemporary with Jeremiah, who was born 645 B.C. or a little before.

3. Sargon's captive lists show only 27,280 prisoners taken, whereas reasonable estimates based on the vast tribute paid in 2 Kings 15:19 would put the adult male population of those tribes at the time around 60,000.

4. For example, the early Nephite prophets continually worked to combat priestcrafts (see 2 Nephi 10:5; 26:29; Alma 1:16), advocated the reunification of all Israel (see Jacob 5; 2 Nephi 3:13), and encouraged devotion to religious law (see 2 Nephi 5:10; Mosiah 2:31).

5. Nothing more is known of Uriah's message. He, like Lehi, was not native to Jerusalem but came from Kiriathjearim (the fields of Jaar), where the ark of the covenant had stood until it was taken into Jerusalem. (See 1 Samuel 7:1-2.) How many others like Uriah and Lehi were there?

6. The event can now be dated precisely from the Babylonian Chronicle. These are cuneiform tablets written in journal form from 626 to 539 B.C. They were translated in 1956. See D. Winton Thomas, ed., *Documents from Old Testament Times* (New York: Thomas Nelson & Sons, 1958), p. 80.

7. Jeremiah 52:28-30 sets the total figure at only 4,600, even though adding his subtotals yields 4,897.

8. The dating footnotes in the Book of Mormon are based on internal evidence and are perfectly self-consistent. However, the date 600 B.C. for Lehi's departure from Jerusalem is based on verses predicting that "even six hundred years from the time that my father left Jerusalem" the Lord would "raise up" a Savior among the Jews. (1 Nephi 10:4.) The figure of 600 years may be only an approximation, or the current dating of the fall of Jerusalem may be faulty. In any event, the dating footnotes in the Book of Mormon were not part of the original text.

9. For example, see "Chiasmus in the Book of Mormon," *New Era* (Feb. 1972), pp. 6-11.

Father Lehi

Marshall R. Craig

The Book of Mormon begins with Lehi—his vision of the destruction of Jerusalem, his family's journey in the wilderness, and their voyage to America. But because his son Nephi wrote the narrative, we often do not realize father Lehi's dominant role as prophet and patriarch in the heaven-directed exodus: Nephi is giving us an account of his own proceedings, his own "reign and ministry." (1 Nephi 10:1.) Thus Lehi, the man whose actions started the magnificent saga of the Book of Mormon, remains shadowy, his personality much less clearly defined than that of Nephi, Jacob, or other major figures in the scripture.

Although Lehi says little about himself in the record we have, we do see him functioning as prophet and patriarch. We glimpse him as a patriarch calming his wife, struggling with his disobedient sons, rejoicing in his obedient ones, and finally blessing his sons and through them his descendants. As a prophet he sees the future of his people and risks his own life to warn them, plunges into seemingly impossible missions when the Lord commands, and receives a vision of the struggle of all men to overcome ignorance, pride, and temptation in order to eat the fruit of the tree of life.

Lehi is a great prophet, paralleling in his mission the experiences of other prophets. He shows the devotion, the openness to the Lord's will, and the determination to follow the Lord's direction that we look for in the ideal of a prophet. In answer to earnest prayer, Lehi is dramatically called to prophesy through a vision of a pillar of fire. Like Zephaniah and Jeremiah, he is a prophet of doom to his nation, and like many Old Testament prophets he predicts the coming of the Messiah. He is rejected by his hearers, his life is endangered, and like Abraham and Moses he leaves his homeland to establish a new nation.

But Lehi is more than a "typical" prophet. And despite the lack of information, he is a man whose personality, at least in part, can be discovered. Lehi himself gives one key to his character. When Sariah, supposing that her sons have "perished in the wilderness," accuses Lehi of being a "visionary man," Lehi agrees: "I know that I am a visionary man; for if I had not seen the things of God in a vision I should not have known the goodness of God, but had tarried at Jerusalem, and had perished with my brethren." (1 Nephi 5:2, 4.)

Dreams and visions dominate Lehi's life; he is called by the Lord in a vision in which he sees Christ and the Twelve. (1 Nephi 1:6-14.) In another prophecy he foretells the Babylonian captivity, the ministry of the Messiah, and the preaching of the gospel to the gentiles. (1 Nephi 10:3-14.) Even the journey into the wilderness was commanded in a dream. (1 Nephi 2:1-3.) In other dreams Lehi was commanded to send his sons back to Jerusalem to obtain the plates of Laban and later to persuade Ishmael and his sons and daughters to join them. (1 Nephi 3:2-4; 7:1-2.)

Lehi does not distinguish between dreams and visions—he begins his report concerning the tree of life by saying, "Behold, I have dreamed a dream; or, in other words, I have seen a vision." (1 Nephi 8:2.) He is indeed a "visionary man."

Jeremiah, who prophesied at the same time, left behind a body of teachings: fifty-two chapters of prophecy and five chapters of lamentation when his darkest prophecies were fulfilled. Lehi was completely lost to the world until 2,430 years after he left Jerusalem, when his life and words were again published. Yet at the time Lehi also was such a powerful voice for the Lord that the people of Judah sought to kill him. (1 Nephi 1:18-20.) We are fortunate to have some of his prophetic utterances made available again.

And Lehi was not the only prophet of that time whose name the Old Testament has forgotten. Nephi says that just prior to his father's call "there came many prophets, prophesying unto the people that they must repent, or the great city Jerusalem must be destroyed." (1 Nephi 1:4.) These were among the messengers of God that the Bible tells us were "mocked," their messages "despised," and themselves "misused." (2 Chronicles 36:15-16.) No prophet who sees beyond the immediate situation to the fall of a nation is ever popular with the people of that nation; and most of the time, unfortunately, he is ignored.

Such prophets seem to gather around themselves small groups of followers, while the majority of their hearers go carelessly to their predicted doom. Noah, with part of his family, and Abraham, with his family and servants, foresaw coming destruction and took their few followers with them to safety. Likewise Lehi took his followers—some of them reluctant to accompany him—into the wilderness, across an ocean, and into a new land. But even in that chosen land, Lehi saw that after the development of a great nation would come its fall: "If the day shall come that they will reject the Holy One of Israel, . . . he will take away from them the lands of their possessions, and he will cause them to be scattered and smitten." (2 Nephi 1:10-11.)

Until his death Lehi is lamenting, "O that ye would awake; awake from a deep sleep, yea, even from the sleep of hell, and shake off the awful chains by which ye are bound, which are the chains which bind the children of men, that they are carried away captive down to the eternal gulf of misery and woe." (2 Nephi 1:13.) He does not rejoice in the fall of the wicked. Instead his compassion makes him grieve: "My heart hath been weighed down with sorrow from time to time." (2 Nephi 1:17.)

Lehi is not a carefree man, but he is a man finely tuned to the Spirit of the Lord, one who asks for knowledge with faith that he will be answered, and that whatever happens, he and his loved ones will be protected by the Lord. Only once does Nephi tell us that his father complained about misfortune. When the wanderers in the wilderness were without food after Nephi had broken his bow, Lehi "began to murmur against the Lord his God." Later the Lord spoke to Lehi and chastened him, "insomuch that he was brought down into the depths of sorrow." (1 Nephi 16:20, 25.) But except for this moment of frustration, Lehi again and again shows his trust in the Lord.

Of the many prophets who spoke for the Lord at that time, most went into captivity with the Jews or made some accommodation with the Babylonians. Lehi, however, was stopped in the middle of his prophetic career in Jerusalem and told to leave. Apparently he never wavered. His reliance was on the Lord alone, and he turned from a dangerous and important task to pursue an even more dangerous and important task. No longer would he try to change a nation. Now he would create one; he would raise up a righteous people for the Lord.

Lehi's family had always been important to him, but now his entire calling focused on his children and their children. His own sons and daughters were his mission, with no distractions. And suddenly the role of patriarch and the role of prophet became one. It was for the benefit of "his seed" that he was commanded to send his sons for the plates of Laban (1 Nephi 5:19), and when he asked Ishmael and his family to share the journey, he was choosing the mothers who would help shape his righteous progeny (1 Nephi 7:1-2). And at the end of his life, when he learned in a vision that Jerusalem had been destroyed, he did not mourn for the city he had loved and served so well. Instead, he reminded his children that they lived in "a land of promise, a land which is choice above all other lands." (2 Nephi 1:5.) He had been a prophet to his family, and he was satisfied. (2 Nephi 1:14-15.)

A "visionary man" sounds impractical to us; a dreamer seems unsuited for tasks demanding decision, strength, and directness. But Lehi's dreams were not daydreams. They were the word of the Lord to one of his few children faithful and strong enough to obey him in all things. It was no weakling who led his strife-torn family through the wilderness. Nephi makes it clear that no matter how close Nephi came to the Lord, the revelations as to where the family should go came to Lehi. The Lord spoke to Lehi "by night, and commanded him that on the morrow he should take his journey into the wilderness." (1 Nephi 16:9.) The "ball of curious workmanship" that directed them on their way appeared before Lehi's tent. (1 Nephi 16:10.) When Nephi's bow broke and he made another to keep the group alive, he went to his father to find out where he should go to get meat. (1 Nephi 16:23-26, 30-31.) And though the Lord spoke to Nephi to command him to build a ship (1 Nephi 17:8), Lehi received the Lord's direction to enter it and begin the voyage (1 Nephi 18:5).

Lehi was too righteous a man to resent Nephi's emerging leadership. He rejoiced that one of his sons was following the Lord so faithfully. Nephi had his father's complete trust when, "being stricken in years, and having suffered much grief because of their children, [Lehi and Sariah] were brought down, yea, even upon their sick-beds. . . . They were brought near even to be carried out of this time to meet their God." (1 Nephi 18:17-18.) It must have been a comfort to Lehi to watch his godly son direct the ship the rest of the way to the promised land, and when he saw Nephi stop the wind and calm the storm, he knew that the Lord had provided a leader for the next generation. (1 Nephi 18:21-22.) He counselled his other sons, "Rebel no more against your brother, whose views have been glorious, and who hath kept the commandments. . . . He hath not sought for power nor authority over you, but he hath sought the glory of God, and your own eternal welfare. . . . And it must needs be that the power of God must be with him, even unto his commanding you that ye must obey." (2 Nephi 1:24-25, 27.)

Yet even as Nephi gradually assumed leadership, Lehi remained as the patriarch until the end. Despite all the quarrels and struggles within the family, the family members did not split up until after Lehi died. (2 Nephi 4:12-13; 5:5.)

Lehi longed for all his descendants to be as righteous as Nephi (2 Nephi 1:28), but he suspected that they would not. The Book of Mormon proves that Laman and Lemuel, not Nephi, represented the major future of Lehi's seed. For a thousand years the people of Lehi vacillated, first righteous, then proud and sinful—repenting when they were brought up short by the Lord's judgments, and sinking into sin again when the Lord blessed them and they prospered. When Lehi spoke to Laman and Lemuel, he was speaking to all future generations: "My heart hath been weighed down with sorrow from time to time, for I have feared, lest for the hardness of your hearts the Lord your God should come out in the fulness of his wrath upon you, that ye be cut off and destroyed forever. . . . O my sons, that these things might not come upon you. . . ." (2 Nephi 1:17, 19.)

He pled with them to "be like unto this river, continually running into the fountain of all righteousness!" and to "be like unto this valley, firm and steadfast, and immovable in keeping the commandments of the Lord!" (1 Nephi 2:9-10.) Like many prophets after him, Lehi had to speak with the power of the Spirit, so that his sons' "frames did shake before him." Thus did Lehi "confound them, that they durst not utter against him." (1 Nephi 2:14.) But as soon as they were away from the prophet, they rebelled.

Even Lehi's last blessing to Laman and Lemuel is a plea repeated over and over that they forsake their unrighteousness: "That my soul might have joy in you, and that my heart might leave this world with gladness because of you, that I might not be brought down with grief and sorrow to the grave, arise from the dust, my sons, and be men, and be determined in one mind and in one heart, united in all things, that ye may not come down into captivity." (2 Nephi 1:21.)

In all that Lehi does, he looks to the future. He knows that Jacob's "soul shall be blessed," that his "days shall be spent in the service of . . . God." (2 Nephi 2:3.) The remainder of Jacob's blessing is a sermon, for Jacob's descendants and for us. The blessing of Joseph, Lehi's "last-born," is a prophecy for Joseph's seed and for the seed of Joseph who was sold into Egypt. (2 Nephi 3.)

Like Abraham, Isaac, and Jacob, Lehi was a prophet known only to his children; but through them he influenced nations for thousands of years. In his words to his children he also speaks to us: "Inasmuch as ye shall keep my commandments ye shall prosper in the land; but inasmuch as ye will not keep my commandments ye shall be cut off from my presence." (2 Nephi 1:20.) He explains a cardinal principle of progression: "For it must needs be, that there is an opposition in all things." (2 Nephi 2:11.) Then he applies this principle to the fall of man: "If Adam had not transgressed he would not have fallen, but he would have remained in the garden of Eden," and he and Eve "would have had no children; wherefore they would have remained in a state of innocence, having no joy, for they knew no misery; doing no good, for they knew no sin." (2 Nephi 2:22-23.)

Lehi was a strong man, not because he relied on his own wealth, power, or talents, but because he relied completely upon the Lord. From his earliest vision to the end of his life, Lehi expressed that confidence. His greatest joy in life came from the works of God, and he exclaimed, "Great and marvelous are thy works, O Lord God Almighty! Thy throne is high in the heavens, and thy power, and goodness, and mercy are over all the inhabitants of the earth; and, because thou art merciful, thou wilt not suffer those who come unto thee that they shall perish!" (1 Nephi 1:14.)

Though by following the Lord Lehi tasted suffering many times in his life, he had a greater reward than many who outwardly seem more successful and content. Just before his death he said, "Behold, the Lord hath redeemed my soul from hell; I have beheld his glory, and I am encircled about eternally in the arms of his love." (2 Nephi 1:15.) He followed his visions all his life, knowing that the giver of those dreams would eventually give him eternal life, where, with those of his family who would follow him, he could taste the white fruit of the love of God forever. (1 Nephi 8:11, 13, 16; 11: 21-22.)

Marshall R. Craig, an emeritus professor of English at Brigham Young University, has been a foreign expert in the People's Republic of China.

Nephi, a Universal Man

Allen E. Bergin

Nephi was that rare combination: a great prophet who is also a founder of a nation. As prophet, he succeeded his father Lehi as spiritual leader in ancient America and laid the groundwork for the heights of righteousness later achieved. As ruler of a new nation, he was so beloved of his people that when "he anointed a man to be a king and a ruler over his people," the people insisted on calling his successors "second Nephi, third Nephi, and so forth." (Jacob 1:9-11.) And his influence was so great that for a thousand years the people called themselves *Nephites*. Near the end of that millennium, Mormon took pride in declaring himself to be a descendant of Nephi. (Mormon 1:5.)

Like Enoch, Moses, Joseph Smith, and Brigham Young, Nephi led his people to physical safety, organized them into a new society, and stood at the head of a unique era in scriptural history. Like Enoch, Moses, and Joseph Smith, he received panoramic visions and great spiritual powers, including a visitation by the Lord. (1 Nephi 2:16; 2 Nephi 11:2-3.) And like Joseph the son of Israel, his righteousness provoked his rebellious older brothers to try to kill him. (See Genesis 37:18-20; 1 Nephi 7:16; 16:38; 2 Nephi 5:4.) Yet, like all of God's prophets, Nephi courageously carried out the will of the Lord, doing that which he was directed to accomplish.

Familiar with his spiritual stature, however, we sometimes fail to recognize that Nephi was one of the "universal men" of this world's history, a person of multiple talents and skills. He led the establishment of a major civilization in the "new" world (2 Nephi 5:6, 10-11, 13); he possessed the intellect, skills, insight, and leadership capacities that class him among the great colonizers of all time. We do not usually apply the term "pioneer" to him, but we should. Indeed, in that way, as in others, he seems to identify with Moses at several points in his writing. (1 Nephi 4:2; 17:23-47.) This analogy seems especially fitting, for both men not only were great colonizers but also were men of great spiritual capacity; both saw visions and both wrote scripture that had great impact on their own as well as other civilizations.

Not only did Nephi personally refine the ore, design the shape, and make the metal plates on which he wrote, but he was also a skilled craftsman in a dozen other areas. (1 Nephi 19:1.) When his steel bow broke, he made one of wood. (1 Nephi 16:23.) Taught by the Lord, he smelted ore, fashioned metal tools, and built a ship of "exceedingly fine" workmanship. (1 Nephi 17:16; 18:1-4.) In the promised land he established a city, built a temple "after the manner of the temple of Solomon," and taught his people to build buildings and to work in wood, iron, copper, brass, steel, gold, silver, and precious ores. (2 Nephi 5:15-16.) For the defense of his people he made weapons, with the sword of Laban for a model. (2 Nephi 5:14.) And in a land where the Lamanites became an "idle people" who subsisted on hunting, Nephi caused his people to be industrious and to labor with their hands. (2 Nephi 5:17, 24.) All this he managed in virgin wilderness, without any help from a civilization base.

We have no portraits of Nephi, but we know he was large and powerful (1 Nephi 4:31), an excellent hunter (1 Nephi 16:31-32), uncomplaining despite pain and hardship. A skilled warrior, he was "a great protector for" his people, wielding "the sword of Laban" in their defense. (Jacob 1: 10.) Even as a youth he overpowered Zoram, a mature man. (1 Nephi 4:31.) Yet despite his strength he did not use force as an argument with his brothers, relying instead on spiritual means. (1 Nephi 3:28-29; 7:16-18; 16:24, 39; 17:48, 52-54.) And even when commanded by the Lord, he struggled greatly to bring himself to kill another man. (1 Nephi 4:10, 18.) This powerful combination of spirituality and personality, coupled with his physical impressiveness, must have made his impact extraordinary.

Imagine a man with the mantle of a prophet, an athletic man who appears to be able to do anything and make anything, and who seems to possess supreme self-confidence, having been "highly favored of the Lord." (1 Nephi 1:1.) In the face of frequent and stiff, even murderous, opposition, he would characteristically meet it with steel resistance. Fearless, he answered doubters with the words, power, and success that the Lord gave him. In modern terms, he was unflappable and unstoppable.

These personality traits also emerged in his teaching style. His approach was frank, direct, even blunt. "My soul delighteth in plainness," he acknowledged (2 Nephi 31:3), and he minced no words in his prophecies of the latter days (see 2 Nephi 28; 29; 33). When his rebuke roused a keen sense of guilt in his brothers, they protested, "Thou hast declared unto us hard things, more than we are able to bear." Nephi answered, "I knew that I had spoken hard things against the wicked, according to the truth; . . . wherefore, the guilty taketh the truth to be hard, for it cutteth them to the very center. . . . If ye were righteous, . . . then ye would not murmur because of the truth, and say: Thou speakest hard things against us." (1 Nephi 16:1-3.)

We've seen this kind of intense confrontation before; it is the eternal conflict between good and evil. Personalities and family rivalries are involved, true enough, but they do not mask a polarity so vivid that it attains classic proportions. The

Book of Mormon stage sees another act of the drama that began with Lucifer's struggle to overcome Christ and continued as Cain opposed Abel. Satan's agents in every dispensation have tried to bring down the servants of the Lord. Laman and Lemuel had more than a normal case of sibling rivalry; their struggle was as much with truth and their own consciences as with Nephi.

Just as Abel's righteousness aroused Cain's hatred, so Nephi's righteousness aroused the hatred of Laman and Lemuel. The record indicates that Nephi spoke up when his brothers' doubts and complaints seemed to interfere with the work of the Lord. Though Laman and Lemuel attacked Nephi, saying, "We will not that our younger brother shall be a ruler over us" (1 Nephi 18:10), it was not his wish to be their ruler. In fact, when Laman and Lemuel, shaken by the power of God, fell down before Nephi and were about to worship him, he protested, "I am thy brother, yea, even thy younger brother; wherefore, worship the Lord thy God, and honor thy father and thy mother." (1 Nephi 17:55.)

Nephi's purity, his father's love for him, and his closeness to the Lord must have been a constant irritation to Laman and Lemuel as they compared themselves to him and always found themselves lacking. They were often humbled: by an angel (1 Nephi 3:29), by their own consciences when Ishmael's wife and a daughter and a son pleaded with them (1 Nephi 7:19-20), by the words of the Lord written on the Liahona (1 Nephi 16:27), by the voice and power of God (1 Nephi 16:39; 17:54-55), and finally by a storm at sea (1 Nephi 18:13-16). But their memories were short, and humility was never strong enough in them to drown out their pride. They rebelled again even more quickly than they had "repented."

Nephi's crystal purity and sterling character set a clear standard for his apparently proud, self-indulgent, and less energetic brothers. He was a mirror they preferred not to look at, for he reflected their true natures back to them with merciless clarity.

But to explain the whole drama as a mere personality clash is assuming too much—the counters are cosmic, the scope eternal. Let's view the situation in terms of both psychology and theology. Human personality is influenced by both theological and psychological principles. Our personality is an offshoot of how an eternal free agent (an intelligence, spirit, and soul) deals with doctrine (eternal law). Thus, like all of us, Laman and Lemuel were born with some personality predispositions developed in the preexistence. We cannot attribute their reactions to Nephi's righteousness only as sibling rivalry. Nor can we interpret Nephi's staunchness as self-righteousness or arrogance toward his brothers. Nephi, in his direct manner, accused them: "Ye are murderers in your hearts. . . . Ye are swift to do iniquity but slow to remember the Lord your God." (1 Nephi 17:44-45.) The conflict takes place on a grander scale. It is the human, mortal expression of a contest between right and wrong. The opposing forces are magnified here until the differences are unmistakable. I have often thought that Nephi was inspired to document this opposition in detail as a lesson to all mankind. The perfection of his character was a necessary element in the story. It helps to heighten the drama and thereby make the Lord's message to us strong and clear. How else but through a Nephi and a Laman and a Lemuel could this message be told so well?

There is another virtue in Nephi's character that has always been compelling to me. He did not emotionally cut off his brothers; that is, he seems not to have held grudges. Love followed rebuke and exhortation. We sense some of his sorrow when his brothers rejected the invitation to embrace the gospel of Jesus Christ. "I did frankly forgive them all that they had done," he says of his early life (1 Nephi 7:21), and years later he wrote, "I pray continually for them by day, and mine eyes water my pillow by night, because of them" (2 Nephi 33:3).

Because of both plainness and love, Nephi possessed a remarkable ability to persuade those he instructed—if they desired righteousness. It was Laman's and Lemuel's failure, not Nephi's, when they turned away from the Lord. Numerous others chose righteousness under Nephi's influence, established his program on the new continent, and "loved Nephi exceedingly." (Jacob 1:10.)

As to Nephi's mind, it is apparent that he was an intelligent person, clear in exposition and lucidly logical, as we see from his theological interpretations of the olive tree and the tree of life. (See 1 Nephi 15.)

For me, one of the tenderest revelations of Nephi's personality comes in the special relationship between him and Lehi. While their beliefs and messages were the same, their personalities were surely different. Both are prophets of heroic proportions, but it is enlightening for fathers and sons of our day to note that Nephi, despite his precociousness, was totally obedient to his father. He observes every rule of decorum in relation to his father's patriarchal role. He believes all that his father declares and seeks his direction before launching into his inspired enterprises. At the same time, Lehi has high regard—even deference—for Nephi, recognizing true greatness in his son. Here we have an exemplary standard for all fathers and sons, one that has not been obscured at all by the centuries, but which is made even more relevant in our time by the dissolution of proper love and authority in many modern families.

Ultimately, Lehi bestows blessings of the greatest magnitude upon Nephi. As he blessed his sons just before his death, Lehi told them: "It must needs be that the power of God must be with [Nephi], even unto his commanding you that ye must obey. . . . And now my son, Laman, and also Lemuel and Sam, and also my sons who are the sons of Ishmael, behold, if ye will hearken unto the voice of Nephi ye shall not perish." (2 Nephi 1:27-28.)

It might have seemed to Laman and Lemuel that their father loved Nephi more than he loved them, but like the Lord, Lehi was no respecter of persons. He made it clear to them that if they had sought the Lord as diligently as Nephi did, they would have deserved and received as many blessings. (2 Nephi 1:27-29.)

Nephi's unusual spiritual endowment may be measured by looking at the special gifts, messages, and powers he received. As with Joseph Smith, he obtained spiritual knowledge at an "exceedingly young" age and was given a preview of his destiny. Like the Prophet Joseph Smith, he had "great desires to know of the mysteries of God, wherefore, I did cry unto the Lord; and behold he did visit me." (1 Nephi 2:16.) Also, the Lord "spake unto me, saying . . . ye . . . shall be led to a land of promise . . . [and] thou shalt be made a ruler and a teacher over thy brethren." (1 Nephi 2:19-20, 22.) He knew his divine calling even before he received the brass plates of Laban.

There then followed a series of revelations and dispensations of power to Nephi that place him among the great prophets of all ages:

"I am filled with the power of God, even unto the consuming of my flesh." (1 Nephi 17:48.)

"If God had commanded me to do all things I could do them." (1 Nephi 17:50.)

"And after I had prayed the winds did cease, and the storm did cease, and there was a great calm." (1 Nephi 18:21.)

"Behold, he hath heard my cry by day, and he hath given me knowledge by visions in the nighttime. . . . My voice have I sent up on high; and angels came down and ministered unto me. And upon the wings of his Spirit hath my body been carried away upon exceedingly high mountains. And mine eyes have beheld great things, yea, even too great for man; therefore I was bidden that I should not write them." (2 Nephi 4:23-25.)

It is not easy to attempt an assessment of the length and breadth of this great man's faith, a faith so strong that ordinary characteristics seem obliterated by an overwhelming heavenly influence. Most of us can't imagine being transported to the tops of mountains, or shaking our enemies by pointing at them, or seeing 2,600 years into the future, but

Nephi's faith was sufficient for these physical wonders as well as the visitations, voices, and visions we most frequently associate with the prophetic calling.

Indeed, Nephi's faith is so singular that our Latter-day Saint culture has been greatly influenced by his example. Our congregations sing of "Nephi, seer of olden time." (*Hymns,* no. 186.) When we want a scripture on faith (and works) we turn to what has become a classic statement by Nephi, probably declared during his teens: "I will go and do the things which the Lord hath commanded, for I know that the Lord giveth no commandments unto the children of men, save he shall prepare a way for them that they may accomplish the thing which he commandeth them." (1 Nephi 3:7.) What greater message to modern youth than to know that the young can receive such spiritual influences. The Lord spoke to Nephi in his youth, saying: "Blessed art thou, Nephi, *because of thy faith,* for thou hast sought me diligently, with lowliness of heart." (1 Nephi 2:19; italics added.) The Lord can and will speak to us as well. If we can exercise faith as did Nephi and obtain a similarly humble "lowliness of heart," then we can have strength to face our problems as he did—and few in history have had greater problems than he.

Imagine, for example, how incredibly unreal and even depressing it would be to an ordinary person with no experience or tradition of seafaring skills to see the great waves of the ocean for the first time and to be told to cross the mighty deep. Nephi, however, had the faith to obtain a vision of what was possible and then to pursue that vision without hesitation before incredible obstacles. He found ore deposits and mined and smelted the ore, fashioning his own metal tools for shipbuilding. His brethren began to complain and taunt him. After subduing his brothers' opposition, he returned to building a ship "after the manner which the Lord had shown unto me." (1 Nephi 18:2.)

Completing this ship was, however, just the beginning of difficulty. Each step of crossing the ocean and establishing a civilization in the promised land was fraught with both physical and spiritual trial. Only an extraordinary human being could have retained his equilibrium and faith in the face of such opposition. Reading Nephi's account is a good antidote for depression, self-pity, and loss of faith, for the magnitude of his difficulties tends to make our own seem more manageable. Indeed, his success may stand as a witness against us if we do not cope with our simpler trials, particularly when he informs us so frequently that the Lord was the source of his succor and strength.

Not only did Nephi exercise complete faith, but his faith was correctly fixed upon Jesus Christ. When we read on the title page of the Book of Mormon that its purpose is to convince "Jew and Gentile that Jesus is the Christ, the Eternal God," and then turn to the books of Nephi we find this promise fulfilled in some of the most vivid testimonies of the Savior in all of sacred writ. Among these is the panoramic vision given to Nephi of the Savior's mission on earth. (See 1 Nephi 11; 12.) His closeness to the Lord and the spirit of testimony he radiates vivify his account.

In my opinion, there is nothing more powerful in these first two books of the Book of Mormon than Nephi's continuing testimony of Jesus, that he "is the Christ, the Eternal God, manifesting himself unto all nations." I recall very clearly how some years ago, as a young college student investigator, I read and reread these challenging testimonies. My initial approach had been skeptical, even cynical, and I wrote critical remarks along the margins as I read, commenting upon the weaknesses in logic, grammar, and philosophy. When I came to those last two pages (2 Nephi 33), however, I was stunned by the power of Nephi's words. They seemed to penetrate my brain and scatter my previously systematic, critical thoughts. I could not avoid the impact of his words. It was almost as physical as if Nephi were using his shock technique on me, pointing his finger and shaking my mind. I read his words again, and they seemed to grip me. Briefly and involuntarily, a sweet feeling came over me that I later recognized as having been the Spirit of Christ, the witness of his reality and his loving closeness.

After a healthy dose of repentance, I was baptized; and

since baptism I have reread that chapter perhaps a hundred times. There, in a few words, we have the fulness of a true testimony written by an old man who had been in the demanding and involving service of the Lord for fifty-five years. Nevertheless, his witness there is as strong as or stronger than anywhere else. Here again his pure character permits the Lord to speak through him to our own age. There is no way to capture the feeling of this chapter by quoting only part of it, so I commend it to all readers for an unusual experience of edification and renewal. I commend it especially to nonmembers, particularly those of Lamanite descent, for I think Nephi's heart was drawn out powerfully to them as he wrote with his mind fixed in vision upon the latter days. If ever there were spiritual power in the written word, it is here. I feel that my own knowledge of Jesus Christ was magnified immeasurably by this message. It prepared me, during those college days, for spiritual enlargement as I continued to read and pray. The feelings Nephi's writing brought into my own life, the life of one man, demonstrate why these golden writings were made, preserved, and brought forth.

It seems to me that Nephi was remarkable, head and shoulders above most of mankind in his vision and his achievement. Thus, he comes across almost as a superman. But we should note the profound expressions of his humanity when he laments his weaknesses: "O wretched man that I am! Yea, my heart sorroweth because of my flesh; my soul grieveth because of mine iniquities. I am encompassed about, because of the temptations and the sins which do so easily beset me." (2 Nephi 4:17-18.)

In this poetic lamentation, Nephi spontaneously discloses another self, a self with weaknesses, a self that is not apparent anywhere else in his writings. This openness is profoundly encouraging to readers like me who hope to improve but are so dazzled by Nephi's perfection that we simply doubt our capacity to bridge the gap. Nephi gives just enough of his own struggle to give us hope that we can achieve self-mastery, too. Some might wonder what "hidden iniquity" prompted this confession; I tend to think that he had none, but rather regretted anger against his enemies and strength-slackening because of his afflictions. In light of his ability to literally will himself into righteousness under extremely adverse conditions, these modest vulnerabilities, serious to him, only add to his stature in our eyes.

So we have in Nephi the almost complete human being—prophet, teacher, ruler, colonizer, builder, craftsman, intellect, writer, poet, military leader, father of nations, son, husband, and physical powerhouse. Measured against mankind, he belongs where he is, in the company of the greatest men of every age. He was incomparable, a universal man who chose to be the Lord's servant above all else. Few have spoken so well in behalf of one age and to another: "And now, my beloved brethren, and also Jew, and all ye ends of the earth, hearken unto these words and believe in Christ; . . . for they are the words of Christ . . . and they teach all men that they should do good . . . And I pray the Father in the name of Christ that many of us, if not all, may be saved in his kingdom at that great and last day. . . . I speak unto you as the voice of one crying from the dust: Farewell until that great day shall come." (2 Nephi 33:10, 12-13.)

Allen E. Bergin is a professor of psychology at Brigham Young University.

Jacob

C. Terry Warner

Few people appreciate the greatness of Jacob among the prophets. This is partly because his story is scattered over 125 pages of the Book of Mormon, and partly because he wrote little about himself. Nevertheless, from what we do know, a picture emerges of a shepherd of his people who also loved us, the Saints of future years, and who by that love calls forth our love for him.

During the first part of his ministry, Jacob was one of three witnesses through whom the testimony of Christ was borne to the early Nephite church. Nephi used Jacob's teachings, together with the prophecies of Isaiah from the brass plates of Laban, to establish the truth of what he himself taught concerning Christ. They, like him, had seen the Redeemer and had received revelations concerning his future ministry. (2 Nephi 11:2-3.) Jacob's role thus seems to have been similar to that given to Hyrum Smith in the latter days, to stand as "second elder" beside a prophet-leader and proclaim a special witness. (See Joseph Fielding Smith, *Doctrines of Salvation* 1:216-22, 258.)

In the second part of his ministry, from the age of about fifty onward,[1] Jacob himself presided over the Church.

(Though Jacob does not say explicitly that this was so, the evidence that we have for it is strong.[2]) He labored in this calling to consolidate the Church against forces of corruption and apostasy. Only one of the discourses he delivered during his administration survives, together with a sermon that Nephi recorded and one that Jacob wrote for posterity; but the three together form one of the most important doctrinal contributions ever made. Besides this, Jacob was a successful father. His immediate posterity became church leaders and keepers of the small plates; in this respect, too, he was like Hyrum Smith.

Jacob and his younger brother, Joseph, were born of Lehi and Sariah during the eight-year journey in the deserts of the Arabian peninsula. (1 Nephi 18:7.) Though their family had been prosperous in Jerusalem (1 Nephi 3:16, 22-25), all that Jacob and Joseph had experienced was hardship and privation. The coastal desert was hot and humid. Their food, for a period, was the raw flesh of animals. But it was not the physical difficulty of the trek that made Lehi call these "the days of my tribulation in the wilderness" and caused Jacob to suffer "afflictions and much sorrow." (2 Nephi 2:1.) Indeed, the Lord blessed the two-family party so that the raw meat was "sweet" (1 Nephi 17:12), and the "women did give plenty of suck for their children, and were strong, . . . and they began to bear their journeyings without murmurings" (1 Nephi 17:2).

What afflicted them through the journey—in the desert, during the shipbuilding, on the ocean voyage, and in the new land—were rebellions, disputes, and contentions provoked by Laman and Lemuel (Jacob's oldest brothers) and by the sons of Ishmael. These men complained constantly, threatened their parents, tried to return to Jerusalem, refused to work, physically abused Nephi, and several times even tried to kill him. Their rebellion and faithlessness more than once caused the Lord to withdraw his providences, so that it seemed the company would perish in the desert or on the high seas. (1 Nephi 16:18-29, 34-39; 18:9-20.)

Jacob and Joseph lived through all this. They saw their father and mother "stricken in years, and having suffered much grief because of their children, they were brought down, yea, even upon their sickbeds." (1 Nephi 18:17.) The two boys, "being young, having need of much nourishment, were grieved because of the afflictions of their mother." (1 Nephi 18:19.)

This sort of emotional and spiritual tribulation never ended for Jacob, who at the end of his life wrote, "Our lives passed away like . . . a dream, we being a lonesome and a solemn people, wanderers, cast out from Jerusalem, born in tribulation, in a wilderness, and hated of our brethren, which caused wars and contentions; wherefore, we did mourn out our days." (Jacob 7:26.)

In the strife that divided this little society, which was the only one Jacob had known, good and evil were sharply polarized. The battle lines were almost always drawn. Jacob could not be indifferent to moral issues; he had to declare himself. He saw conflicts as old as mankind. Laman and Lemuel contended that the Jerusalem Jews whom they had left and who kept the Law of Moses hypocritically, as a cover for sin, were a righteous and happy people. (1 Nephi 17:22.) They said that their father, who condemned the Jews in the name of the Lord for their overripe iniquity, was a fanatical visionary.

Think about a boy in Jacob's situation trying to sort out what was right. To appreciate what it took to stand beside his nearly broken father and embattled brother Nephi, consider how persuasive Laman and Lemuel's position was. They pointed to the enjoyable life they had left. They sorrowed sincerely for the hardships endured by their wives, who carried, bore, and nursed children on the journey. Look what we have given up and what we have endured, they said, in order to trudge year after year—aimlessly, it seemed, and at the risk of life—in a wasteland. (1 Nephi 17:20-21.) Why should they be blamed for their resistant attitude in a situation like this? What was more natural?

But more important than what Laman and Lemuel said was what they left out. They had the evidence of divine manifestations that this journey was not simply their father's escapade, and they were untrue to this evidence. They hated Nephi, not because he differed from them in religious things, but because inwardly they knew he was right. (1 Nephi 17: 45-46.) Like their consciences, he was a reproach to them. Jacob was different from Laman and Lemuel; he yielded his heart to the truth that they all knew.

In times of peril Jacob exercised his faith and saw miraculous deliverances. He fasted and prayed for storms to abate, for food to be found, and for the Liahona to point their way. In the pitched moral battle that surrounded his childhood, he committed himself. Because of this, his father promised him, all his afflictions would be consecrated for his gain. (2 Nephi 2:2.) While still in his youth he beheld the glory of the Savior, saw in prospect "that in the fulness of time he [the Lord] cometh to bring salvation unto men" (2 Nephi 2:3), received blessings "even as they unto whom he shall minister in the flesh," and was himself redeemed from the fall (2 Nephi 2:3-4). At times unidentified in his life, he also enjoyed the ministration of angels, heard the voice of the Lord, and received "many revelations, and the spirit of much prophecy." (Jacob 1:6; see also 2 Nephi 10:3; Jacob 2:11; 4:6.)

It is little wonder that Lehi, in giving instruction to Jacob (2 Nephi 2), spoke of opposition, freedom, and Christ. These concerns were always at the fore in the experiences Jacob had had.

Lehi treated these topics with a profundity unsurpassed in any literature. One of the principles Lehi taught was that living the law without yielding one's heart to God cannot justify anyone. The law points to Christ and the redemption he offers, which can be received only by a person whose heart is broken and whose spirit is contrite. This attitude reminds us of the sacrifice of the Messiah—a person must figuratively lay down his life according to the flesh and take it up again by the power of the Spirit. That is what Jacob did, which is why redemption came to him "in and through the Holy Messiah." (2 Nephi 2:6.) All of this lay behind Jacob's reply in later life when Sherem, the anti-Christ, accused him of perverting the law of Moses by preaching Christ. Jacob said, "Then ye do not understand [the scriptures]; for . . . none of the prophets have written, nor prophesied, save they have spoken concerning this Christ." (Jacob 7:11.)

Another principle Lehi taught Jacob was that there is purpose in opposition. (2 Nephi 2:11.) There was a reason for the presence of Laman and Lemuel on that arduous journey just as there was for the beguiling voice of Satan in the Garden of Eden. Without the opposition and the opportunity for sin and sorrow it presents, there can be no voluntary resistance to evil and therefore no virtue; and if there is no virtue, there can be no happiness.

Finally, Lehi made it clear that there is a kind of freedom enjoyed only by those who, against opposition, yield their hearts to Christ. Whereas everyone who has received the law is morally free either to yield to the will of the Holy Spirit or to pursue his own carnal purposes, only the former course will lead to this special freedom, which Lehi called "liberty and eternal life"; all others, through the exercise of their agency, choose to suffer "captivity and death, according to the captivity and power of the devil." (2 Nephi 2:27.)

These themes describe Jacob's ministry as well as his boyhood. The texts available give evidence that he gained the ultimate victory of mortality: he sought no advantage for himself, but labored with all his time, energy, and devotion "for Christ's sake, and for the sake of our people." (Jacob 1:4.)

The evidence is briefly this. From the time he and Joseph were consecrated "priests and teachers" (2 Nephi 5:26) unto their people (Jacob was then about twenty-five), his desire was for the welfare of their souls. In this Melchizedek Priesthood calling (see Bruce R. McConkie, *Mormon Doctrine,* pp. 598-99), he labored under a constant, preoccupying anxiety for the people. (2 Nephi 6:3.) A quarter century later, when Nephi charged him to keep the sacred small plates, he was still driven by the same anxious charity. He wrote of that time: "We labored diligently among our people, that we might persuade them to come unto Christ. . . . And we did magnify our office unto the Lord, taking upon us the responsibility, answering the sins of the people upon our own heads if we did not teach them the word of God with all diligence." (Jacob 1:7, 19.)

In this he found delight and peace. (2 Nephi 9:49.) Moreover, he "often" spent time teaching his family "in the nurture and admonition of the Lord." (Enos 1:1. It was those remembered teachings that moved his youthful son Enos, who revered him, to pray day and night for forgiveness of sins.) Yielding to the will of the Holy Spirit rather than to the will of the flesh, Jacob became one of those rare people who are free of the unseemly and insistent motivations that drive men to do what they despise themselves for doing. This is the special sort of freedom Lehi spoke of. In the demanding bonds of Christ, Jacob lived the perfectly liberated life.

Jacob's commitment to these principles can be appreciated only in light of the three discourses that have been preserved. Indeed, one reason he is not an outstanding leader for many Book of Mormon readers is that the message of these sermons is seldom brought into focus. If their interlocking themes were to converge in a single statement, it might be this: Though Israel may reject its Holy One and be scattered in tribulation and captivity, he is mighty to deliver them because of the sacrifice he made, if they turn to him again with their hearts. And what is true of Israel as a people is also true of individuals: each can and must shake himself from his spiritually scattered condition and return, alive again, to Christ.

The first surviving sermon is the longest in scripture, three pages longer than King Benjamin's, and so long indeed that Jacob took two days in delivering it. This is the sermon that Nephi engraved on the small plates as a witness to the truth of his own teachings. The text for this sermon is drawn from Isaiah. Jacob uses it to speak of the Lord's covenants with Israel. We learn of Christ's power and desire to deliver Israel's people from captivity, to recover them from dispersion, and to redeem them from sin, and of the suffering Christ would undergo in accomplishing this. All Israel, both Zion and Jerusalem, are commanded to awake, flee uncleanness and captivity, and return to him.

The first main section (2 Nephi 9:1-26) of Jacob's commentary on this text concerns Israel's Holy One: his Palestinian ministry, his death in behalf of mankind, his power of atonement to deliver men—by resurrection and spiritual rebirth—from death and hell, and his promise to the righteous of a heavenly inheritance and joy forever.

Next (2 Nephi 9:27-54), Jacob calls to repentance those who know the truth and reject it. There is a world of difference between such unbelief and the ignorance of those who have not been given the law of God. The latter are guaranteed the benefits of the atonement. But the former, if they remain and die in their sins, have a terrible destiny. Their deafness and blindness to the truth are deliberate, hypocritical; and yet they puff themselves up in pretension of wisdom and self-sufficiency as they despise the poor and persecute the meek. Remembering their "awful guilt in perfectness" (v. 46), they will one day be smitten by the knowledge of their iniquities. They will exclaim, "I know my guilt; I transgressed thy law, and my transgressions are mine." (V. 46.) Jacob pleads with them, as an ordinary man would plead for his life, to shake off the devil's chains, confess the lie they have been living, and humbly receive the overflowing abundance of life that the Lord gives freely.

Finally (2 Nephi 10), on the following day Jacob links his counsel on how the individual may come again to Christ (an angel had told him the night before that this would be the Redeemer's name) to the theme of God's covenants with Israel. Like the Jews, the children of the Nephites would, he teaches, reject the Savior and perish in unbelief; but ultimately, according to the promises, they would be restored again to their inheritance.

The second of Jacob's surviving discourses (Jacob 1:17–3:12) was delivered in the temple while (as we have supposed) he was presiding over the Church. It is an even more exercised call than the earlier one for his people to awaken from the troubled, self-deceiving slumber of sin. Under their second king, many of the Nephite brethren were becoming mired down in two kinds of sin. First, they were obsessed with ostentatious clothing and riches (to the point of spending much time in search of precious metals). This preoccupation with acquisition and social station left them calloused to the destitute; indeed, they persecuted their humbler neighbors. Their pride, aggressive and mean, was destroying them.

Some of Jacob's most stirring teachings concerned pride, particularly the pride of riches and of learning. He thought wealth and education good, provided they are acquired and used in obedience to God and in service to others. But most men pervert these opportunities, exalting themselves, despising the humble, and afflicting the poor. Jacob's sayings on these things illustrate his gift for rich and ringing statement. (See 2 Nephi 9:28-30, 42-43; Jacob 2:12-21.)

The second and grosser sin was lust. The brethren tried to rationalize their dark desire to have many wives and concubines by supposing themselves no different from David and Solomon of old. But beneath this veneer was nothing more than a lust for whoredoms. In a revelation that is explicitly so called, the Lord denounces them: "Ye have broken the hearts of your tender wives, and lost the confidence of your children." (Jacob 2:35.) Though we are not told how many Church members had taken additional wives or concubines, we are given to understand that lust itself is abominable to God. Whether he acts upon his evil imaginings or not, a man with an unfaithful heart reduces his capacity for affection and distresses his family, for they cannot find security in a polluted love.

In their spiritual condition the Nephite men were worse than the Lamanites whom they, in their insufferable pride, despised; for the Lamanites, though indolent and filthy, were faithful to their wives and loved their families. The Lord tells the Nephites that he brought them out of Jerusalem to raise up a righteous people and would therefore not suffer them to defile their posterity in whoredoms. Whether pure-hearted men had ever been commanded to practice polygamy was irrelevant for the Nephites; their case was wholly different, for their hearts were not pure and they had been commanded to have but one wife and no concubines.

Jacob calls upon the victimized pure in heart to look to God for consolation in these afflictions, and he commands the guilty impure to "shake yourselves that ye may awake from the slumber of death." (Jacob 3:11.)

The third discourse (Jacob 4-6) was never spoken, but was written to us—indeed, to all whom Jacob hoped would read his record (Jacob 4:3; 7:27). It sheds light on Jacob to think of him slowly inscribing the characters of this lengthy document on the recalcitrant metal and addressing his audience as "my beloved brethren." Again, he is impelled by "over anxiety" for the welfare of souls—in this case, the souls of people far removed from him in time. As before, his theme is how, after rejecting the Lord, a people may return to Him and build upon the sure foundation that He provides. (Jacob 4:17.) And once more, Jacob relates the up-and-down career of Israel to the spiritual lives of individuals.

The sermon consists mainly in quoting Zenos's allegory of the olive grove. (Jacob 5.) This may be the most profound allegory in literature. It seems to hold the key for understanding the vicissitudes of God's covenant people on the earth, the principles upon which a righteous people may be established, and the Lord's intensified latter-day work of gathering and nourishing the choice branches of Israel while pruning away those branches—of Israel or otherwise—that bear bitter fruit. And besides all this, though too rich and complicated to be outlined here, the allegory enables us to feel the pains the Lord has taken for the nurturing and reclamation of Israel. What looks like punishment—the scattering of Israel as branches cut off from their main trunk and the roots whose nourishment they could not assimilate—was not punishment at all, but the Lord's devoted effort to do the one thing that could save his people. This explains an otherwise puzzling aspect of the Book of Mormon. It shows, to use but two examples, how Lehi could read of Jerusalem's destruction and its inhabitants' dispersion and, immediately thereafter, rejoice and praise God because of it. (1 Nephi 1:14.) It shows why Jacob, fully aware of the afflictions that awaited Israel, could nonetheless write, "And how merciful is our God unto us, for he remembereth the house of Israel, both roots and branches; and he stretches forth his hands unto them all the day long; and they are a stiffnecked and a gainsaying people; but as many as will not harden their hearts shall be saved in the kingdom of God." (Jacob 6:4; compare 2 Nephi 9:17-22.)

Jacob closes this sermon by once again pleading with his audience—with us this time—not to wither, not to bring forth evil fruit after we have been nourished so lovingly, not to make a mockery of the redemption or reject the revealed words that speak of it or quench the Holy Spirit that testifies of it.

After Jacob thought he had finished his record and bid his readers farewell, something occurred that brought his people a blessing for which he had long labored and prayed. It restored "peace and the love of God . . . again among the people." (Jacob 7:23.) The event was an encounter with Sherem, the anti-Christ who had seduced many into apostasy. Sherem's was an aggravated case of living a lie. Through Jacob's faith, Sherem was brought to confess the truths that he had denied. The astonished multitude was overcome and began again to live the gospel. Because it brought this blessing, Jacob was moved to add to his record the story of this event.

Jacob ends his record by handing the plates on to his son, Enos, and, with the loving hope that many of us would read it, bids us a second farewell. (Jacob 7:27.)

C. Terry Warner is a professor of philosophy at Brigham Young University.

Notes

1. Because it was about thirty years after Lehi's departure from Jerusalem that Jacob was consecrated a priest and teacher (2 Nephi 5:26, 28), he would have been between twenty-three and twenty-nine at this time. It was just twenty-five years later that he received custody of the small plates. (Jacob 1:1.)

2. Jacob was entrusted with stewardship of the Church record (Jacob 1:1), received revelations on behalf of the Church (Jacob 2:11, 23; 3:9), and was the authority of last resort sought out by a powerful enemy of the Church (Jacob 7:3).

Benjamin, the Great King

Eugene England

"What really lifts him to [the level of the world's greatest men] is the moral grandeur of his life. He lived solely for the good of his people. He is the first instance in the history of Christendom of a ruler who put aside every personal aim or ambition to devote himself wholly to the welfare of those whom he ruled."

This is historian J. R. Green's description of Alfred (A.D. 849-901), the only English king who has come to be known as "the Great." But the words are actually more appropriate to a king who lived a thousand years before Alfred, one whose deeds and concerns—in uniting his people, winning victories over their barbaric enemies, and developing their language and culture—remarkably parallel the English king's, though his prophetic power and insight go far beyond King Alfred's. His name was Benjamin, the figure in the Book of Mormon we most often mention with the title *King*. And to a degree almost beyond our imagination, he "put aside every personal aim or ambition to devote himself wholly to the welfare of those whom he ruled"—not only their temporal and social welfare, but also their eternal welfare.

King Benjamin comes into view as a great light after the

dark ages of his people. Following the great spiritual outpourings of Nephi and his brother Jacob—and even of Jacob's son Enos and his grandson Jarom—the book of Omni reveals a long period, from before 400 B.C. to after 200 B.C. when the small plates of Nephi, designed to record the religious experience of the people, are no more than an outline. The sacred record is passed from father to son for five generations, essentially without addition, until Abinadom tells us why the record is so sparse in a haunting commentary on his nation's spiritual decline: "I know of no revelation save that which has been written, neither prophecy [the last recorded was to Enos nearly 300 years before]; wherefore, that which is sufficient is written." (Omni 1:11.)

But the next record keeper, Abinadom's son Amaleki, has much more to tell us, because during his life the Lord warned the Nephite king, Mosiah I, to flee the land of Lehi-Nephi with "as many as would hearken unto the voice of the Lord" (Omni 1:12)—whether to escape the Lamanites or the decline and corruption of other Nephites is uncertain. They are led through the wilderness to Zarahemla, where they find a people more numerous than themselves—yet more barbaric and spiritually in need. It turns out that these are descendants of the people of Mulek, who fled Jerusalem when it was destroyed shortly after Lehi's departure. But because Mulek had left in such desperate haste, or perhaps because of a lack of prophetic foresight, he had brought no records—nothing like the brass plates of Laban that the Lord told Lehi to bring, which provided the Nephite civilization with a crucial source of language, literature, culture, and, most significantly, the moral and religious teachings of the prophets, especially concerning the holy Messiah who would come.

We can see here most dramatically a central theme of the Book of Mormon: records, especially scriptural records, must be kept and preserved, valued and taught from generation to generation, or a people will dwindle in unbelief—and in every other way. In a mere four hundred years without written records, the Mulekites had become warlike and contentious, their language had become corrupted so that they and the Nephites could not even understand each other, "and they denied the being of their Creator." (Omni 1:17.) But Mosiah began a marvelous work, completed by his son Benjamin, of making these separate, semibarbaric tribes into a civilized, Christian nation.

Amaleki tells of Mosiah first teaching the people of Mulek the Nephite language and then of the two groups uniting culturally and politically under his kingship. The record keeper lived to see Mosiah's death and the beginning of King Benjamin's reign, a time of "serious war and much bloodshed." (Omni 1:24.) The young King Benjamin had to repulse invading Lamanites; he led his armies personally, fighting "with the strength of his own arm, with the sword of Laban." (Words of Mormon 1:13.) Then there was a profound turning point as the vigorous fighter for freedom turned to the arts of peace.

Amaleki, having no son and "knowing king Benjamin to be a just man before man before the Lord" (Omni 1:25), turned the small plates of Nephi over to him, bringing the separate religious record to a close because now one man was both prophet and king, recording all events on the large plates. Then, for an all-too-short period of time—until the end of the reign of his son, Mosiah II—there is a great "golden age," a time when the ancient ideal is realized of uniting power and righteousness in a single leader to form a theocracy, that perfect but difficult and extremely rare form of government we have seen under Enoch, Abraham, Moses, and in modern times for a while under Brigham Young.

Over five hundred years later, when Mormon abridged and edited the Nephite records into the Book of Mormon, he included a chapter of editorial commentary—The Words of Mormon—at the end of the small plates of Nephi to explain why he had included them and to make a transition to his continued abridgment of the large plates, a secular record Nephi had started and which under Benjamin would become the religious record as well. Mormon tells how King Benjamin, having won several generations of peace from his external enemies, turned to internal problems. He established civil order, punishing false teachers "according to their crimes" (Words of Mormon 1:15) and dealing with others who caused "contention and many dissensions away unto the Lamanites." (Words of Mormon 1:16.) Then he built up a core of supporters, teachers of righteousness, "holy men [who] did speak the word of God with power and with authority. . . . Wherefore, with the help of these [holy men], king Benjamin, by laboring with all the might of his body and the faculty of his whole soul, and also the prophets, did once more establish peace in the land." (Words of Mormon 1:17-18.)

Like his father, Mosiah, Benjamin also paid great attention to language: his son Mosiah commented that Benjamin caused that his sons "should be taught in all the language of his fathers, that thereby they might become men of understanding." (Mosiah 1:2.) Benjamin forcefully explained to his sons that if God, through his prophets, had not preserved the brass plates from Jerusalem and the plates of Nephi, which contained the acts and teachings of the American prophets, "we must have suffered in ignorance, . . . not knowing the mysteries of God. . . . Even our fathers would have dwindled in unbelief, and we should have been like unto our brethren, the Lamanites." (Mosiah 1:3, 5.) He therefore commanded his sons to search the records diligently.

But the importance of language to King Benjamin and his profound, inspired skill with words are revealed best in his famous last address. Seeing that he was approaching death, Benjamin had his son Mosiah, who was to be his successor, call the people together so he could announce the succession and give a final message of transcendent importance. That sermon, given to all the citizens of Zarahemla gathered at the temple, is one of the longest and most powerful in the Book of Mormon. The very preservation of the speech itself testifies to the success of Benjamin and his father in making language an effective resource, because it was possible for King Benjamin to have the speech "written and sent forth among those that were not under the sound of his voice" (Mosiah 2:8) and then to include what is probably an abridgment in the large plates. Thus we have before us much of the speaker's own words and exact thought, which enables us to analyze the speech with attention to Benjamin's skill of organization and specific imagery and wording.

King Benjamin's language immediately establishes him as a secure, authoritative king: "I have not commanded you to come up hither to trifle with the words which I shall speak." (Mosiah 2:9.) But at the same time his words show him to be amazingly realistic and humble: "I am like as yourselves, subject to all mannner of infirmities in body and mind; yet I have been . . . kept and preserved . . . to serve you with all the might, mind and strength which the Lord hath granted unto me." (Mosiah 2:11.) He seems determined to dispel the superstitious awe that the people have had for him and his father, perhaps because if they thought he was "more than a mortal man" his own example would be useless to them. He emphasizes how much he is like them so that they must accept as relevant to *them* both the great qualities of his life and the force of his own humble message—that with all his great work he is yet in God's debt. He reminds them that he has not exploited them in any way with taxes or unjust laws and punishments, but has labored with his own hands for his support. Yet he has served them mightily. He explains this, not to boast, but to teach them the great lesson "that when ye are in the service of your fellow beings ye are only in the service of your God." (Mosiah 2:17.)

King Benjamin then uses a series of powerful rhetorical devices to touch the souls of his hearers and bring them toward the meekness and lowliness of heart essential to their acceptance of Christ. His framework is a simple but devastating argument: If I your king have served you, you should serve one another, and if I deserve any thanks, "O how you ought to thank your heavenly King!" (Mosiah 2:19.) But no matter how much you thank the Lord and try to serve him by serving each other, Benjamin tells them, you will always be profoundly in his debt. He strengthens the emotional force of this rational argument by a series of rapid parallels in verses 20 and 21. The words "I say . . . if" introduce three crescendoing statements of what we might do to repay God: "I say . . . if you should render all the thanks and praise . . . —I say . . . if ye should serve him who has created you from the beginning, and is preserving you from day to day . . . —I say, if you should serve him with all your whole souls. . . ." We read these words in increasing hope, only to be profoundly shocked at the climax with the flat announcement that no matter how much we serve him, "yet ye would be unprofitable servants." (Mosiah 2:20-21.) King Benjamin ultimately builds up to the fact that because our very lives are a gift and because when we obey him God immediately blesses us more, we are so indebted to God "and will be, forever and ever," that we "cannot say that [we] are even as much as the dust of the earth." (Mosiah 2:24-25.) And he anticipates anyone's defense that at least we are created of the dust of the earth by noting that "behold it belongeth to him who created you."

Then in a marvelous transition he begins to move from this emotional sense of our utter dependence to a consideration of our sinfulness: he combines that same image of dust with an earlier theme by reminding his people that even he, their king, whom they have thought of as more than mortal, is "also of the dust" (Mosiah 2:26) and in fact is about to return to the dust. But first he must cleanse himself of their sins by declaring repentance to them. (Mosiah 2:27-28.)

King Benjamin then carefully defines sin as a person's "having transgressed the law of God contrary to his own knowledge" (Mosiah 2:33) and reminds his people that under his leadership they have all, except their little children, been taught the law and are thus without excuse (Mosiah 2:34). He evokes just the right combination of guilt and hope in them before announcing that the resolution to their dilemma is a forthcoming Savior. Benjamin does not directly accuse anyone, but uses two general "if" propositions that leave the hearers free to look, without defensiveness, into themselves at their own individual sins and desires: "If ye should transgress and go contrary to that which has been spoken, . . . the man that doeth this, the same cometh out in open rebellion against God; . . . if that man repenteth not, [he] remaineth and dieth an enemy to God." (Mosiah 2:36-39.) At the same time he portrays first the awful fate of those who thus "withdraw [them]selves from the Spirit of the Lord," become enemies "to all righteousness," and thus lay themselves open to a final doom of "never-ending torment" (Mosiah 2:36-39), and then "the blessed and happy state of those that keep the commandments of God, . . . hold out faithful to the end," and are able to "dwell with God in a state of never-ending happiness" (Mosiah 2:41).

With this careful foundation, King Benjamin moves to his central message. He reports that an angel from God had visited him to declare "glad tidings of great joy," so that he might rejoice and declare them to his people "that they may also be filled with joy." (Mosiah 3:3-4.) King Benjamin was thus one of a long line of Book of Mormon prophets, "wise men," as Helaman calls them (Helaman 16:14), to hear directly from heavenly messengers the most glorious announcement in human history. And he gives us more extensively than we have anywhere else the actual declaration of the angel.

King Benjamin's report of the angel's message includes a full and clear statement of the nature and purpose of Christ's mission. He emphasizes what an angel who visited Nephi nearly 500 years before had called the "condescension of God" (1 Nephi 11:16)—the Lord's literal descent with us into the depths of our temporal and spiritual pain, experiencing the fullness of our earthly trial, in order to love us with a direct comprehension that would have power to redeem us. In a meaningful and dramatic statement of our Savior's incarnation, King Benjamin announces, "The time . . . is not far distant, that with power, the Lord Omnipotent . . . shall come down from heaven among the children of men, and shall dwell in a tabernacle of clay." (Mosiah 3:5.) The words emphasize the disparity between what Jesus was—"Lord Omnipotent"—and what he was willing to become—"clay"—in order to identify with us and move us to repent.

After a short review of the Lord's ministry, King Benjamin turns to the central act of the Atonement: "He shall suffer temptations, and pain of body, hunger, thirst, and fatigue, even more than man can suffer, except it be unto death; for behold, blood cometh from every pore, so great shall be his anguish for the wickedness and the abominations of his people." (Mosiah 3:7.)

The account goes on to announce the name of Jesus Christ and that of his mother, Mary. Then the angel declares the Lord's resurrection, that his blood atones for all who sinned ignorantly, and that salvation can come to "him who knoweth that he rebelleth against God" only "through repentance and faith on the Lord Jesus Christ." (Mosiah 3:8, 11-12.) And then King Benjamin gives us an astounding perspective: these people, and probably other individuals and peoples as well, could become Christians in every sense, including fully experiencing redemption, 158 years before our Redeemer's death on the cross: "The Lord God hath sent his holy prophets among all the children of men, to declare these things to every kindred, nation, and tongue, that thereby whosoever should believe that Christ should come, the same might receive remission of their sins, and rejoice with exceeding great joy, even as though he had already come among them." (Mosiah 3:13.)

Because this fact has not been available to traditional Christianity, most theories of the working of Christ's atonement have supposed that what he did literally changed the universe so that only people after that time could be saved. King Benjamin's sermon and its recorded effect on his people show us that when Christ descended from his heavenly position and lived and suffered and died in mortality, he ransomed all those who would have faith in his atonement and repent of their sins, whether they lived before or after it happened. In the words of the prophet Amulek some fifty years after Benjamin, the Lord's achievement for *all* mankind was "to bring about the bowels of mercy, which overpowereth justice, and bringeth about means unto men that they may have faith unto repentance." (Alma 34:15.)

And that is precisely what happened to King Benjamin's people when the angel's message again harrowed up their souls with a vision of their great need to accept the Savior. The angel quoted the Lord as saying, "If they be evil they are consigned to an awful view of their own guilt and abominations, which doth cause them to shrink from the presence of the Lord." (Mosiah 3:25.) The people responded by humbling themselves "to the earth" in true repentance (Mosiah 4:1), and they "received a remission of their sins, and... peace of conscience, because of the exceeding faith which they had in Jesus Christ who should come" (Mosiah 4:3). Seeing that the process of redemption had begun in them, King Benjamin responded by reviewing his message of salvation through the Savior's atonement. He taught them that by continually humbling themselves in daily meditation on God's goodness and their relative unworthiness, and by "standing steadfastly in the faith of that which is to come"—Christ's life and suffering for them—they "shall always rejoice, and be filled with the love of God, and always retain a remission of [their] sins." (Mosiah 4:11-12.)

King Benjamin then continues with a series of very specific teachings about how, after being thus saved by the Atonement, a person must continue to live a Christlike life, growing "in the knowledge of the glory of him" that created him. (Mosiah 4:12.)

First, he gives us one of the finest teachings in all scripture about the duty of parents, in which we probably hear the voice of his own personal experience as a father: "And ye will not suffer your children that they go hungry, or naked; neither will ye suffer that they transgress the laws of God, and fight and quarrel one with another, and serve the devil, who is the master of sin.... But ye will teach them to walk in the ways of truth and soberness; ye will teach them to love one another, and to serve one another." (Mosiah 4:14-15.)

Then King Benjamin conveys to us one of the most extraordinary views in all literature of the ultimate demands of Christlike love when he requires that we as individuals give of what substance we have to those who *ask* without judging what they "deserve." It is painful for us to see our own rationalizations in King Benjamin's picture of those who say of beggars and others who are needy, "The man has brought upon himself his misery; therefore I . . . will not give unto him, . . . for his punishments are just." It is even more painful to know we share their condemnation: "Whosoever doeth this the same hath great cause to repent; and except he repenteth . . . he perisheth forever." (Mosiah 4:17-18.) But King Benjamin's logic is inescapable. He goes back to his central image, that all of us, including himself, the king, are actually beggars, utterly dependent upon a generous God for all the substance we have, for our very lives, and finally for our forgiveness and joy: "And now, if God, who has created you, . . . doth grant unto you whatsoever ye ask that is right, in faith, believing that ye shall receive, O then, how ye ought to impart of the substance that ye have one to another." (Mosiah 4:21.)

Benjamin's third specific teaching reveals the humble, practical nature of his own daily life—which he has obviously kept simple and sweetly responsive to the everyday concerns and experience of his people: "And I would that ye should remember, that whosoever among you borroweth of his neighbor should return the thing that he borroweth, according as he doth agree, or else thou shalt commit sin; and perhaps thou shalt cause thy neighbor to commit sin also." (Mosiah 4:28.)

Confirmed in their repentance by these teachings, the people assure King Benjamin that they "have no more disposition to do evil, but to do good continually" (Mosiah 5:2), and that they are willing to "enter into a covenant with our God to do his will, and to be obedient to his commandments in all things" (Mosiah 5:5).

King Benjamin accepts their covenant, formalizing it by having their names recorded. (Mosiah 6:1.) Benjamin tells them that as they have taken the name of Christ upon them, they have become his adopted children, spiritually born of him and made free. (Mosiah 5:7-8.) In a beautiful last image he pleads with them to never let that name be blotted out of their hearts by transgression, but "to retain the name written always in your hearts, . . . that ye hear and know the voice by which ye shall be called, and also, the name by which he shall call you." (Mosiah 5:11-12.)

The old king lived three more years and died about 121 B.C. But with characteristic attention to practical needs, he had added to his many achievements one of the finest—and rarest—legacies a king can provide: an orderly succession to the next king. At the time of his great speech, Benjamin had given his son Mosiah "all the charges concerning the kingdom, and also had appointed priests to teach the people, that thereby they might hear and know the commandments of God, and to stir them up in remembrance of the oath which they had made." (Mosiah 6:3.)

The list of Benjamin's achievements is long and to some degree paradoxical. Though he had the power and could have had the riches of a king, he set a different example and left us our finest teachings on humility and service. Though he lived long before Jesus' coming, he left us one of the fullest, most moving accounts of the nature and power of Jesus' mission. Even while occupied with the enormous political and social tasks of uniting two different peoples and establishing a common language and culture among them, he labored humbly with his own hands to support himself, and at the same time developed great literary and theological skills, providing us with one of the world's great sermons, which contains not only great imagery and skillful oratory but also marvelous and unique insights: that in the final judgment we judge ourselves (Mosiah 3:25); that the punishment of hell is an internal torment like "a lake of fire and brimstone" (Mosiah 3:27); that service to others is the same as service to God and should be given without judging them

(Mosiah 2:17; 4:16-26); and so on. Benjamin has blessed all the generations of his own people and all modern generations who have the Book of Mormon.

King Benjamin's son Mosiah later decided—because his own sons, who had turned to missionary work among the Lamanites, did not want to take over the throne after his death (Mosiah 29:3-4)—to change the government from a monarchy to a republic. At that time he told the people, "If it were possible that you could have just men to be your kings, who would establish the laws of God, and judge this people according to his commandments, yea, if ye could have men for your kings who would do even as my father Benjamin did for this people— . . . then it would be expedient that ye should always have kings to rule over you." (Mosiah 29:13.) And almost 100 years after King Benjamin's death the great Nephite prophet Helaman taught his sons, "Remember . . . the words which king Benjamin spake unto his people; yea, remember that there is no other way nor means whereby man can be saved, only through the atoning blood of Jesus Christ, who shall come; yea, remember that he cometh to redeem the world." (Helaman 5:9.)

Obviously King Benjamin was one of those rare mortals who take upon themselves so fully the divine nature that they become direct models for Christlike living—even bringing others to know Christ himself. Probably one reason he could move his people so quickly and profoundly to a newness of being was that they actually saw in him a prototype of Jesus Christ, whose future coming he taught them about. And this may explain why the angel was sent to convey so fully and precisely to his mind what the nature and spirit of the Lord's earthly mission would be: he understood these glad tidings in such a way as to be able to teach them with such immediate effectiveness—and in language that can still, two thousand years later and in translation, leave us breathless with insight and conviction.

Because of his great leadership, held in long remembrance, King Benjamin ranks with the great rulers of history who have blessed their people with peace and civilizing influences. But because he also brought his own people to redemption and left for all men one of history's most powerful testimonies of salvation through the atoning blood of Jesus Christ, he may well be the greatest king who has ever lived.

Eugene England is an associate professor of English at Brigham Young University.

Three Kings and a Captain

Orson Scott Card

The land of Nephi was a frontier outpost of Nephite civilization during the time spanned by the latter part of the book of Omni and the book of Mosiah. From their twelfth year in the land, the colonizers were often under attack or threat of attack from the Lamanites in the neighboring land of Shemlon. This almost constant stress may have been part of the reason that this group of Nephites produced some of the greatest men—and some of the worst—in the Book of Mormon.

Two great prophets came from the colony in the land of Nephi: The martyr Abinadi denounced a wicked king and was burned to death for it. And Alma, a priest of the wicked king, recognized the truth he had heard from Abinadi's lips and led a righteous group of people out of the land into the wilderness. (See Mosiah 18:32-35.)

But the people of Nephi also had notable men for their political and military leaders. They ranged from Gideon, a sometime military leader who lived and died for the principles of righteousness, to Noah, a king who lived for his own pleasure and power, and who died at the hands of men he had led in cowardly flight. Zeniff, the first king in the Nephite colony, was the staunch and sturdy leader of his people against a treacherous enemy, while Limhi, his grandson, was a king who gave his trust even to his enemies, when they asked for it.

These four men and the people they led show us that righteousness and the love of God are the foundation of freedom and happiness.

Zeniff

The land of Nephi had been the homeland of the Nephites before they left and joined the people of Zarahemla. (See Omni 1:12-19.) After their departure the land had been occupied by Lamanites—but there were "a large number" of the Nephites who wanted to return "to possess the land of their inheritance." (Omni 1:27.)

Zeniff was in the first expedition sent to win back the former Nephite lands. He had been "sent as a spy among the Lamanites," looking for their strengths and weaknesses so that the Nephite army "might come upon them and destroy them." But as he studied the Lamanites, he "saw that which was good among them," and he "was desirous that they should not be destroyed." (Mosiah 9:1.)

So Zeniff argued with the leader of the expedition, trying to persuade him to make a treaty with the Lamanites. But the leader was "a strong and mighty man, and a stiffnecked man" (Omni 1:28), and he commanded the Nephites to kill Zeniff (Mosiah 9:2).

Perhaps Zeniff had persuaded others to his point of view, or perhaps others simply rebelled at the idea of having him killed. Whatever the reason, Zeniff was "rescued by the shedding of much blood." (Mosiah 9:2.) Most of the expedition was killed in the fight, so that only fifty souls returned to Zarahemla. (Omni 1:28.)

But Zeniff had seen the land, and he wanted to possess it. In later years he looked back on his younger self and wrote, "I [was] over-zealous to inherit the land of our fathers." (Mosiah 9:3.) But at the time many others felt as he did, and a second expedition left Zarahemla for the land of Nephi.

After many difficulties in the wilderness—caused, Zeniff

wrote, because "we were slow to remember the Lord our God" (Mosiah 9:3)—they reached the place where the first expedition had ended in disaster. This time Zeniff was able to carry out his plan to make a treaty, and with four other men he went to King Laman to see if he could "go in with my people and possess the land in peace." (Mosiah 9:5.)

Cunning and crafty King Laman agreed. Though he made a covenant with Zeniff and ordered his own people to leave the lands of Lehi-Nephi and Shilom, events revealed that Laman really planned to bring the Nephites into bondage. (See Mosiah 9:6-7, 10.) He stirred up his people to war against the Nephites, and though Zeniff and his people were able to resist successfully, they were repeatedly forced to fight to survive.

Once, when Zeniff discovered a Lamanite army about to descend on his people, he ordered that the women and children hide in the wilderness, while all the men, old and young, who could bear arms, went to battle against the Lamanites. (Mosiah 10:9.) "Putting their trust in the Lord," they fought mightily. At the end of the battle the Lamanites were driven out of the land, and Zeniff wrote, "We slew them with a great slaughter, even so many that we did not number them." (Mosiah 10:19-20.)

By this time Zeniff was an old man (Mosiah 10:10), yet his courage was undimmed, and he didn't flinch from fighting even when the odds seemed against him. But he did not seek war. Even when the Lamanites attacked he was able to view them with understanding. Though he called his enemies a "wild, and ferocious, and a blood-thirsty people" (Mosiah 10:12), Zeniff understood that their hatred of the Nephites came from the false traditions of their fathers, and he still desired to live in peace beside them. (See Mosiah 10:12-17.)

After having served his people well, always relying on the Lord to preserve them in battle, Zeniff gave up the kingship in his old age. He chose one of his sons to follow him. It is ironic that his heir, Noah, would systematically try to destroy the faith, the standards, and eventually the strength and courage of the people of Nephi—everything that Zeniff had labored all his life to build.

Noah

It is an understatement when the scripture says, "Noah . . . did not walk in the ways of his father." (Mosiah 11:1.)

After being led by Zeniff, a righteous man, the people might have been disgusted by a king who took many wives and concubines, committed whoredoms, set his heart upon wealth, spent his time in riotous living, and became a winebibber. (See Mosiah 11:2, 14-15.) But when Noah sinned, the people did not hold fast to the principles taught by Zeniff. Instead they joined King Noah in his sins, becoming idolatrous, drinking wine, and committing "whoredoms and all manner of wickedness." (Mosiah 11:2; see also 11:7, 15.)

Noah tried to create the physical signs of civilization. With the people's taxes he "built many elegant and spacious buildings; and he ornamented them with fine work of wood, and of all manner of precious things." (Mosiah 11:8.) He didn't stint on the palace or the temple either, and like many kings and government leaders in other ages of mankind, he used impressive monuments and elegant facades to persuade the people that they were a wealthy and mighty kingdom.

And the people "were deceived by the vain and flattering words of the king" and his hand-picked priests. (Mosiah 11:7.) Perhaps they relished their new "freedom" from the restraints of God's laws. Perhaps they believed that Noah had made them a great people. But if they had not allowed themselves to be blinded, they might have seen some danger signs.

When the problems with the Lamanites began, Noah "*sent* guards round about the land to keep them off"; for the major battle, Noah "*sent* his armies against them, and . . . drove them back." (Mosiah 11:17-18; italics added.) Perhaps the Nephites had forgotten that King Zeniff was not content to *send* his armies—he fought with his own arm, even in his old age. (See Mosiah 9:16; 10:10.) When his people fell,

Zeniff, with his "own hands, did help to bury their dead." (Mosiah 9:19.) But Noah did not walk in the ways of his father, and he stayed at home when the battles were fought.

When the Nephite army drove the Lamanites back "for a time" (Mosiah 11:18), they used their victory as an excuse for more pride. "They did boast in their own strength, saying that their fifty could stand against thousands of the Lamanites." (Mosiah 11:19.) In the days of Zeniff, the Nephites had remembered that their strength depended on the Lord. But under the influence of King Noah and his priests, they "did delight in blood, and the shedding of the blood of their brethren." (Mosiah 11:19.)

The people were so steeped in wickedness that when Abinadi came preaching repentance "they were wroth with him, and sought to take away his life" (Mosiah 11:26)—even before Noah heard of the prophet and ordered his capture. Instead of realizing their errors, the people sided with King Noah: "They hardened their hearts against the words of Abinadi, and they sought from that time forward to take him." (Mosiah 11:29.) And when at last Abinadi was captured, the people "carried him bound before the king" and denounced him as a traitor and a false prophet. (Mosiah 12:9.) In their pride they said, "O king, behold, we are guiltless, and thou, O king, hast not sinned. . . . We are strong, . . . and thou shalt also prosper." (Mosiah 12:14-15.)

Eventually—after Abinadi's martyrdom and Alma's departure into the wilderness—a sizable portion of the people began to rebel against King Noah. But almost to the very end Noah was able to lead at least a part of his people into actions that brought them only shame.

Despite Noah's power, which he used to get rich, to commit adultery, and to protect himself, he was weak in character. Even surrounded by his guards and his priests, he was so frightened by Abinadi's testimony that he "was about to release him, for he feared his word." (Mosiah 17:11.) Yet when his priests goaded him he reversed himself and ordered Abinadi's death.

Both Noah and his father, Zeniff, faced a massive Lamanite invasion at the end of their reigns. But the difference between them is pointed up most clearly by the ways they handled similar situations. Zeniff armed even the "old men that could bear arms, and also all [the] young men that were able to bear arms" (Mosiah 10:9), and stood himself with his armies to fight off the attack. Noah, on the other hand, "commanded the people that they should flee before the Lamanites," and instead of making sure all were safe in the retreat, Noah "himself did go before them." (Mosiah 19:9.)

Zeniff sent the women and children into the wilderness to hide while the men fought to protect them. But Noah, seeing that the Lamanites were overtaking his people, "commanded them that all the men should leave their wives and their children, and flee before the Lamanites." (Mosiah 19:11.) It is to the credit of the people that many of them "would not leave" their families, "but had rather stay and perish with them." It is to their shame that "the rest left their wives and their children and fled." (Mosiah 19:12.)

But the men who joined Noah in cowardly flight soon realized that their families and their honor were more important than their lives: "Now they [swore] in their hearts that they would return to the land of Nephi, and if their wives and their children were slain, and also those that had tarried with them, that they would seek revenge, and also perish with them." (Mosiah 19:19.)

These men might have found their courage, but Noah had not. Foolishly disregarding their resolve, he "commanded them that they should not return." At last the people felt the disgust they should have felt long before. "They were angry with the king, and caused that he should suffer, even unto death by fire." (Mosiah 19:20.) Noah learned, too late, that his power over his people lasted only as long as they were willing to follow him. When he commanded them to do something too contemptible for them to bear, they finally rebelled.

But there was another side to the story. By proving that

Noah could not make them do something they did not want to do, the people also proved that their own wickedness was not entirely King Noah's fault. He had pointed out an evil path, but they had followed him willingly. Abinadi, in his dying moments, had told King Noah, "Ye shall suffer, as I suffer, the pains of death by fire." (Mosiah 17:18.) That promise was fulfilled. But another promise remained: "Ye shall be smitten on every hand, and shall be driven and scattered to and fro, even as a wild flock is driven by wild and ferocious beasts." (Mosiah 17:17.) The people had at last rid themselves of a wicked king. But they had yet to suffer the penalty of their own sins—affliction at the hands of the Lamanites.

Limhi

When Noah ordered the Nephites to leave their families and run, many disobeyed him and stayed behind with their loved ones. Outnumbered as they were, they had to surrender, and to stop the bloodshed they sent their fair daughters to "plead with the Lamanites that they would not slay them." (Mosiah 19:13.)

Zeniff had seen much that was good among the Lamanites. His people now had a chance to see for themselves that even though they may have been "wild, and ferocious" (Mosiah 10:12), the "Lamanites had compassion on" the Nephites (Mosiah 19:15).

The Lamanites allowed the Nephites to return to their homes, but the terms of the peace treaty were harsh. The Nephites had to covenant that they would pay the king of the Lamanites half of all they possessed every year. They also had to "deliver up king Noah into the hands of the Lamanites." (Mosiah 19:14.)

One of King Noah's sons had stayed behind to defend the women and children. His name was Limhi, and he "was desirous that his father should not be destroyed" (Mosiah 19:17)—for that is probably what the Lamanites intended to do once they got Noah in their hands. But Limhi was a righteous man, and he knew that his father was wicked: the Book of Mormon does not say he refused the Lamanites' terms, and Limhi did comply with the rest of the treaty. (Mosiah 19:26.)

One wonders how a righteous man like Limhi survived to adulthood in Noah's court. What did Limhi go through as a boy, watching his father assemble a harem, promote drunkenness, squander the people's money, and corrupt the laws of the kingdom? Perhaps Limhi knew his grandfather, Zeniff, before he died. Certainly Limhi's life more closely followed his grandfather's. Perhaps he read Zeniff's own record, and learned from him that the people must depend on the Lord, and that it is the king's place to serve his people, not to profit from them.

Whatever Limhi's life had been like before, he was such a man that the people, defeated and in bondage, chose him to be their king. His reign began as he "made oath unto the king of the Lamanites that his people should pay tribute unto him, even one half of all they possessed." (Mosiah 19:26.)

Limhi ruled his people in peace for two years. But at the end of that time, the wicked priests of King Noah, who had escaped into the wilderness, kidnapped twenty-four of the "daughters of the Lamanites" when they "gathered together to dance." (Mosiah 20:5.) The Lamanites, thinking that the people of King Limhi had committed the crime, became angry, and their king led an army against the Nephites. (Mosiah 20:6-7.)

Limhi saw their preparations for war from a high watchtower that Noah had built. Even though he didn't know why the Lamanites were attacking, he gathered his people together, and they were lying in wait when the enemy arrived. (See Mosiah 20:6-9.) The battle was savage, "for they fought like lions for their prey" (Mosiah 20:10), but at the end the Nephites drove the enemy away, even though the Lamanites outnumbered them by more than two to one (see Mosiah 20:11). When the Lamanites retreated, their king was left wounded on the field.

Limhi had the Lamanite king brought before him, after his wounds had been treated, and found out from him about the kidnapping of the Lamanite girls. Limhi was a just man, and he said, "I will search among my people and whosoever has done this thing shall perish." (Mosiah 20:16.) Fortunately, however, they became convinced that the priests of King Noah had committed the crime, and the Lamanite king "was pacified towards" the Nephites. (Mosiah 20:24.)

If Limhi had accomplished a great deal in winning the trust of his enemy, the Lamanite king asked even more trust in return. He actually asked the Nephites to "go forth to meet my people, without arms, and I swear unto you with an oath that my people shall not slay thy people!" (Mosiah 20:24.)

Go unarmed to face the Lamanites! What guarantee did the Nephites have that the Lamanites, furious at the taking of their daughters, would pay any attention to their king? It probably occurred to more than one Nephite that if the Lamanite king were determined to utterly destroy the Nephites, the best possible way to accomplish it would be to have an unarmed Nephite army meet a well-armed and angry Lamanite army.

But Limhi trusted the Lamanite king as much as the Lamanite king trusted him. And Limhi's people followed their king—not into wickedness, as they had followed Noah, but into danger and possible death, all for the chance of ending the war by convincing the Lamanites that they were innocent of any crime. It wasn't a sure thing, either, for the Lamanite king, keeping his oath, had to bow down before his army and "plead in behalf of the people of Limhi." (Mosiah 20:25.)

It is hard to imagine such a diplomatic feat today. Two warlike peoples with a memory of years of bloody battles faced each other, and one of the armies did the incredible: on the strength of the promise of the enemy king, they completely disarmed themselves and threw themselves on the mercy of their enemies. And their enemies, when they saw "the people of Limhi, that they were without arms, . . . had compassion on them and were pacified towards them, and returned with their king in peace to their own land." (Mosiah 20:26.)

Limhi did not rule as a dictator. He knew what his father seems never to have realized: that if the people are determined to do something, not even a king can stop them, except by persuasion. For example, when Lamanite harassment provoked the Nephites to go to war, Limhi at first did not consent. But "they did afflict the king sorely with their complaints," until finally Limhi "granted unto them that they should do according to their desires." (Mosiah 21:6.)

The Nephites went to battle three times, and three times they were slaughtered. There "was a great mourning and lamentation among the people of Limhi." (Mosiah 21:9.) Abinadi's promise that they would be "smitten on every hand, and . . . driven" (Mosiah 17:17; see also 12:2) had been fulfilled as a direct consequence of their own pride.

But their defeats had at least one good effect: "They did humble themselves even to the dust, subjecting themselves to the yoke of bondage, submitting themselves to be smitten, and to be driven to and fro." (Mosiah 21:13.) Limhi watched his people turn to the Lord: "They did cry mightily to God; yea, even all the day long did they cry unto their God that he would deliver them out of their afflictions." (Mosiah 21:14.)

At last their prayers were answered when a group of men from Zarahemla were discovered outside the city walls. Limhi learned from their leader, Ammon, that they had been sent by the second King Mosiah to find Zeniff's people. Ammon taught King Limhi "the last words which king Benjamin had taught" (Mosiah 8:3; see Mosiah 2-5), and King Limhi "entered into a covenant with God, and also many of his people" (Mosiah 21:32).

Limhi addressed his people at the temple, telling them that the Lord had delivered them: "Therefore, lift up your heads, and rejoice, and put your trust in God." (Mosiah 7:19.) They followed an inspired plan of escape (see Alma 1:8), abandoned the land they had fought for generations to keep, "joined Mosiah's people, and became his subjects" (Mosiah 22:13).

In all of Limhi's words recorded in the Book of Mormon

there is not a hint that he was reluctant to give up his throne. His people's safety, righteousness, and happiness were more important to him, apparently, than power. When Ammon came, offering the possibility of escape from the land of Nephi and a return to Zarahemla, Limhi said, "I will rejoice; and . . . I will cause that my people shall rejoice also"—rejoice even if they became slaves to the Nephites, for almost anything was better than their current situation! (Mosiah 7:14-15.) Limhi didn't hesitate. As he had used his power wisely, for the benefit of his people, so now, for the benefit of his people, he gladly began a series of events that led to his giving up that power.

Gideon

Zeniff, Noah, and Limhi were kings. But the Book of Mormon also tells us about Gideon, a man who represented the finest among the common people. After Abinadi's martyrdom and Alma's flight into the wilderness, Gideon was one of the group that began to oppose King Noah. A strong man, "he drew his sword, and swore in his wrath that he would slay the king." (Mosiah 19:4.) He very nearly succeeded, too, but Noah fled from him to the watchtower and saw the Lamanite army approaching. "Gideon, spare me," King Noah cried, "for the Lamanites are upon us, and they will destroy us; yea, they will destroy my people." (Mosiah 19:7.) The Book of Mormon tells us that the people actually meant little to Noah (Mosiah 19:8), but apparently Gideon cared very much about their safety, and he let Noah live.

Gideon stayed with the women and children when Noah ran away. He must have been a leader of some sort, for when the Lamanites demanded that the Nephites turn over King Noah to them, it was Gideon who "sent men into the wilderness secretly, to search for the king." (Mosiah 19:18.)

The strong soldier was highly regarded: by the time of the battle in which the Lamanite king was captured, Gideon was "the king's captain." Once again his concern was for the people. When King Limhi commanded that the people be searched to find and punish those who had kidnapped the Lamanite girls, Gideon said, "I pray thee forbear, and do not search this people, and lay not this thing to their charge." (Mosiah 20:17.) He reminded the king about the priests of King Noah, and Limhi realized that the crime was undoubtedly their work.

Years later, when Ammon came to lead the people out of bondage, it was Gideon who spoke up and suggested the plan of escape. (See Mosiah 22:3-9.) He undoubtedly was among those who accepted baptism in Zarahemla when "king Limhi was desirous that he might be baptized; and all his people were desirous that they might be baptized also." (Mosiah 25:17.)

Gideon surfaces one more time, again because of his remarkable courage in defending righteousness. In his old age he was a teacher in the church of God. (Alma 1:7-8.) He met Nehor, a teacher of false doctrine, and as Nehor began to "contend with him sharply," Gideon "withstood him, admonishing him with the words of God." (Alma 1:7.) Nehor "drew his sword and began to smite" Gideon. And because Gideon was now an old man, "he was not able to withstand his blows, therefore he was slain by the sword." (Alma 1:9.)

Gideon entered history with a sword in his hand, and died by the sword as well. But always he acted in defense of righteousness, striking out against evil and on behalf of the people he loved. A righteous king found Gideon to be a steadfast, valuable servant. A wicked king found him to be his enemy. If all the people of King Noah had been as firm in righteousness as Gideon, perhaps their suffering might have been avoided.

The People

The people of the land of Nephi were righteous under good King Zeniff. But they allowed King Noah to lead them astray. It took years of suffering, much bloodshed, and virtual slavery before they finally learned the lesson the Lord had for them. Limhi lamented at their weakness: "How blind and impenetrable are the understandings of the children of men; for they will not seek wisdom, neither do they desire that she should rule over them!" (Mosiah 8:20.)

But the people learned at last. When Ammon came, Limhi reminded the people of their experiences, saying, "For behold, the Lord hath said: I will not succor my people in the day of their transgression; but I will hedge up their ways that they prosper not." (Mosiah 7:29.) And now he was able to promise them, "If ye will turn to the Lord with full purpose of heart, and put your trust in him, and serve him with all diligence of mind, . . . he will . . . deliver you out of bondage." (Mosiah 7:33.)

Orson Scott Card is a book editor at Compute! Publications Inc. in North Carolina. He is also a freelance writer.

Ammon

Robert A. Rees

The story of Ammon is one of the most dramatic and heroic in scriptural literature. From a rebellious prince, one of "the very vilest of sinners" (Mosiah 28:4), fighting against the church of God in the kingdom of his father, Mosiah, Ammon underwent a transcendent conversion and dedicated the next fourteen years of his life to a perilous and difficult mission among the Lamanites. With his brothers, Ammon was instrumental in converting thousands of Lamanites to Christ, thereby changing the course of Lamanite history. At the end of his mission, Ammon became the high priest over these same people (see Alma 30:20), who were called after him—the people of Ammon (see Alma 27:26).

There is enough in Alma's recounting of Ammon's mission to the Lamanites to suggest that he recognized that such a story, with its many examples of great faith, repentance, courage, and love, would well support the expressed purpose of the Book of Mormon: "To show unto the remnant of the House of Israel what great things the Lord hath done for their fathers; and that they may know the covenants of the Lord, that they are not cast off forever." (Title page.) How well we see the response of part of that "remnant of the

House of Israel," the Lamanites of today, to that message of welcome return to the kingdom of God, and the great blessings they have received as a result. And how well we see the good fortune of the "Jew and Gentile," who have participated in those blessings and received another powerful witness "that Jesus is the Christ, the Eternal God, manifesting himself unto all nations."(Ibid.)

Our first encounter with Ammon in the Book of Mormon finds him trying to destroy the Church. With his brothers and with Alma the Younger, he rebelled not only against the commandments of God but also against the proclamations of his father, King Mosiah, who had established a law prohibiting persecution of the believers. What is said of Alma could undoubtedly also be said of Ammon: "He became a great hinderment to the prosperity of the church of God; stealing away the hearts of the people; causing much dissension among the people; giving a chance for the enemy of God to exercise his power over them." (Mosiah 27:9.) Later, in recounting this period of their lives to his brothers, Ammon said, "Behold, we went forth even in wrath, with mighty threatenings to destroy his church." (Alma 26:18.)

Alma the Elder was so troubled by the rebellion of his son Alma that he prayed with great faith that the Lord would show him the error of his ways. In response, the Lord sent an angel, who appeared to Alma and Ammon and the rest of Mosiah's sons and spoke "with a voice of thunder" (Mosiah 27:11), causing the earth to shake beneath them. Like Paul, who had a similar experience on the road to Damascus, Ammon and his companions were astonished and frightened, for they recognized this as a demonstration of the power of God, which they had been denying. Following the angel's departure, they fell to the earth, doubtless overpowered by a realization of their perilous position before the Lord. In this state they began to repent, and the Lord, as Ammon said, "snatched us from our awful, sinful, and polluted state. . . . In his great mercy [he] hath brought us over that everlasting gulf of death and misery, even to the salvation of our souls." (Alma 26:17, 20.)

So grateful were they for being redeemed from their iniquity that Ammon, his brothers, and Alma set out to make restitution for the wrongs they had done, "zealously striving to repair all the injuries which they had done to the church, confessing all their sins, and publishing all the things which they had seen, and explaining the prophecies and the scriptures to all who desired to hear them." (Mosiah 27:35.) In spite of being persecuted and abused by nonbelievers, they "did impart much consolation to the church" (Mosiah 27:33) and brought many to a knowledge of Christ.

Not content simply to rectify the wrongs they had done among their own people, Ammon and his brothers were so grateful for the mercies of the Lord that they each declined an invitation to succeed their father as king of the land of Zarahemla. (See Alma 17:6.) They relinquished a worldly kingdom to labor in the kingdom of God, devoting their lives to preaching the gospel to the Lamanites, "for they could not bear that any human soul should perish; yea, even the very thoughts that any soul should endure endless torment did cause them to quake and tremble." (Mosiah 28:3.)

The faith, courage, and especially the love that this mission to the Lamanites required are a wonder to comprehend. Their fellow Nephites did not believe they could succeed and, in Ammon's words, "laughed [them] to scorn" for even suggesting such an idea. (Alma 26:23.) Not only that, but the Nephites also proposed to Ammon that they all take up arms and destroy the Lamanites, for they greatly feared them. (See Alma 26:24-25.) And they had good reason for that fear, for as Alma says, Ammon and his brothers "had undertaken to preach the word of God to a wild and a hardened and a ferocious people; a people who delighted in murdering the Nephites, and robbing and plundering them." (Alma 17:14.)

The Lamanites were not only hostile and hardened, but they had also lost almost all understanding of the Lord and his ways. King Lamoni, to whom Ammon first preached the gospel, didn't even have an understanding of the words *God* and *heaven*. (See Alma 18:24-32.) In fact, he mistook Ammon for "the Great Spirit." (See Alma 18:2, 4, 11.) The record further indicates that "notwithstanding they believed in a Great Spirit," their moral system was such that "they supposed that whatsoever they did was right." (Alma 18:5.) And the traditions of their fathers, Laman and Lemuel, still held sway over their beliefs. King Lamoni's father, who was king over all the land of the Lamanites, called Ammon "one of the children of a liar [Nephi]," who "robbed our fathers [evidently referring to the sacred records—compare Mosiah 10:11-17]; and now his children are also come amongst us that they may, by their cunning and their lyings, deceive us, that they again may rob us of our property." (Alma 20:10, 13.)

In the face of this deeply ingrained enmity, Ammon and his companions set out to teach the gospel to their brethren, the Lamanites. After journeying into the wilderness, and perhaps sensing for the first time the difficulty of their undertaking, they became discouraged and disheartened. Ammon said, "Our hearts were depressed, and we were about to turn back." At this moment the Lord comforted them and said, "Go amongst thy brethren, the Lamanites, and bear with patience thine afflictions, and I will give unto you success." (Alma 26:27.) Emboldened by this witness, they set out to accomplish their mission, going their separate ways into the various areas of the land inhabited by the Lamanites. Before doing so, Ammon administered to each of them, blessing them and giving them their instruction from the Lord. It is interesting to note that while Ammon apparently was not the eldest of Mosiah's sons (the kingship was first offered to Aaron; see Mosiah 29:1-3), he was "chief among them," possibly because of his great faith and leadership. (See Alma 17:18.)

Among the Lamanites they encountered many obstacles and endured great hardships. Ammon says that they "suffered every privation; . . . and we have been cast out, and mocked, and spit upon, and smote upon our cheeks; and we have been stoned, and taken and bound with strong cords, and cast into prison; . . . and we have suffered all manner of afflictions." But they endured all of this with patience "that perhaps we might be the means of saving some soul." (Alma 26:28-30.)

Of Ammon's fourteen-year sojourn among the Lamanites, Mormon chose to give us a detailed account of only one experience, Ammon's visit to the land of Ishmael. Why he chose this one out of what must have been a rich and varied record we can only surmise, but it is hard to imagine a more dramatic example of a person accomplishing great things by putting his complete trust in the Lord. Indeed, the conversion of King Lamoni and his people, which the Lord brought about through the efforts of His servant Ammon, ranks with the great stories of faith and courage in the scriptures. Ammon is like David going against Goliath, or Joseph in the court of Pharaoh; he is like Nephi going up to Jerusalem to get the brass plates: he is the man of God courageously facing seemingly insurmountable odds that he might accomplish a righteous task.

As he entered the land of Ishmael, Ammon was bound and taken before the king. When the king asked what he wanted, Ammon replied, "I desire to dwell among this people for a time; yea, and perhaps until the day I die." (Alma 17:23.) King Lamoni was so impressed with Ammon that he offered him his daughter's hand in marriage—an extraordinary turn of events when one considers that Ammon was a Nephite intruder among a people who traditionally had "an eternal hatred towards the children of Nephi." (Mosiah 10:17.) What could have prompted King Lamoni to offer to draw Ammon so close to his own family? Perhaps he recognized Ammon's royal bearing, his personal qualities, and his eagerness to serve as the attributes of an extraordinary person and one rare in any kingdom. But Ammon, having already forsaken one position of royalty, declined the offer, saying, "Nay, but I will be thy servant." (Alma 17:25.)

As a servant, Ammon was given the task of helping to watch the king's flocks and to feed his horses. When a band of Lamanite herdsmen scattered the flocks in hopes of stealing some of the strays for themselves (see Alma 18:7), Lamoni's other servants feared that the king would put them to death as he had other servants (Alma 17:28); but Ammon rejoiced, for he saw this as an opportunity to demonstrate the power of God to his "fellow-servants," thus winning their hearts and making it possible to them to believe his words (Alma 17:29). Ammon urged the other servants to find the scattered sheep and gather them together. Once the flock was contained, he told them to guard it while he went to contend with the robbers.

Again, consider Ammon's faith: alone, with only a sling and a sword, he defended the king's flocks against a sizable number of the enemy. Single-handedly he slew six with his sling and with his sword killed the enemy leader and cut off the arms of "not a few" of those who came against him with raised clubs. (See Alma 17:33-38.) Such a heroic display of courage and strength so impressed the other servants that they felt Ammon had supernatural powers and could not be slain.

King Lamoni, on hearing of Ammon's feats, said, "Surely, this is more than a man. Behold, is this not the Great Spirit?" (Alma 18:2.)

The servants, who later called Ammon "Rabbanah," meaning "powerful or great king" (Alma 18:13), replied that they did not know whether Ammon was a man or the Great Spirit but they knew that he was "a friend to the king" (Alma 18:3).

While his heroic deeds were being recounted with enthusiasm and wonder at court, Ammon was off feeding the king's horses. The king was as astonished by this faithful service as by the account of Ammon's physical prowess. "Surely," he said, "there has not been any servant among all my servants that has been so faithful as this man." (Alma 18:10.)

As Ammon had hoped, his faithfulness to the king resulted in an opportunity to teach him the gospel. Starting with the Creation, Ammon recounted to Lamoni the scriptural history from Adam to Lehi and from Lehi down to their own time. (See Alma 18:36-39.) When Ammon told Lamoni of the plan of redemption, Lamoni cried to the Lord for forgiveness and was "carried away in God" (Alma 19:6), falling to the earth as though dead. For two days Lamoni lay unconscious (see Alma 18:43; 19:1), and then, symbolic of his spiritual resurrection, he rose on the third day to exclaim, "Blessed be the name of God.... Behold, I have seen my Redeemer" (Alma 19:12-13). His joy was so full that he was again overpowered by the Spirit, and his testimony was so powerful that his wife, and Ammon, and his servants also fell to the earth overcome. While they were thus overcome, one of Lamoni's servants, Abish, who was a believer, saw her opportunity to help others "believe in the power of God." (Alma 19:17.) She ran from house to house gathering the people.

Through Abish's efforts, a "multitude" was present when Ammon and the king and his household arose and testified to the astonished and perplexed citizens of Lamoni's kingdom. They said that "their hearts had been changed; that they had no more desire to do evil" (Alma 19:33), and many believed and were converted. Thus from the powerful conversion of Lamoni, the Church was established among the Lamanites for the first time in more than four hundred years. So significant was Lamoni's conversion that it led not only to the establishment of the Church in the land of Ishmael but also, through its influence on his father, the king of the Lamanites in all the land of Nephi, to a much more widespread teaching of the gospel.

Like his son, Lamoni's father was spiritually awakened by "the generosity and the greatness of the words of... Ammon." (Alma 22:3.) Upon hearing the gospel from Ammon's brother Aaron, he said, "I will give up all that I possess, yea, I will forsake my kingdom, that I may receive this great joy." "(Alma 22:15.) When Aaron invited him to ask the Lord for forgiveness, the king prayed, "I will give away all my sins to know thee." (Alma 22:18.) Because of the king's testimony, the queen and all the household were converted, and he sent forth a proclamation throughout his land that

Ammon and his brothers were to be permitted to teach the word of God unmolested.

These events bring up an interesting point. It seems from the scriptures and also from latter-day experience that we usually find the gospel carried by the poor and humble to the poor and humble—and then to the powerful and strong, if they are to accept it at all. Ammon's experiences are all the more unique, then, because here we have a son of a king going out and converting kings and their households first, making it then possible to take the gospel to everyone—including the poor and humble. That doesn't happen often, especially in the modern world.

With the support of the Lamanite king, Ammon and his brothers and their companions were able to convert thousands of the Lamanites to the gospel. But what is more remarkable, "as many of the Lamanites as believed in their preaching, and were converted unto the Lord, never did fall away." In fact, so total was the conversion of those previously wicked and murderous Lamanites who did accept the gospel that they covenanted with the Lord that they would never again take up weapons of war, even to defend their own lives. So grateful were they for the forgiveness of their sins that they chose to suffer death, if necessary, rather than risk sinning again. (See Alma 24:5-16.) When their enemies came against them, many of these new converts were slain, but "more than a thousand" of the enemy were so moved by their faith and courage that they threw down their weapons, repented, and joined the Church. (Alma 24:27.)

The extent to which Ammon's influence on the lives of these Lamanites was recognized may be seen in the fact that shortly afterward, when they moved into the Nephites' land of Jershon, they were called "the people of Ammon." (Alma 27:26.) Because of "the pity and the exceeding love which Ammon and his brethren had" for the people of Ammon, they brought them down to the land of Zarahemla where they could be protected by the Nephites. (Alma 53:11-12.)

It is fitting that Ammon became a high priest over the Ammonites. (See Alma 30:20.) Having forsaken a throne to be a servant in the household of King Lamoni, and having declared that he desired to live among these people, "perhaps until the day I die" (Alma 17:23), Ammon continued to serve them, presumably until the day of his death. From tending the king's flocks and feeding his horses, Ammon rose to the highest position of spiritual leadership in that part of the land.

Near the end of their missionary journey Ammon and his brothers were reunited, and on one occasion Ammon summarized their experiences and rejoiced at their blessings, celebrating their great success among the Lamanites. (See Alma 26.) Ammon's expression is similar in style and tone to the hymns of Moses and Deborah in the Old Testament (see Exodus 15; Judges 5), the Magnificat in the New Testament (see Luke 1:46-55), and Nephi's "psalm" in the Book of Mormon (see 2 Nephi 4:15-35). It is an outpouring of joy and rejoicing, an extended song of praise to God.

Ammon's "glorying in the Lord" is replete with words and phrases that have a ring of recognition. Such phrases as "blessed be the name of our God," "let us sing to his praise," "let us give thanks to his holy name," "my joy is full," "I will rejoice in my God," "sing redeeming love," "we will praise him forever," "a great and marvelous work" are only some of the phrases Ammon uses that can be found repeatedly in the Book of Mormon and the Bible. Having been a serious student of the scriptures and therefore being familiar with the language of the great poet-prophets, and having learned to seek the inspiration of the Holy Ghost (see Alma 17:2-3), Ammon voices a memorable song to the Lord.

C. S. Lewis says the image we get of the great epic poets is "the picture of a venerable figure, a king, a great warrior, or a poet inspired by the Muse, seated and chanting to the harp a poem on high matters before an assembly." But Ammon's poem differs from secular poetry in that its purpose is not to celebrate his own accomplishments, but God's. Typically the epic poet made a boast of his prowess in battle or of his great deeds, but Ammon exulted in the Lord. His brother Aaron misunderstood Ammon's great rejoicing in the things they had accomplished and rebuked him: "Ammon, I fear that thy joy doth carry thee away unto boasting." (Alma 26:10.) But Ammon replied that he was not vaunting his own strength and wisdom but the Lord's: "Therefore I will not boast of myself, but I will boast of my God, for in his strength I can do all things." (Alma 26:12.) After reviewing their successes among the Lamanites and praising God for his goodness and mercy, Ammon reiterated the fact that he was glorying in the Lord: "Now if this is boasting, even so will I boast; for this is my life and my light, my joy and my salvation, and my redemption from everlasting wo. Yea, blessed is the name of my God." (Alma 26:36.)

Mormon's inclusion of this great poetic statement in the record preserved for our day is greatly appreciated when we consider the extent to which we have come to trust in our own strength and to take the glory for our own accomplishments. Too often we lose sight of the wonders and mysteries of God in the face of our technological and scientific discoveries. Ammon's hymn reminds us that we owe all to God, who alone has the power to help us overcome sin and Satan's power.

The story of Ammon speaks to those of us in Christ's kingdom today. It reminds us that repentance takes courage and sacrifice; it inspires us to share the gospel with others, no matter how hardened their hearts or how foreign their way of life; it teaches us that heroism inspired of God is possible for all of us and that with faith we can perform great miracles. The way is not easy, as Ammon continually reminds us, but the joy is unspeakable and the peace past understanding. Finally, Ammon reminds us that those who have tasted of the love of the Father and the Son should *praise* him. Again and again Ammon expressed his love to the Lord in paeans of praise and thanksgiving: "How great reason have we to rejoice" (Alma 26:1), "Let us sing to his praise, yea, let us give thanks to his holy name" (Alma 26:8), "Behold, my joy is full, yea, my heart is brim with joy, and I will rejoice in my God" (Alma 26:11), "Blessed be the name of my God" (Alma 26:36). Those of us who, like Alma and Ammon, have "felt to sing the song of redeeming love" (Alma 5:26) could well take Ammon's concluding expression as our own: "Now this is my joy, and my great thanksgiving; yea, I will give thanks unto my God forever. Amen." (Alma 26:37.)

Robert A. Rees is the assistant dean of the College of Fine Arts at the University of California at Los Angeles. He is also director of the department of the arts at the UCLA Extension Service.

Alma, Son of Alma

Jeffrey R. Holland

There are multitudes of men and women—in and out of the Church—who are struggling vainly against obstacles in their path. Many are fighting the battle of life—and losing. Indeed, there are those among us who consider themselves the vilest of sinners.

We have all known such people. We have all spoken with someone who does not think he has been forgiven—or worse, who does not think he can be forgiven.

How many broken hearts remain broken because those people feel they are beyond the pale of God's restorative power? How many bruised and battered spirits are certain that they have sunk to a depth at which the light of redeeming hope and grace will never again shine?

To these the story of the younger Alma comes like water to a parched tongue, like rest to a weary traveler. From the depths of hellish iniquity, from rebellion and destruction and utter wickedness, the younger Alma returned—and therein lies again the "miracle of forgiveness." It *is* a miracle. In fact, it is the greatest of all miracles. It is the miracle at the heart of the atonement of Jesus Christ.

Surely that is the "good news" of the gospel—that there is a way back, that there is repentance and safety and peace because of Christ's gift to us. The good news is that the nightmares—large ones, little ones, every fear and concern—can end, and a safe loving light can shine in that "dark place, until the day dawn[s]," clean and clear and gloriously bright, and "the day star arise[s] in your hearts." (2 Peter 1:19.)

That is the message all the world must hear.

The process of repenting, of course, is not an easy one. The experience of young Alma is a frightening testament of that. Wrongs must be made right, and there is no painless way to accomplish it. But it must be done, and with Alma we can all thank our Heavenly Father that it can be done. However weary or wicked we may feel, the story of the younger Alma is an open invitation to every child of God. It is the promise that, with the psalmist, we too may sing, "The Lord is my shepherd, I shall not want. . . .

"He restoreth my soul. . . .

"Yea, though I walk through the valley of the shadow of death, I will fear no evil. . . .

"Surely goodness and mercy shall follow me all the days of my life: and I will dwell in the house of the Lord for ever." (Psalm 23:1, 3-4, 6.)

The sons of strong fathers provide many of the messages given in the Book of Mormon: Nephi and Jacob, sons of Lehi, recorded almost all of the material given on the small plates of Nephi. Moroni, son of Mormon, concluded his father's work and some fourteen hundred years later delivered it to the young prophet Joseph Smith. Other sons who learned great lessons from their parents provide commentary throughout this sacred scripture.

Perhaps no son, however, captures our imagination as does the younger Alma. More pages are devoted to the span of his life and ministry than to any other person in the Book of Mormon, and the book that bears his name is nearly two-and-a-half times longer than any other in the record. He strides with prophetic power onto the great center stage of the Book of Mormon, appearing near the precise chronological midpoint of the record—five hundred years after Lehi leaves Jerusalem, five hundred years before Moroni seals up the record.

The centrality of Alma's life is not limited simply to chronology or pagination, however. The significance of his life is in the course that it took. The gospel of Christ is literally "the glad tidings . . . that he came into the world, even Jesus, to be crucified for the world, and to bear the sins of the world, and to sanctify the world, and to cleanse it from all unrighteousness; that through him all might be saved." (D&C 76:40-42.)

The life of the younger Alma portrays the gospel's beauty and reach and power perhaps more than any other in holy scripture. Such dramatic redemption and movement away from wickedness and toward the permanent joy of exaltation may not be outlined with more compelling force anywhere else. In him is symbolized the task of the whole human family, which must, as Paul commands, "leave your former way of life, . . . lay aside that old human nature which, deluded by its lusts, is sinking towards death. You must be made new in mind and spirit, and put on the new nature." (Ephesians 4:22-24, New English Bible.)

The first mention of young Alma tells us of a difficult time. (Mosiah 27:8.) We might wish to know more of the causes for such difficulties, but we are told little of his early life. Was he born in the land of Nephi? If so, was it before or after his father's conversion? Or was he born in Zarahemla, in the presence of third- and fourth-generation Christians? What training did he have? Who influenced him? What were his hopes and fears and aspirations?

We do not have the answers to these questions; but we know something went very, very wrong. Unlike most other father and son relationships noted in the Book of Mormon, the bond between the two Almas is characterized, when we first learn of it, by anguish and opposition.

The elder Alma had not been born into church activity, and had it not been for the dramatic message of Abinadi before the court of Noah, perhaps the light of the gospel would never have penetrated the darkness of his world.

But that light had come, and Alma the Elder immediately

chose to walk by it. He began to build the Church despite the threat of danger to his own life and the lives of those who followed him. With great difficulty he led his little group of followers out of the then-apostate land of Nephi and established them with the faithful body of the church in Zarahemla. (See Mosiah 23–25.) Surely only those who have paid such a price for the gospel can appreciate what deep meaning the Church has in their lives. Of course, the emotion of that commitment is often intensified when others do not recognize that same meaning or sense the same importance. So it was with the elder Alma. As he now directed the affairs of the Church in Zarahemla (see Mosiah 26:8), he found that "there were many of the rising generation that . . . did not believe the tradition of their fathers. . . . And now because of their unbelief they could not understand the word of God; and their hearts were hardened. And they would not be baptized; neither would they join the church. And they were a separate people as to their faith, and remained so ever after, even in their carnal and sinful state; for they would not call upon the Lord their God." (Mosiah 26:1, 3-4.)

This group brought great difficulty and deep heartache to the elder Alma, and he was "troubled in his spirit." (Mosiah 26:10.) He labored faithfully, however, inviting such young people to repent as he himself had done. Some did number themselves among the people of God. Others, however, "would not confess their sins and repent of their iniquity" (Mosiah 26:36), and the names of these were stricken from the records of the Church.

An ecclesiastical problem became a personal tragedy when the elder Alma found that his own son, "called Alma, after his father," was numbered among these unbelievers. (Mosiah 27:8.) Perhaps no anguish of the human spirit matches the anguish of a mother or father who fears for the soul of a child. Through this travail the elder Alma, and undoubtedly his beloved wife, waded—and waited.

We do not know how sinful the young Alma really was, but the scripture records he was "a very wicked and an idolatrous man" (Mosiah 27:8), who, with the sons of Mosiah, was "the very vilest of sinners" (Mosiah 28:4). We know he conscientiously worked at destroying the Church of God, "stealing away the hearts of the people" and causing dissension among them. (Mosiah 27:9.) He was in every way "a great hinderment to the prosperity of the church of God." (Mosiah 27:9.)

Years later, the younger Alma recounted these events in order to save his own sons from walking such a painful path: "I had rebelled against my God, and . . . had not kept his holy commandments. Yea, and I had murdered many of his children, or rather led them away unto destruction; yea, . . . so great had been my iniquities, that the very thought of coming into the presence of my God did rack my soul with inexpressible horror." (Alma 36:13-14.)

Yet Alma returned from such terrible sin and its consequences to become a noble example of faith, service, and righteousness. How did he do it? Can we do it? What can we learn?

We learn that there is majestic, undeniable power in the love and prayer of a parent. The angel who appeared to Alma and the sons of Mosiah did not come in response to any righteousness on their part, though their souls were still precious in the sight of God. He came in response to the prayers of a faithful parent.

"The Lord hath heard the prayers . . . of his servant, Alma, who is thy father," declared the angel with a voice of thunder that shook the earth, "for he has prayed with much faith concerning thee that thou mightest be brought to the knowledge of the truth; therefore, for this purpose have I come to convince thee of the power and authority of God, that the prayers of his servants might be answered according to their faith." (Mosiah 27:14.)

Parental prayer is an unfathomable source of power. Parents can never give up hoping or caring or believing. Surely they can never give up praying. At times prayer may be the only course of action remaining—but it is the most powerful of them all.

We learn that there is great power in the united faith of the priesthood. It is not only the elder Alma who prays when his son is laid helpless and insensible before him, but also the priests and, we might assume, other faithful friends and neighbors. With the support of more private prayers, the priesthood assembled and "began to fast, and to pray to the Lord their God that he would open the mouth of Alma, that he might speak, and also that his limbs might receive their strength—that the eyes of the people might be opened to see and know of the goodness and glory of God." (Mosiah 27:22.)

Here is a majestic example of Christlike love. No one in this group seems delighted that devastating recompense has finally come. No one here seems pleased to imagine the torment of this young spirit. Yet this is the young man who has despised their faith, harmed their lives, attempted to destroy the very church of God which they hold dearer than life itself. But their response is the response of the Master: "Love your enemies, bless them that curse you, do good to them that hate you, and *pray for them which despitefully use you,* and persecute you." (Matthew 5:44; italics added.) These Saints are wise enough to know that they and every other human soul are wholly dependent on the merciful gift of God's forgiveness, "for all have sinned, and come short of the glory of God." (Romans 3:23.) What we all need we cannot in good conscience or integrity deny another. So they prayed for him who had despitefully used them.

We learn that repentance is a very painful process. By his own admission Alma says he wandered "through much tribulation, repenting nigh unto death," that he was consumed with an "everlasting burning." (Mosiah 27:28.) "I was in the darkest abyss," he says. "My soul was racked with eternal torment." (Mosiah 27:29.) "My soul was harrowed up to the greatest degree and racked with all my sins. . . . I was tormented with the pains of hell. . . . The very thought of coming into the presence of my God did rack my soul with inexpressible horror." (Alma 36:12-14.)

Then this most appalling cry: "Oh, thought I, that I could be banished and become extinct both soul and body, that I might not be brought to stand in the presence of my God, to be judged of my deeds." (Alma 36:15.)

For three seemingly endless days and nights he was torn "with the pains of a damned soul" (Alma 36:16), pain so real that he was physically incapacitated and spiritually terrorized by what appeared to be his ultimate fate. No one should think that the gift of forgiveness is fully realized without significant effort on the part of the forgiven. No one should be foolish enough to sin willingly or wantonly, thinking forgiveness is easily available.

Repentance of necessity involves suffering and sorrow. Anyone who thinks otherwise has not read the life of the young Alma, nor tried to personally repent. In the process of repentance we are granted just a taste of the suffering we would endure if we failed to turn away from evil. That pain, though only momentary for the repentant, is the most bitter of cups. No man or woman should be foolish enough to think it can be sipped, even briefly, without consequence. Remember the words of the Son of God himself of those who don't repent: "Therefore I command you to repent—repent, lest I smite you by the rod of my mouth, and by my wrath, and by my anger, and your sufferings be sore—how sore you know not, how exquisite you know not, yea, how hard to bear you know not. . . . Which suffering caused myself, even God, the greatest of all, to tremble because of pain, and to bleed at every pore, and to suffer both body and spirit—and would that I might not drink the bitter cup, and shrink." (D&C 19:15, 18.)

We learn that when repentance is complete, we are born again and leave behind forever the self we once were. To me, none of the many approaches to teaching repentance falls more short than the well-intentioned suggestion that "although a nail may be removed from a wooden post, there will forever be a hole in that post."

We know that repentance (the removal of that nail, if you will) can be a very long and painful and difficult task. Unfortunately, some will never have the incentive to undertake it.

We even know that there are a very few sins for which no repentance is possible. But where repentance *is* possible and its requirements are faithfully pursued and completed, there is no "hole left in the post" for the bold reason that it is no longer the same post. It is a new post. We can start again, utterly clean, with a new will and a new way of life.

Through repentance we are changed to what Alma calls "new creatures." (Mosiah 27:26.) We are "born again; yea, born of God, changed from [our] carnal and fallen state, to a state of righteousness, being redeemed of God, becoming his sons and daughters." (Mosiah 27:25; see also 5:1-12.) Repentance and baptism allow Christ to purify our lives in the blood of the Lamb, and we are clean again. What we were, we never have to be again, for God in his mercy has promised that "he who has repented of his sins, the same is forgiven, and I, the Lord, remember them no more." (D&C 58:42.)

We learn that the teachings and testimonies of parents and other good people have an inevitable, inexorable effect. Those lessons are not lost on even the most wayward soul. Somewhere, somehow, they get recorded in the soul and may be called upon in a great moment of need.

It was in such a moment that the young Alma "remembered also to have heard my father prophesy." (Alma 36:17.) That prophecy may have been uttered in a day when Alma was taunting his father, or jeering at those who believed, or willfully denying the reality of revelation. It may have come at a time when his father assumed Alma did not care or hear or understand. Or it may have come so early in life that his father might have thought he had forgotten. We do not know when the lesson was taught. But somewhere, sometime, one or more or a dozen of those teachings had been heard and had been implanted somewhere in his heart. Now it was being called forth for the very protection it had intended to give. Like Enos, who was haunted by "the words which I had often heard my father speak" (Enos 1:3), Alma also remembered—and believed. Parents, friends, teachers—none must ever stop teaching and testifying. There will always be a great power—even latent, delayed, residual power—in the words of God we utter.

We learn above all else that Christ is the power behind all repentance. We have noted above that Alma had been touched by the teaching of his father, but it is particularly important that the prophecy he remembered was one regarding "the coming of one Jesus Christ, a Son of God, to atone for the sins of the world." (Alma 36:17.) That is the name and that is the message that every man must hear.

Alma heard it, and he cried out from the anguish of a hell that kept burning and a conscience that wouldn't heal, "O Jesus, thou Son of God, have mercy on me." (Alma 36:18.) Perhaps such a prayer, though brief, is the most significant one that can be uttered in this world. Whatever other prayers we offer, whatever other needs we have, all somehow depends on that plea: "O Jesus, thou Son of God, have mercy on me."

He is prepared to provide that mercy. He paid with his very life in order to give it. The least we can do is ask for it and be worthy of it and love it and appreciate the magnitude of its meaning. "There is none other name under heaven given among men, whereby we must be saved." (Acts 4:12.)

If Alma's may be the central *human* story in the Book of Mormon, surely Christ's is the central name to the story within the story. It is in exactly this way that the Book of Mormon testifies that Jesus is the Christ—not only in terms of theology and doctrine and precept, which are important, but also in the very power of his name, the reality of his life, and the reach of his priesthood, which are even more important.

We learn, then, that through repentance the earlier sorrow and darkness are transformed into joy and light. Calling out to Christ for salvation from the gall of bitterness and the everlasting chains of death, Alma found his pain being lifted. Replacing it were peace and new possibilities. "And oh, what joy, and what marvelous light I did behold; yea, my soul was filled with joy as exceeding as was my pain! . . . There can be nothing so exquisite and sweet as was my joy." (Alma 36:20-21.)

With that wonderful transformation comes another intriguing, even more revealing, change. This young man who was so tormented and horrified at the thought of coming back into the presence of God—who literally wished to be annihilated so he would not have to face the great Judge of the quick and the dead—now had opened to him a vision of God sitting upon his throne, and with his newly cleansed soul he cried, "My soul did long to be there." (Alma 36:22.)

Not only does our spiritual record change and our physical life become clean, but also our very desires are purified and made whole. Our will quite literally changes to receive *His* will.

We may have avoided Church attendance, the sacrament, the bishop, our parents, our worthy companions—avoided anyone we had sinned against, including God himself—but now that repentant heart longs to be with them. That is part of the joy and light of the Atonement—the "at-one-ment"—which not only binds us back to God but also brings us back to a special unity with our best natural self and our most beloved human associates.

We learn last of all that the ultimate proof of our repentance is in its permanence. (See D&C 58:43.) Its blessings should be in our memories constantly, compelling us to continue in the cause of truth and to lend our best efforts to the work of God. Alma's testimony is that from the very hour of his conversion "until now, I have labored without ceasing, that I might bring souls unto repentance; that I might bring them to taste of the exceeding joy of which I did taste; that they might also be born of God, and be filled with the Holy Ghost. . . . Because of the word which he has imparted unto me, behold, many have been born of God, and have tasted as I have tasted, and have seen eye to eye as I have seen; therefore they do know of these things of which I have spoken, as I do know; and the knowledge which I have is of God. And I have been supported under trials and troubles of every kind, yea, and in all manner of afflictions; yea, God has delivered me from prison, and from bonds, and from death; yea, and I do put my trust in him, and he will still deliver me. And I know that he will raise me up at the last day, to dwell with him in glory; yea, and I will praise him forever." (Alma 36:24, 26-28.)

And so he lived. From the depths of sin Alma repented and became a prophetic model of virtue and valor, becoming one of the greatest missionaries of any dispensation of the world. There is so much that should be said of him: his political role, his high priestly power, his missionary trials, his concern for his own sons. He saw people repent at great social and political cost. Some paid with their very lives. He met others, even anti-Christs, who would not repent, and he testified boldly against them. He saw faith as a seed that will grow if we nourish it, and he wished he were an angel that all could hear his word. He taught deep doctrines, he lived by sublime personal values, and he rejoiced in his own missionary success and the success of his brethren. But these all came after—and finally only because of—his willingness to undergo what one twentieth-century writer has called "the ordeal of change"—movement from night to day, from pain to peace, from sin to the joy of salvation—that monumental process of the soul called repentance. "O Jesus, thou Son of God, have mercy on me" is the cry that changed Alma's world forever.

Then one day he was taken home. He left to join his brethren, men like Adam, Abraham, Nephi, and Jacob. But surely he went first to seek the companionship of his Savior, who had made it all possible and so perfect. After a long and beautiful life of service, the great desire of his soul was finally granted to him: he "did long to be there" with his Master. Perhaps no personal journey gives more encouragement to you or me that peace and joy are possible, that it can—and must—be so.

Jeffrey R. Holland is president of Brigham Young University.

Encounter in Ammonihah

Francine Bennion

What is it to be blessed?

Why does our loving, powerful Father allow some innocent children and women to suffer an unjust and anguishing death?

Can man obtain God's power to control the elements and perform miracles? Can man know when and how to use that power?

In what ways do men use and misuse laws in their dealings with each other? In what ways can human civilization keep people from reality and truth? What happens to people living in a world of their own creation when they are confronted with higher realities? What are my own realities?

These questions, typical of some asked by people contemplating man's relationship with God and with other men, were also faced by Amulek and Zeezrom, two men living in Ammonihah in 82 B.C. To me, their story suggests some powerful answers.

Amulek and Zeezrom lived in a city with a diverse population. A large portion of the people were descendants of Nephi, Zoram, Sam, Jacob, Joseph, Nephi's sisters, and others who had separated themselves from the Lamanites five hundred years earlier. (2 Nephi 5:6.) Also living among the Nephites in Ammonihah in 82 B.C. were some of the people of Zarahemla—Mulekites who forty years earlier outnumbered the Nephites and could still be distinguished from them. (Omni 1:19; Mosiah 25:2, 4.) Descendants of the priests of Noah and daughters of the Lamanites were another segment of the population. (Mosiah 25:12.) It is entirely possible that full-blooded Lamanites were also in Ammonihah at this time: missionary work by the sons of Mosiah had instigated friendly relations between some Lamanites and Nephites, and Ammonihah was apparently close to the border between Nephite and Lamanite land. (See Alma 23:18. For the location of Ammonihah, see Alma 8:3, 6; 22:28; 25:2.) The diversity of peoples in Ammonihah was great enough that when Amulek introduced himself to Alma, he first identified himself by saying, "I am a Nephite." (Alma 8:20.)

When Alma came to Ammonihah to preach, apparently some of these diverse peoples were still righteous. (Alma 10:22-23.) But most of the people had abandoned the ways of God to follow leaders who were "after the order and faith of Nehor," committed to personal gain at the expense of love for fellowmen, for truth, or for God. (Alma 14:16, 18; 10:32; 11:20; 15:15.)

Nehor, who loved costly apparel and riches, had preached ten years earlier that priests and teachers should be supported by the people, and that all mankind would be saved and have eternal life without any need for obedience or repentance. (Alma 1; 15:15.) After his execution for the murder of Gideon, Nehor's followers went forth preaching false doctrine for the sake of their own riches and honor. (Alma 1:15-16.) Some of those followers, led by Amlici, fought for power over the people; and after their defeat, Amlicite survivors scattered to the wilderness in the area of Ammonihah. (Alma 2; 8:3, 6.)

Presumably for gain of personal riches and power, the people of Ammonihah planned to destroy the liberty of the Nephites. (Alma 8:17.) We are told that this same seeking for riches was evident in the life of Zeezrom (Alma 10:31-32); of

Amulek we are told that he was of "no small reputation" and had "acquired much riches."

Before Amulek met the angel and Alma, he had apparently given little attention to the things of God. When he preached with Alma to the people, he began by identifying himself in the terms they valued. He established his genealogy and then continued: "And behold, I am also a man of no small reputation among all those who know me; yea, and behold, I have many kindreds and friends, and I have also acquired much riches by the hand of my industry. Nevertheless, after all this, I never have known much of the ways of the Lord, and his mysteries and marvelous power. I said I never had known much of these things; but behold, I mistake, for I have seen much of his mysteries and his marvelous power; yea, even in the preservation of the lives of this people. Nevertheless, I did harden my heart, for I was called many times and I would not hear; therefore I knew concerning these things, yet I would not know." (Alma 10:4-6.)

For Amulek, it seems that reputation and riches had become the important realities, the things he *knew. (What are my own realities?)*

For Zeezrom also, personal gain had become the object of life and the badge of identity. With cunning and skill, he manipulated words and thereby people. His talk clouded reality rather than casting light on it. (See his confrontation with Amulek, Alma 11:26-46, wherein he twists Amulek's words in an attempt to distort his message.) Debate and argument, for him and for his people, were means not of discovering truth but of exhibiting personal skill. Indeed, truth seemed to be altogether ignored, and debate was only a matter of wits, rules, and trickery—a dangerous game with rich prizes for the winner. (*Do we see such game-playing today?)*

In such debates, neither Zeezrom nor his associates ignored the just laws established by King Mosiah ten years earlier. (See Mosiah 29.) Rather, they used and misused the laws in order to gain their riches. (*Is it easier to deceive oneself and others if it seems to be done according to law?)*

In Ammonihah, lawyers and judges were paid according to the time they spent trying "offenders." (Alma 10:32; 11:1-3.) The more offenders, the greater the gain: "They received their wages according to their employ, therefore, they did stir up the people to riotings, and all manner of disturbances and wickedness, that they might have more employ, that they might get money according to the suits which were brought before them." (Alma 11:20.)

The people, like the lawyers, knew the law and used their own interpretation of it to suit their purposes. When Alma first tried to teach them, they challenged his jurisdiction over them. They were not so interested in *what* he had to say as they were in trying to establish that he had no *right* to say it to them: "Behold, we know that thou art Alma; and we know that thou art high priest over the church which thou hast established in many parts of the land, according to your tradition; and we are not of thy church, and we do not believe in such foolish traditions. And now we know that because we are not of thy church we know that thou hast no power over us; and thou hast delivered up the judgment-seat unto Nephihah; therefore thou art not the chief judge over us." (Alma 8:11-12.)

When Alma preached in Ammonihah a second time, the people challenged the validity of his testimony because he was only one witness, and their law (based on Mosaic law) required at least two: "Who art thou? Suppose ye that we shall believe the testimony of one man, although he should preach unto us that the earth should pass away?" (Alma 9:2.)

They were not so interested in knowing whether the earth would pass away as they were in knowing whether the man who warned them did so by their own rules. And if there was a God, they would hold even him to their own understanding of rules: "Who is God, that sendeth no more authority than one man among his people, to declare unto them the truth of such great and marvelous things?" (Alma 9:6.)

Zeezrom and his people were so occupied with rules and laws of their own interpretation that they had forgotten the principles for which the rules were established—although, as Alma suggested, they *could* remember if they *would*. They dealt with absolute truth as though no such thing really existed. (See Alma 9:13-14; 10:25.) They no longer looked beyond the world of their own understanding.

Both Amulek and Zeezrom were going about their usual business in the usual way when unexpected confrontations with truth and reality took them beyond Ammonihah—and beyond themselves.

Amulek had his confrontation while "journeying to see a very near kindred": he met an angel who told him to go home and "feed a prophet of the Lord." Amulek tells us, "I obeyed the voice of the angel, and returned towards my house." (Alma 10:7-8.) He met Alma and took him to his home.

Amulek was promised, and believed, that he would be *blessed* for his obedience. The angel said of Alma, "He shall *bless* thee and thy house; and the *blessing* of the Lord shall rest upon thee and thy house." (Alma 10:7.) That Amulek believed is demonstrated by his words to Alma: "Thou wilt be a *blessing* unto me and my house." (Alma 8:20.) We are told that after eating bread at the house of Amulek, Alma *"blessed* Amulek and his house," saying, "Amulek, . . . thou art *blessed.*" (Alma 8:22, 26.) Later, Amulek testified to the people of Ammonihah, "He hath *blessed* mine house, he hath *blessed* me, and my women, and my children, and my father and my kinsfolk; yea, even all my kindred hath he *blessed,* and the *blessing* of the Lord hath rested upon us." (Alma 10:11; all italics in paragraph added.)

Amulek, this *blessed* man, thereafter lost all his possessions; he was rejected by his friends, his father, and his kindred; he was scorned, smitten, insulted, imprisoned, bitten, spat upon, stripped naked, and given no food or water for many days. These experiences are not what we generally think of as blessings. In what ways was Amulek blessed?

To me, it is blessed to be free of bondage to possessions and peer pressures, to food and comfort.

To me, it is blessed to know truth, to be free from the limitations of ignorance and false perception.

To me, it is blessed to receive power from God, and direction from the Spirit in using it. Amulek received this power and direction after developing enough faith to consecrate himself and all that he had to God's work.

To me, it seems more blessed to temporarily lose friends or family, even by fiery anguish, than to give them a lifetime of deceptive comfort and possibly lose them in eternity.

To me, it is blessed to love as Amulek loved. He loved his neighbors, his kin, and the people of Ammonihah enough to preach repentance to them, even though he knew many would reject him. He loved God enough to trust him. He loved Zeezrom, who helped cause his suffering and loss, enough to go to him immediately when he was asked to help cure him. He loved himself enough to commit himself and all that he possessed to the ways of God.

I find Amulek's blessings great, but not easily come by. They involved effort and sacrifice and pain. So did the Savior's. And so do ours.

In contemplating the general experience of Amulek, I am stirred by an understanding of other blessings. To me, it is blessed to know a just God who does not intervene every time evil men choose to inflict suffering, so that men can be judged for what they are, not for what they might have become if God hadn't intervened. Without freedom to be evil, or to be hurt by evil, there would be no freedom (see D&C 93:30); man would be a mere puppet with no identity—a piano to be played upon by God, in the words of my children. (I find it enlightening to read Mosiah 12:17; 13:1-7; 17:1, 13, 20, and then Alma 8:31; 9:32-34; 14:13, asking, "When does God intervene to prevent evil men from hurting the righteous?")

Furthermore, I think we are mistaken when we speak of health and wealth and success as unquestionable blessings. For me, the real blessing lies in what we become from our experiences: health or sickness, wealth or poverty, success or failure can bless us. Of course, most of us would prefer to be blessed by health and wealth and success—it usually *seems* easier that way. But Amulek, hearing reality and truth in the gospel, abandoned the many attractions of "success" and called himself blessed in losing wealth and security to serve man and God. I love Amulek for his commitment to truth in the face of many kinds of personal human pain.

When Amulek began to preach to the people, he was challenged by Zeezrom, one of Ammonihah's most expert lawyers. (Alma 10:31.) Zeezrom, deaf to Alma's call to repentance, saw in Amulek an adversary to be used for personal gain. He underestimated Amulek, however, and mistook his true adversary. (See Alma 12:3-6.)

In many ways, the two men came from a common cultural background, one in which riches, success, skill, and wit were very important. Each in the past had neglected the things of God. Each was aware of his observers. Each was debating for what he perceived to be the highest of rewards.

Although the two were well matched in ability and intensity, their resources were different. Zeezrom used a bag of tricks: traps and snares, premature commitments, leading questions, suppositions, omissions, subtly perverted quotes, semantic contradictions, calculated appeals to observers' emotions. But Amulek responded to trickery with truth. He carefully gave answers that prevented the use Zeezrom intended to make of them—answers that taught his listeners those principles which Amulek wanted to teach them.

The debate ended when Amulek spoke of the resurrection and that final judgment when a man's guilt will be evident both to himself and to God. Zeezrom, accustomed to deceit and pretense and to living by appearances, was convinced that both Amulek and God knew his very thoughts. He could no longer deceive even himself, and he trembled with a knowledge of his guilt.

Unlike Ananias and Sapphira in Jerusalem a century later (see Acts 5), Zeezrom was not rendered lifeless by that knowledge. Neither did he join those neighbors who turned their guilt to anger against their accusers. Instead he repented. He inquired diligently, he confessed, and then he pled with the wicked for the sake of Alma and Amulek and their new converts. But Zeezrom learned he had helped to create a monster he could no longer control—his society: "And they spit upon him, and cast him out from among them, and also all those who believed in the words which had been spoken by Alma and Amulek; and they cast them out, and sent men to cast stones at them. And they brought their wives and children together, and whosoever believed or had been taught to believe in the word of God they caused that they should be cast into the fire; and they also brought forth their records which contained the holy scriptures, and cast them into the fire also, that they might be burned and destroyed by fire. And it came to pass that they took Alma and Amulek, and carried them forth to the place of martyrdom, that they might witness the destruction of those who were consumed by fire." (Alma 14:7-9.)

Like Amulek, Zeezrom became a new man. Unlike Amulek, however, Zeezrom was so harrowed up by his guilt that he became very ill. Cast out from Ammonihah, he lay at Sidom scorched with a burning fever, "his mind . . . exceedingly sore because of his iniquities." (Alma 15:3-5.) He believed in the Redeemer and his atonement and in all the words of Alma and Amulek. (Alma 15:6-9.) He knew that the Savior could heal and redeem him. In faith he sent for Alma and Amulek, who had the authority to heal in the name of Christ. Upon receiving an immediate healing from the Lord, Zeezrom leapt to his feet and walked. After his rebirth was furthered by baptism, he began to preach to the people.

Led by the Holy Spirit, Amulek and Zeezrom had abandoned wealth and pride to become "humble, meek, submissive, patient, full of love and all long-suffering." (Alma 13:28.) And their conversions were not short-lived: we read of their preaching to the Zoramites eight years later, and Amulek's words to Zeezrom were still being quoted by Nephite leaders fifty-two years after they were spoken in Ammonihah. (See Alma 31:6 and Helaman 5:10.)

These were not perfect men. But Amulek and Zeezrom, at great cost, made the changes in their lives to which baptism entitles us all. In our present time of profane "realities," I pray that we will, like them, escape our Ammonihahs.

Francine Bennion is a homemaker and a part-time instructor at Brigham Young University.

King Lamoni

Lenet H. Read

It is recorded in 2 Samuel, chapter 23, that the last words of King David as a psalmist, given to him by God, were these: "He that ruleth over men must be just, ruling in the fear of God. And he shall be as the light of the morning, when the sun riseth, even a morning without clouds; as the tender grass springing out of the earth by clear shining after rain." (2 Samuel 23:3-4.)

That beautiful tribute could easily be given to the Lamanite king Lamoni, a descendant of Ishmael and king over the land of Ishmael, a Lamanite territory. (See Alma 17:21.) Lamoni had been raised in the darkness of the Lamanite tradition, but his life was to change immensely the day Ammon, one of the sons of Mosiah, crossed the borders into his land.

It was the custom of the Lamanites in the land of Ishmael to bind all Nephites who trespassed into their lands and carry them before the king to be imprisoned, cast out, or even slain, according to the king's desire. (See Alma 17:20.) But when Ammon was brought bound before him, King Lamoni did none of these things to Ammon; instead, he gave him an opportunity to explain his intentions. In doing so, Ammon was either extremely impressive or King Lamoni possessed much basic goodness, or both—or perhaps Lamoni had learned that Ammon was the son of a kind and saw the possibility of some kind of political opportunity. In any event, upon hearing of Ammon's desire to dwell for a time within the land, Lamoni was very pleased and granted him that privilege. Not only that, but he also offered him one of his daughters to be a wife. (See Alma 17:22-24.)

In spite of these acts of generosity to Ammon, we learn that Lamoni had not always hesitated in the past to misuse his powers as king. For after thieving Lamanites scattered the king's flocks, those servants responsible for his flocks feared exceedingly for their lives, and with just cause. King Lamoni had previously slain those who failed in that stewardship. (See Alma 17:28.) But when the servants returned to inform King Lamoni of all that Ammon had done in defense of his flocks at the watering place, he was "astonished exceedingly." (Alma 18:2.) From this reaction and from subsequent actions by Lamoni, we discover a number of things about the character of this remarkable king. We find him to be an individual of basic faith within his own traditions, for we see that he did believe in the tradition of a "Great Spirit," which had been taught by his fathers, and he wondered if Ammon was that Great Spirit. (See Alma 18:2, 5, 11.) We also find him receptive to the first small shafts of light that began to penetrate the Lamanite traditions. For although the Lamanite belief in the Great Spirit seems to have required righteous action only to the extent that "they supposed that whatsoever they did was right," Lamoni began to fear, and his conscience began to wrestle with good and evil—specifically regarding the slaying of servants who had failed to protect his sheep.

The scriptures indicate that Lamoni was so unsettled by the events surrounding Ammon's defense of his flocks that he dared not even call Ammon into his presence. (See Alma 18:11.) However, that fear was not jealous fear that his power was somehow threatened, but righteous fear that his own actions had been unworthy—certainly a mark of justice in his character.

To appreciate more fully Lamoni's reaction, it might be helpful to contrast it with that of King Saul when David's great feats were lauded before him. Saul's major reaction *was* one of jealousy, seeing David's greatness as a threat to his own power and glory and brooding upon that jealousy until he sought over and over again to take David's life. The thought that came to dominate Saul was: ". . . and what can he have more but the kingdom?" (1 Samuel 18:8.)

Yet we see none of this kind of jealousy in Lamoni. When he was told that this Ammon who had demonstrated such power over the king's enemies was at that moment preparing the king's horses as commanded, he was pleased. It seems really to be a matter of righteousness responding to righteousness. He marveled that one of such power would also serve faithfully in a lowly task. (See Alma 18:8-10.)

When Ammon appeared on his own before Lamoni, there was a great change in Lamoni's countenance, and he was unable to speak in Ammon's presence. At length when Ammon perceived the king's thoughts and spoke of the cause of his awe, Lamoni's amazement grew even more until it broke forth in an abrupt question: "Who art thou? Art thou that Great Spirit, who knows all things?" (Alma 18:18.)

Ammon's reply to the contrary does not seem to generate much emotion one way or another, but only central driving questions: "How knowest thou the thoughts of my heart? . . . Tell me by what power ye slew and smote . . . my brethren that scattered my flocks." (Alma 18:20.) Again, Lamoni's motivation seems to be governed not by jealousy or covetousness, nor by fear at this point, but by one simple great desire: to know the truth. And because Lamoni's mind was apparently free of selfishness, jealousy, and covetousness and was filled with a desire for truth, he received that truth in all its beauty and power. When Ammon said to Lamoni, "Wilt thou hearken unto my words, if I tell thee by what power I do these things?" Lamoni replied, "Yea, I will believe all thy words." (Alma 18:22-23.)

Ammon then proceeded to expound the gospel to him—

the identity of God, the Creation, the Nephite-Lamanite history, the doctrine of Christ, and so on. Lamoni's response was, "I believe all these things which thou hast spoken." (Alma 18:33.) This is obviously sincere belief, not hasty or false words elicited by force or trickery.

Again, we must recognize Lamoni's readiness to believe as a remarkable quality of greatness. Much of what Ammon said must have been hard for him to hear. It was counter to everything the Lamanites had been taught to believe. Especially when Ammon "rehearsed unto them concerning the rebellions of Laman and Lemuel, and the sons of Ishmael, yea, all their rebellions did he relate unto them" (Alma 18:38)—that was certainly not the kind of thing anyone would want to hear or believe about his fathers. And this version of past history came from a Nephite. The traditional teachings handed down by Lamoni's fathers had been that Nephi had usurped the place of honor belonging to the older sons of Lehi, and thereby the right and power to rule over the people. (See Mosiah 10:12-17.) We realize how much hatred toward the Nephites this tradition had engendered among the Lamanites, and we also get some idea of how strongly these ideas must have been urged upon Lamoni, when we later hear his father say, "Whither art thou going with this Nephite [Ammon], who is one of the children of a liar? . . . Behold, he [Nephi] robbed our fathers; and now his children are also come amongst us that they may, by their cunning and their lyings, deceive us, that they again may rob us of our property." (Alma 20:10, 13.) Yet Lamoni chose to listen to Ammon, and after all of Ammon's teachings it is recorded that Lamoni "believed all his words." (Alma 18:40.)

In addition to the fact that Ammon's teachings must have been hard for the ordinary Lamanite to forthrightly accept, remember too that it is not usually the way of kings to humble themselves before others to a state of teachableness. It is true that Ammon had just demonstrated remarkable powers. But we would greatly underestimate Lamoni's character if we were to believe that his conversion was attributable only to that demonstration of power. Actually, power in others has traditionally been construed by rulers as a threat to their own powers. Pharaoh beheld Moses' power, and the Sadducees knew of Christ's miracles; yet selfishness and jealousy in both instances vanquished humility and belief. And consider again the case of Saul when he beheld David's growing power: "*And Saul saw and knew that the Lord was with David.* . . . And Saul was yet the more afraid of David; and Saul became David's enemy continually." (1 Samuel 18:28-29; italics added.) Thus Lamoni's humility and belief are doubly noteworthy.

Because of Lamoni's faith and acceptance of the truth, he was blessed with a special and powerful spiritual experience. When Ammon finished teaching him, Lamoni began to cry to the Lord for mercy, for himself and for his people. Then he "fell unto the earth, as if he were dead" (Alma 18:42) and remained that way for three days. Some of his household were convinced that he *was* dead.

Ammon, however, understood that King Lamoni was not dead, but that he was "under the power of God; he knew that the dark veil of unbelief was being cast away from his mind, and the light . . . had infused such joy into his soul . . . that this had overcome his natural frame, and he was carried away in God." (Alma 19:6.)

If any of us can recall the joy we have felt when just a small portion of darkness regarding a simple principle has been replaced by light and understanding, perhaps we can begin to sense the vast joy that became Lamoni's as the burden of darkness and ignorance gave way to great and beautiful light. Particularly we must be sensitive to the joyful transition from belief in a vague "Great Spirit," with an indeterminate effect on people's everyday lives, to a knowledge of the glory and goodness of the true and living God, who created man in his image, suffered with and sustained him through all tribulation, and would offer his Son to redeem him, then promise him all that is promised in eternal life. There was indeed cause to be overcome with joy.

But there was more to the experience than even that. We learn from Lamoni himself upon his arising that he had been active while "carried away in God": "As sure as thou livest, behold, I have seen my Redeemer; and he shall come forth, and be born of a woman, and he shall redeem all mankind who believe on his name." (Alma 19:13.)

This whole experience seems to fall into a pattern that may be recognized elsewhere in the scriptures. Consider, for example, the blindness of the New Testament Saul on the way to Damascus. Why was he stricken blind for a period of three days, his vision restored only after Ananias came to him? Was the Lord merely punishing him? Was there no larger purpose in his blindness? Did not Paul suffer physical blindness that gave way under priesthood blessing to sight as a memorable physical witness that he was undergoing the great change from *spiritual* blindness to *spiritual* sight? "Receive thy sight," his blessing reads, "and be filled with the Holy Ghost. And immediately there fell from his eyes as it had been scales: and he received sight forthwith, and arose, and was baptized." (Acts 9:17-18; see also Acts 9:8-16.)

Consider also the younger Alma's experience with the angel, which occurred not long before Ammon's encounter with King Lamoni. After the angel commanded Alma and his companions (one of which was Ammon) to cease their work of destroying the Church, Alma fell to the earth in astonishment and became so weak that he could not move, nor could he speak. (See Mosiah 27:11-19.) But after three days and three nights, he arose and declared that he had been "born of the Spirit," just as all people must be "born again; yea, born of God, changed from their carnal and fallen state, to a state of righteousness." (Mosiah 27:24-25.) Similarly, the subsequent "deaths" and then reawakenings of Lamoni and later his wife and servants, Ammon, and others may be seen as manifestations or witnesses of the rising from spiritual death to spiritual life. It may very well be that there is purposeful witness in these events, just as there was purposeful witness in Jonah's three days of "death" in the belly of the fish and his subsequent "resurrection." (Matthew 12:40.) Ultimately, all these events testify of Christ's atoning death and resurrection, the forerunner of the resurrection and spiritual salvation of all men. Bringing life out of death was what Christ's coming was to be all about. The hope and belief in that coming and its promise had been previously lost to the Lamanites.

It is significant that after the "death" and reawakening experiences recorded in Alma 18 and 19, the lives of those involved underwent fundamental changes that were *lasting,* making these "power of God" acts of much more worth than mere signs. It is beautifully recorded that as a part of their "new life" they arose declaring "that their hearts had been changed; that they had no more desire to do evil." Having "seen angels and . . . conversed with them," they went forward and "became a righteous people, and they did establish a church among them." (Alma 19:33-35.)

After his conversion, Lamoni's faith did not dwindle in passivity, but flourished through activity. His immediate desire was to take Ammon and the light he had come to know to his father, who was king over all the Lamanites. However, Ammon convinced him that the Lord's will was that he should go instead to the aid of his "brother and brethren" who were imprisoned in another part of the land. Without hesitation, Lamoni prepared to go with Ammon to help him with the task the Lord had given him. (See Alma 20:1-7.)

It was on the resulting journey that Lamoni and Ammon happened to cross paths with Lamoni's father. Here we witness the full fury of the traditional Lamanite bitterness against the Nephites, referred to before. Ammon is called a child of a liar, a descendant of robbers, come in cunning and deceit to rob the Lamanites. (See Alma 20:8-13.)

The vise in which Lamoni finds himself at this point is surely torturous. Perhaps he had an instinctive desire to be obedient to his father, or perhaps he was simply afraid, for he "feared to offend him." (Alma 20:11.) And then consider the agony that must have been his to see his father's hatred and to hear his father command him to slay Ammon! Perhaps we can better comprehend the emotional stress this would cause if we recall the similar dilemma confronting Jonathan, who had come to love the soul of David "as his own soul" (1 Samuel 18:3), only to hear his father, Saul, command him to slay his friend. (See 1 Samuel 19:1; also 20:31-32.) In the face of his father's fury, Lamoni was not cowed, but stood boldly, refusing to obey his father's commands and bearing his testimony—not defiantly, because he loved his father, but steadfastly: "I will not slay Ammon, neither will I return to the land of Ishmael, but I go to the land of Middoni that I may release the brethren of Ammon, for I know that they are just men and holy prophets of the true God." (Alma 20:15.)

Lamoni must have anticipated the possibility of the rage his father then felt, and indeed the sword of the father did turn upon the son. And it was only through the intervention of Ammon's power that Lamoni was saved and his father humbled.

Lamoni's father was "astonished exceedingly" at Ammon's love for Lamoni. Because of the capacity to love, both in Ammon and Lamoni, great righteousness came to pass. Ammon had come to bring light to a dark land. His fate would have been the same as that of his brethren in the land of Middoni had it not been for the goodness of Lamoni. At the same time, Lamoni became the vessel through which Ammon could bring the gospel to other Lamanites. Because of Lamoni's influence as king over the land of Ishmael, and because of his father's backing, Ammon's brothers were freed from prison in Middoni. (See Alma 20:28-30.) The gospel was preached to the assembled people of the land of Ishmael. Synagogues were built. Lamoni rejoiced in love over his people, personally teaching them and freeing them from all oppression. In righteousness, Lamoni did not force his new faith upon his people, but taught those who would listen and made them free that they might worship "according to their desires." (Alma 21:18-23.)

Finally the influence of Lamoni's faith extended even to

his father, who exclaimed at the time of his conversion: "Behold, . . . I will give up all that I possess, yea, I will forsake my kingdom, that I may receive this great joy." (Alma 22:15.) This conversion truly opened all the Lamanite lands to preaching. The darkness which had lain upon the Lamanites was rent—and it had all begun with the conversion of one man: King Lamoni. So great was the influence of the Spirit that there began a period of righteousness among the Lamanites for which there would be few equals.

Since it is true that when the wicked rule the people mourn, it is also true that when the righteous rule the people have cause to rejoice. (See Proverbs 29:2.) The value of a great leader and his influence for righteousness upon his people cannot be overemphasized: "He that ruleth over men must be just, ruling in the fear of God. And he shall be as the light of the morning, when the sun riseth, even a morning without clouds; as the tender grass springing out of the earth by clear shining after rain." (2 Samuel 23:3-4.)

Exactly how does Lamoni measure up to those qualities of leadership proclaimed by God through David? Surely his justness and his eager inclination to rule "in the fear of God" are demonstrated by his willingness and ability to "hear" the words of Ammon and then to humble himself and let those words work a change in his life. And after he believed and then sought to help bring the dawn of light to a land and a people long shrouded in darkness, he truly became "as the light of the morning," reigning in the brightness of that light without any clouds to cast shadows of darkness. And after the powerful earthly experience of "death" and reawakening, after having seen his Redeemer and arising "with no more desire to do evil," his state of innocence had to be exceptional. Could any words better describe that kind of innocence than "tender grass springing out of the earth by clear shining after rain"?

Our Lord, Jesus Christ, is, of course, the archetype of the righteous ruler sung of by David; and there is clear evidence in the Book of Mormon that Lamoni grew toward that pattern. His growth reaffirms the faith of every true believer that it *is* possible to achieve a "measure of the stature of the fulness of Christ." (Ephesians 4:13.)

Lenet Hadley Read is a homemaker residing in Gainesville, Florida.

Dissent and Treason

Orson Scott Card

If there had been no traitors among the Nephites during the reign of the judges, the Nephite nation might possibly have been at peace with the Lamanites. Though that's only speculation, one piece of evidence points to it: in the case of each of the nine separate groups of the dissenters during the first ninety-five years of the reign of the judges, their dissent either worked to the advantage of attacking Lamanites or—and this was more usual—the dissenters actively called on or incited the Lamanites to attack the Nephite nation.

In fact, there is no record of the Lamanites ever going to war against the Nephites during this period *except* when they were either incited or led—or both—by Nephite dissenters!

And yet, despite the great danger that these dissenters who turned traitors posed to the Nephites, the righteous majority (while there still was a righteous majority) never broke or bent the law in order to curb the dissenters' freedom. Even when it seemed that the majority vote might go against the righteous—even at the risk of losing everything—they committed themselves to following the will of the majority. For ninety-five years, the majority chose righteously.

The Amlicite Rebellion

Only five years after the judges replaced kings in ruling the Nephites, Amlici, a "cunning man, yea, a wise man as to the wisdom of the world" (Alma 2:1), flattered enough Nephites into wanting him to be their king that he posed a real threat. The people of the church were alarmed, because "according to their law . . . such things must be established by the voice of the people. Therefore, if it were possible that Amlici should gain the voice of the people, he, being a wicked man, would deprive them of their rights and privileges of the church; for it was his intent to destroy the church of God." (Alma 2:3-4.)

But the vote was held. The people gathered and disputed the question and then "did assemble themselves together to cast in their voices concerning the matter; and they were laid before the judges." (Alma 2:6.) Apparently the voting was by voice rather than secret ballot. Whatever the method, the vote went against Amlici. (Alma 2:7.)

But Amlici's followers decided to ignore the majority's vote, and they banded together and declared Amlici king—completely illegally. (Alma 2:9.) One of Amlici's first acts was to command his followers to take up arms against the rest of the Nephites, in order to impose his will on them. (Alma 2:10.)

Alma the younger, who was at that time chief judge over the Nephites, commanded the army that defeated Amlici's insurrection and pursued the rebels to the borders of the land. Spies were sent to see what the Amlicite army was doing—and the report came back: the Amlicites had joined with a large Lamanite force and were harrying the Nephites "in the land of Minon, above the land of Zarahemla." (Alma 2:24.) Guided and strengthened by the Lord, the Nephites fought and overcame a vastly larger (Alma 2:27, 35) Lamanite army. Alma fought with Amlici face to face, and after calling on the Lord for strength, "he was strengthened, insomuch that he slew Amlici with the sword." (Alma 2:31.)

The Zoramite Rebellion

The Zoramites, who lived in a strategically important land, Antionum, apostatized from the Church and at the same time separated themselves from the Nephite nation. (Alma 30:59; 31:1, 3.) Fearing the Zoramites might ally themselves with the Lamanites, a potentially dangerous situation, the Nephites did *not* send an army. Instead, they sent missionaries! Of course, the missionaries' concern was saving souls, but that had a nice side effect: "As the preaching of the word had a great tendency to lead the people to do that which was just—yea, it had had more powerful effect upon the minds of the people than the sword, or anything else, which had happened unto them—therefore Alma thought it was expedient that they should try the virtue of the word of God." (Alma 31:5.)

The poor were very receptive to the preaching of Alma, Amulek, Zeezrom, and three of the sons of Mosiah. The mission failed, however, with the proud, wealthy class of Zoramites, whose Rameumptom, or holy stand, epitomizes self-righteousness and hypocrisy in worship. The wealthy Zoramites "were angry because of the word, for it did destroy their craft." (Alma 35:3.) The Zoramite leaders found out who in their land supported Alma's teachings—and then cast them out of Antionum! The people of Ammon, converted Lamanites who lived in the neighboring land of Jershon, received all the refugees, who were mostly poor, it seems, and gave them food and clothing—and "lands for their inheritance." (Alma 35:9.)

The chief ruler of the Zoramites sent a message to the righteous Lamanites demanding that they should cast the refugees out of their land—and accompanied his demand with threats. (Alma 35:8-9.) When the people of Ammon refused, the Zoramites began to mix with the unconverted Lamanites and prepare for war. (Alma 35:10-11.)

In the ensuing battle, Captain Moroni commanded the Nephite armies in war for the first time. He introduced the first known example of military strategy in the Book of

Mormon as he entrapped and surrounded the Lamanite-Zoramite army. Moroni also introduced body armor into Nephite warfare for the first time. Yet despite the superiority of Moroni's tactics and equipment, he still relied on the Lord: after the Lamanites' initial retreat, Moroni sent messengers to the prophet Alma for guidance, and the Lord told Alma "that the armies of the Lamanites were marching round about in the wilderness, that they might come over into the land of Manti." (Alma 43:24; see whole chapter.) Moroni left part of his army as a rearguard and took the rest of his army to Manti, calling on all the people in that area to arm themselves and join in the defense. (Alma 43:25-26.)

Through strategy Moroni's troops surrounded the Lamanite army; and partly because of the advantage gained through their use of armor, the Nephites caused great damage to their enemies. But the Lamanite leader, Zerahemnah, had placed Nephite dissenters in charge of his forces—Zoramites, Amalekites, and Amulonites (descendants of the priests of Noah)—and inspired by these Nephite-hating Nephites, the Lamanites "did fight like dragons" (Alma 43:44), and the Nephites almost broke. This time, however, Moroni proved himself to be not only a great strategist, but also an inspiring leader of men: he rallied the Nephites, and they fought the Lamanites back to encircle them on the banks of the river Sidon. (Alma 43:48, 52.)

When it was clear that the Lamanites had lost the battle, Moroni ordered the battle to stop, and he offered peace if the Lamanites would all covenant not to take up arms against the Nephites again. (Alma 43:54; 44:1-7.) Though some of Zerahemnah's men made the covenant (Alma 44:15), Zerahemnah refused. The battle was rejoined, and the slaughter continued until at last Zerahemnah was forced to capitulate. So many were killed that the bodies were cast into the river Sidon, just as had been done after the battle with the Amlicites.

After their first defeat, however, the Zoramites did not disappear from history. They kept turning up, along with the

Amalekites and Amulonites, as the most savage fighters against the Nephites. Amalickiah used those Nephite dissenters as spies because they had recently left Nephite lands (Alma 47:36); Jacob, a particularly determined captain of the Lamanite army in a later invasion, was described as "a Zoramite, and having an unconquerable spirit" (Alma 52:33). Even as late as A.D. 3-5, Zoramites were leading away the younger generation of Lamanites converted in a great mission by Nephi and Lehi, persuading them to join the Gadianton robbers. (3 Nephi 1:29.) All in all, the Zoramites built up a tragic record of rebellion, treason, and subterfuge against the Nephite nation and the Church of God.

Amalickiah's Rebellion

Amalickiah became a leader of dissenters from the Church after Alma's departure from the land, only a year after the defeat of the Zoramites. Some of the Nephites began to want a king—and Amalickiah declared himself a willing candidate for the job! (Alma 46:1-4.) Amalickiah wooed away many even in the Church by promising them they would be rulers under him, and support for him became so great that the Nephites were in a very precarious position, despite their recent victory over the Lamanites. (Alma 46:5-10.)

Moroni, loving freedom, immediately took action—but *not* military action. Instead, he raised the famous title of liberty and rallied the freedom-loving Nephites to his cause. Soon it became clear to Amalickiah that he and his supporters were outnumbered, and he led off those of his followers who would come with him, and went to join with the Lamanites. (Alma 46:11-29.) Once again, dissent had turned into treason.

Then, and only then, did Moroni take military action. He headed off Amalickiah's army, but Amalickiah took a small group of men and made good his escape. Without him, his rebellion disappeared. (Alma 46:30-33.) Moroni, having been given authority by the Nephite people, offered Amalickiah's followers the choice between death and covenanting to maintain a free government and support the cause of freedom. (Alma 46:34-35.) Amalickiah went on to take the throne of the Lamanites by murder and treachery, and later launched a bloody war against the Nephites that was carried on by his brother Ammoron even after Amalickiah's death at the hands of Teancum.

Morianton's Revolt

Morianton and his followers waged war against the people of the land of Lehi, trying to gain control of a portion of their land. When the people of Lehi fled to Moroni's army for protection, Morianton and his people took off the other way—northward, toward Bountiful. If they had arrived there, they might have proven a great threat against the Nephites from the rear. However, Morianton was a violent man and beat a maidservant, who went straight to Moroni and told him of Morianton's plans. Moroni sent an army, led by Teancum, which intercepted the would-be rebels. (Alma 50:25-34.)

Morianton aroused his people to stubborn resistance, so that a battle commenced between Morianton's people and Teancum's army. Teancum killed Morianton and defeated his army, and with their leader gone, the people returned to their lands and lived at peace with the people of Lehi. (Alma 50:35-36.)

The Revolt of the King-men

The "king-men" were men of "high birth" who wanted to be kings. When Pahoran, the new chief judge after the death of his father, Nephihah, refused to change some laws to their favor, the king-men began a campaign to abolish the rule of judges. Opposed by the "freemen," the king-men were defeated by the voice of the people. There was no bloodshed during the dispute, and the king-men appeared to acquiesce. (Alma 51:2-8.)

However, at this very time Amalickiah launched his major campaign against the Nephites, bringing a huge Lamanite army to attack. And the king-men "were glad in their hearts; and they refused to take up arms, for they were so wroth with the chief judge, and also with the people of liberty, that they would not take up arms to defend their country." (Alma 51:13.)

The refusal of a large part of the population to fight in defense of the land worried Moroni, but he took no action until the voice of the people gave him "power to compel those dissenters to defend their country or to put them to death." (Alma 51:15.) With the law squarely behind him, Moroni moved against the king-men. Those who did not acquiesce, agree to fight in defense of their nation, and "hoist the title of liberty upon their towers, and in their cities" (Alma 51:20) were either killed in battle against Moroni's army or taken prisoner—without trial, "for there was no time for their trials at this period" (Alma 51:19). And so ended the rebellion of those whose pride and "nobility" led them to welcome an invasion of their country.

The Rebellion of Pachus

During a time when the armies of the Nephites were hard-pressed on several fronts, a group of rebels drove Pahoran from the judgment seat and took over control of the land of Zarahemla. With as much of an army as he could muster, Pahoran fled to the loyal land of Gideon and gathered more support there. (Alma 61:1-7.) Though the rebels, led by their new king, Pachus, did not dare try to extend their rebellion by attacking Pahoran's forces in Gideon, they immediately contacted the Lamanites, offering to keep control of Zarahemla while the Lamanites conquered everything else. (Alma 61:8.) They hoped that they would be given rule over the Nephites after the Lamanites completed their conquest.

And the plan might have succeeded, since not only did the rebels pose a threat behind Nephite lines, but also they had cut off all supplies from the rich land of Zarahemla to the Nephite armies struggling through battles in the wilderness. Pahoran was able to send a little help, but not much.

Likewise, Moroni's armies were so tied down by the Lamanite armies that he could come with only a small force to help Pahoran regain the judgment seat. (Alma 61:16-18; 62:3.) Moroni raised the standard of liberty wherever he went on his way to meet Pahoran, and "thousands did flock unto his standard, and did take up their swords in the defence of their freedom, that they might not come into bondage." (Alma 62:5.)

With this force of loyal freemen, Moroni and Pahoran marched to Zarahemla and ousted the dissenters, killing Pachus and taking his men prisoners. (Alma 62:6-8.) As soon as Pahoran was restored to the judgment seat, "the men of Pachus received their trial, according to the law, and also those king-men who had been taken and cast into prison; and they were executed according to the law." (Alma 62:9.) For the safety of the country, then, Moroni and Pahoran, according to the law, "inflicted death upon all those who were not true to the cause of freedom" (Alma 62:11)—but not until these righteous leaders had thoroughly proved that the dissidents' intent was to overthrow the elected government and turn the nation over to the Lamanites.

Other Dissenting Groups

Over the next sixty-five years, three other groups of dissenters pulled away from the Nephites and incited the Lamanites to attack, including a daring attack right into the heart of Zarahemla itself, led by "Coriantumr . . . a descendant of Zarahemla . . . a dissenter from among the Nephites." (Helaman 1:15.) Coriantumr was successful in capturing the city of Zarahemla, but when he left the city to pillage nearby lands he was surrounded by Nephite troops who had been guarding the borders of the land. Moronihah, Moroni's son, then led the Nephite armies to defeat the Lamanites—whose king, Tubaloth, was the nephew of Amalickiah (Helaman 1:16), a dissenter from the Nephites a generation earlier! (For accounts of two other groups of dissenters during this sixty-five-year period, see Alma 63:14-15 and Helaman 4.)

At last the pattern of open dissent and treason on the part of the Nephite minorities ended—not because the Nephites became completely unified in righteousness, but because even those in the Church became lifted up in pride (Helaman 4:11-13) to such a degree that the Lamanites were able to take over a large amount of the Nephite lands. Even when some of the people began to repent, Moronihah could lead them to recapture only half of what they had lost. (Helaman 4:14-20.) The Nephite people "had altered and trampled under their feet the laws of Mosiah [and] had become a wicked people, insomuch that they were wicked even like unto the Lamanites. And because of their iniquity the church had begun to dwindle; and they began to disbelieve . . . and the judgments of God did stare them in the face. . . . Yea, thus had they become weak, because of their transgression, in the space of not many years." (Helaman 4:22-23, 26.)

Another form of corruption undermined the Nephite nation now—the band of Kishkumen, later called the Gadianton robbers after Kishkumen's opportunistic successor. Instead of open dissent and rebellion, these people made no pretense of idealogy—they were out for wealth and power, and their methods were assassination, theft, and secrecy. They dwelt right among the Nephites, particularly in the "more settled parts of the land." (Helaman 3:23.) And as more and more people joined them, they gradually gained control over the government. Though Gadiantons flourished among the "more wicked part of the Lamanites" (Helaman 6:18), at last even "the more part of the Nephites . . . did unite with those bands of robbers, and did enter into their covenants and their oaths" (Helaman 6:21), which "were put into the heart of Gadianton by that same being who did . . . plot with Cain" (Helaman 6:26-27).

Dissenters could no longer leave the Nephites and appeal to the Lamanites for help, either, for after the great mission of Helaman's sons, Lehi and Nephi, the Lamanites had become so righteous that they even returned to the Nephites the lands they had taken in war! (Helaman 5:52.) "And the Lamanites had become, the more part of them, a righteous people, insomuch that their righteousness did exceed that of the Nephites, because of their firmness and their steadiness in the faith." (Helaman 6:1.)

Why the Dissenters Failed

Until the Nephite people became utterly corrupt and the Lamanites became converted to the faith, the nine different rebellions by dissenters all ended in defeat. Why?

Perhaps the answer is simply that the Lord helped the righteous preserve their freedom. The Book of Mormon seems clear in stating that if there had been no righteous majority, the cause of freedom would have been lost. (See Alma 2:6-7, 28; 46:11-29; 51:6-7, 14-16; 62:4-6; Helaman 4: 14-16.)

Careful examination of the nine accounts of dissent, particularly the six given in detail, reveals several points that the dissenters had in common—and that the righteous majority never had.

1. The dissenters sought to impose kings over the people instead of judges, while the more righteous majority insisted on maintaining their freedom and the system of government in which the voice of the people made the laws.

2. The dissenters were intolerant of any dissent other than their own: as the Amlicites immediately armed themselves against their neighbors, so the Zoramites expelled from their lands all those who believed in the gospel, and Pachus's group forcibly expelled the chief judge. But the more righteous majority felt bound by law: "There was no law against a man's belief; therefore, a man was punished only for the crimes which he had done." (Alma 30:11.) Moroni took no action against the king-men until the voice of the people gave him the power (Alma 51:14-16), and those who tried to change the law and elect a king were never hindered as long as they followed the normal elective process. The people of the Lord, then, tolerated divergent opinions—but took strong action when such opinions became treason and subversion.

3. The dissenters were invariably opposed to the Church

of God, from Amlici to Amalickiah, from the Zoramites to Pachus; while, of course, the more righteous majority showed again and again their reliance on the Lord, and even sent missionaries where a less righteous people might have sent armies. (Alma 31:5.)

4. The unrighteous dissenters exploited the free laws of the Nephites in an effort to subvert or overturn those very laws—and, indeed, it was because the Nephite society was basically just that the Gadiantons were able to flourish: the law required that as long as no one could or would testify against the assassins, they were to be allowed to stay at liberty. (Helaman 6:21-24.) Yet the more righteous majority was not so eager to put down dissent that they allowed those laws protecting the rights of dissenters to be damaged. Only after dissenters proved that their intent was treasonous did the more righteous Nephites take action against them.

5. The dissenters, without exception, once they were legally defeated, turned to the Lamanites to try to overcome the Nephites. Even the mildest rebellion, that of the king-men, turned into treason when the king-men refused to take up arms to defend their country against imminent Lamanite attack. Of course, there may have been many instances of dissent that did *not* turn into treason. Since such dissent was not illegal, there may have been other, less notable, occurrences that were left out of the abridged record of the Book of Mormon. Such loyal dissenters would have fought alongside the rest of the righteous majority in spite of their differences of opinion, and so would never have been considered separate from the righteous!

6. Nephite dissenters, once they had left their homeland, became the most virulent haters of the Nephites. It took the Nephite dissenter Amalickiah to stir up the reluctant Lamanites to war against the Nephites. (Alma 47.) The Lamanite war leader Zerahemnah took advantage of the hatred of the Nephite dissenters by making them commanders over his soldiers. (Alma 43:6.) In contrast, the more righteous Nephites were merciful and tried, where possible, to avoid

bloodshed. Moroni frequently stopped a battle when the outcome seemed clear, offering the Lamanites and the renegade Nephites with them a chance to save their lives if they would covenant not to wage war. The dissenters sought bloodshed; the more righteous Nephites sought peace—but not at the cost of liberty.

7. Pride and wealth seemed to be forerunners to most of the dissenters' rebellions. Either they had too much pride and wealth and sought power as well—as with the king-men, the Amalickiahites, and the Amlicites—or they seemed determined to gain wealth at someone else's expense, as with Morianton and Pachus. The Zoramites were the epitome of empty pride and a ridiculously dominant sense of superiority. The more righteous majority of the Nephites, however, were unselfish and recognized their constant dependence on the Lord. They helped the poor and needy—indeed, it was noted as one of the symptoms of their downfall that they stopped being humble and helpful to the poor. (Helaman 4:12-13.)

8. The leaders of the treasonous dissenters were *not* unselfish idealists. They wooed their followers with flattery or promises of power. Some of them, like Amlici and Pachus, appear to have fought valiantly along with their armies. Others, like Amalickiah, were quick to abandon their armies when it looked as though the fight would go against them. But always they were characterized by a selfish pursuit of their own personal power and influence. The leaders of the more righteous majority, however, were godly men. Moroni, for instance, fought for freedom and then, though he might have pursued rule within the kingdom, quietly retired to "spend the remainder of his days in peace" (Alma 62:43); Moroni's son, Moronihah, refused to lead the Nephites into battle except when he saw they were repentant of their sins (Helaman 4:16); the chief judge Nephihah "filled the judgment-seat with perfect uprightness before God" (Alma 50:37); his son, the chief judge Pahoran, worked fervently "that we may retain our freedom, that we may rejoice in the

great privilege of our church, and in the cause of our Redeemer and our God" (Alma 61:14); and, of course, the prophets Alma, Helaman, Helaman the younger, and Nephi all served as either judges or captains in the service of their country, and as prophets in the service of the Lord.

What finally defeated the Nephites? Not the dissenters, for as long as the righteous majority served the Lord and upheld the law, the dissenters and the enemies from without never prevailed for long. The Nephites were finally brought down when the unrighteous became the majority, oppressing the righteous, perverting the law, waging unjust wars, and allowing secret combinations to prevail. When the majority is wicked, it is the righteous minority that is in dissent—and while the righteous are tolerant, the unrighteous are not. It was in such a time that the Church members were threatened with death until they were saved by the day and night and day without darkness when Christ was born. (3 Nephi 1:4-21.)

What does this mean to us today? We need to examine our own society. Does the majority follow the pattern of the righteous Nephites? Are we dedicated to freedom; tolerant of disagreement; righteously serving God? Do we uphold the law even when our enemies exploit it against us? Are we loyal to our nation whether we agree with particular policies or not? Are we merciful in victory, and humble and sharing to those less fortunate than we? Are our leaders righteous, unselfish men?

If there are dangers and problems, we must act as the righteous Nephites so often did: rallying to oppose the destruction of freedom through every lawful means, without ever losing sight of the rights of those we disagree with, without ever serving our own pride or seeking our own aggrandizement. If the righteous Nephites had been content with passively attending church and had not heeded Moroni's rallying cry and flocked to the banner of liberty, it is quite possible that the treasonous dissenters might have succeeded in their aim.

It was not the dissent itself, but the actual treason that proved to be a danger to the Nephites. Likewise, it was not the force of arms, but rather the righteousness and determination of the members of the Church in standing fast that preserved freedom for so many years against such heavy odds.

Orson Scott Card is a book editor at Compute! Publications Inc. in North Carolina. He is also a freelance writer.

Korihor

Chauncey C. Riddle

Korihor appears out of nowhere, as it were, in the Nephite record. His entire story is contained in Alma 30, where he suddenly appears in the land of Zarahemla, preaching "unto the people against the prophecies which had been spoken by the prophets, concerning the coming of Christ." (V. 6.) What we know of his background is mostly from inference, but his arguments show that he was an educated man, in sophistry if not in the scriptures. But we know from his own final admission that Korihor once had a testimony: "I always knew that there was a God. But behold, the devil hath deceived me. . . . And I have taught his words; and I taught them because they were pleasing unto the carnal mind, . . . insomuch that I verily believed that they were true." (Alma 30:52-53.) Thus Korihor's life teaches us that having the truths of the gospel and being a covenant servant of Christ are in nowise guarantees of salvation. We are also reminded that the most powerful opposition to the work of the Savior on this earth comes from those who know the truth and then deliberately turn from it and seek to destroy others.

Korihor took what might be called a philosophical approach to destroying faith in our Savior, an approach remarkably similar to that taken by many persons today in semiphilosophical attempts to "relieve" believers of what they are pleased to call their "naiveté." His arguments could not hurt those whose belief was born of genuine spiritual experience, but they were powerfully effective among those weak in the faith whose belief had not yet gone beyond words. An analysis of those arguments helps us to see how we can be strong in the faith in Christ. Let us select three of his arguments as examples.

We begin with Korihor's argument for naturalistic empiricism (the belief that it is possible to *know* all truth through the senses—by experience and observation): "Behold, these things which ye call prophecies, which ye say are handed down by holy prophets, behold, they are foolish traditions of your fathers. How do ye know of their surety? Behold, ye cannot know of things which ye do not see; therefore ye cannot know that there shall be a Christ." (Alma 30:14-15.)

Now, it is plain that empiricism has value. It is good for us to observe our surroundings carefully and to appreciate our sensations. How else would we walk or drive an automobile? Without sensation, how could we know beauty or communicate with friends and loved ones or appreciate the marvelous handiwork of the creations of our God? Sense experience is indeed a valuable part of this life; the error comes in supposing that it is the *only* way of knowing what we know.

What can our senses tell us about justice or mercy or the future? Nothing. Indeed, it works the other way. Only when we have acquired by some nonempirical means the concepts of justice and mercy, or an idea about some future event—only then can we recognize the significance of our sensory experiences relating to justice and mercy or the fulfillment of prophecy.

None of the more important questions we ask can be solved or answered by depending solely on sensation. Is there a God? Is man immortal? Is it good to be honest? What should I do next in my life? The answers to each and all of these more important questions must come by faith. Every man answers these questions and makes the great decisions of his life on the basis of his belief in and acceptance of someone or something he cannot see. No man knows by his senses that each man has a spirit separate from his physical body, but some have a testimony of that fact gained by faith.

The answer to Korihor is plain and simple: Our initial acceptance of Christ is not empirical, for we do not see him. But we have received into our lives a Holy Spirit that teaches us to understand the scriptures about Christ and to believe that he lives. We do not pretend that this is yet knowledge. It is faith. We believe in Christ without having seen him because we trust this Holy Spirit that has taught us so many good things.

Korihor might by his argument be able to confuse someone who had never had revelation, but his contention is only a pathetic childishness to those who enjoy the companionship of the Holy Ghost.

A second argument used by Korihor might be called his humanism. In concert with the other humanists of the world, he insists that achievement and success come by human means, such as physical strength, skill, and reason: "And many more such things did he say unto them, telling them that there could be no atonement made for the sins of men, but every man fared in this life according to the management of the creature; therefore every man prospered according to his genius, and that every man conquered according to his strength." (Alma 30:17.)

Korihor would have us believe, like some authors of modern "success" books, that the solutions to our problems lie in sharp thinking and realistic approaches to life. But such persons define success in terms of wealth, social status, political power, and the glutting of the senses; and, as the servants of Christ know, if selfish attainments are one's goal, the world is so constructed that one can indeed ignore the Savior and attain. But Korihor and his fellow humanists think that they are masterfully doing it on their own, not realizing that those who succeed at the expense of faith and love are on a down escalator and are being carefully guided, encouraged, aided, and comforted by their unseen mentor Satan. Their glorying in their own strength and accomplishments is a tribute to the cleverness of Satan, that devil who greases the sluiceway of sin.

Conversely, those who have accepted the gospel see that real success in this world is overcoming selfishness and turning one's strength to righteousness, to blessing others. They know full well that this kind of success is an uphill, strained effort into the very teeth of the forces that make sin so easy. They know that it is not by any human means that one can overcome the world. After all we can do by human power, we are still nothing. It is only when the grace of God touches our lives that we can overcome evil and enact the precious mercies of righteousness. There can be no boasting, no pretension that anything human prospers us. The glory is all given unto God by those who are more than armchair servants of the Master.

The humanist argument is very persuasive to many because it is flattering. We do not naturally like to believe that without Him we can do nothing. Thus part of Satan's entourage includes those who know the gospel is true but who insist they really don't need much help except for a pointer or two and a little assistance in being resurrected. The servant of Christ is not persuaded, however. Long pleading with the Lord has stripped him of all humanistic pride.

A third argument used by Korihor is that of relativism: ". . . and whatsoever a man did was no crime." (Alma 30:17.) A fuller statement of this attack by Korihor is as follows: Since (he claims) there is no God and men do not live after death, and since (he claims) all so-called "laws" and "commandments" are but social conveniences to give power to priests, the only important thing in life is to do what you want to do—if you can get away with it. How modern Korihor sounds! But the argument is timeless, as old as sin itself.

There are, of course, many versions of relativism (one would hardly expect relativism to be absolute). One version encourages enjoyment of the Church social organization without getting uptight about theology or religious commandments. Another kind of relativism says that the commandments are great but open to broad private interpretation. A third acknowledges that there are commandments, but allows indulgence in sin since "nobody's perfect." A fourth version says that the commandments were okay when they were given, but they have become superfluous in our enlightened age. A fifth kind of relativism, that used by Korihor, says that the commandments were bad from the first; they are inhibitions on the soul of man that actually prevent him from ever achieving happiness. A sixth type, also used by Korihor, says that since one act is indifferent from another, it doesn't matter what we do.

The great power of all relativistic approaches is that they allow the individual to judge his own actions. This is why almost any of the approaches strikes a responsive, sympathetic chord in all other relativists. Korihor found many who were pleased with his relativism, even though they may have rejected much else of what he said. "And thus he did preach unto them, leading away the hearts of many, causing them to lift up their heads in their wickedness." (Alma 30:18.)

In stark contrast to the virtually infinite number of personal choices available in the broad way of relativism is the way of the Savior. That strait and narrow way is to do as he did: not to seek our own will, but to do the will of Him who sent us. It is to obey him in all things, obeying his word, which is his law, as it is freshly written in our hearts from revelation to revelation. It is to rely solely upon his merits, counting him as the only fountain of righteousness. It is being willing to die for his sake, crucifying the old person with worldly wants and desires in order to be born again "as a child, submissive, meek, humble, patient, full of love, willing to submit to all things which the Lord seeth fit to inflict upon him, even as a child doth submit to his father." (Mosiah 3:19.)

Thus the gospel teaches a way that is absolute—absolute

in that the formula for righteousness is always the same for every person and for every time and circumstance: take the name of Christ, always remember him, keep all of the commandments that he gives unto us. There is no other way to righteousness, for whatsoever is not of faith in Christ is sin.

Now, it is little wonder that Korihor found much success in commending relativism to the members of the Church in his time. For while the Church is true, the members of the Church here on earth have not yet overcome the world, although most are still trying. For many, the effort is hard, the price too great. Whether they leave the Church or not, they abandon the narrow way and settle for some variety of relativism.

But there is one thing relativism can never do, even within the Church. One who subscribes to any of the versions of relativism just listed will never (unless he repents) be brought to those sacrifices that will prepare his soul to spend an eternity in blessing others. Relativism can never purify heart and mind, or transform body and countenance into the image of the Savior.

Thanks be to our God that there is a way, strait and narrow though it be, to learn to love with a pure love! But the price is great. We must place all of our heart, might, mind, and strength at his disposal—always. We must count as dross and expendable everything of this world, including our own lives. This does not mean to deny life, but to live fully, enjoying the companionship of the Holy Ghost, working in a crescendo of works of love that will take us without faltering through the veil to results understood only in eternity.

Korihor was not unique to Book of Mormon times. His counterparts have always been with the Church, and they will now but increase in flattery and fury until the end of the world. What will prevent us from succumbing to their sophistries? The following are offered as a time-tested prescription against apostasy.

1. *Hunger and thirst after righteousness.* Blessed are they who do so, "for they shall be filled with the Holy Ghost."

(3 Nephi 12:6.) Righteousness is to bless others, to minister to their needs, both temporal and spiritual. The great enemy of righteousness is not only evil; plain old-fashioned evil fools few. A more subtle and therefore more dangerous enemy is self-righteousness, supposing that what pleases us will be good for others.

Perhaps the great divider between the seekers of righteousness and the self-righteous is that those who hunger and thirst after true righteousness cannot rest until satisfaction and happiness come to those whom they strive to help. They hurt when others hurt. The self-righteous are often deed-conscious rather than people-conscious. They seem to glory in forms and traditions, formulas and standards. They cast alms to the poor without loving them or stopping to discern what the real problem might be.

Those who seek true righteousness quickly learn one thing—their own impotence. They find they are not knowledgeable enough, nor wise enough, nor powerful enough to bless others as their hearts desire. Their hunger for righteousness has prepared them for the gospel, and when they hear its good news they leap at the opportunity to make the covenant to love the Savior and to receive his Spirit to be with them.

2. *Learn to live by the Holy Spirit.* The Spirit teaches us the truth of the gospel. But it is another thing to learn to live by the Holy Spirit. The difference is like hearing a violin concert expertly performed and acknowledging its merit, then personally mastering the violin to be able to play as expertly ourselves.

This mastery is a matter of constant, faithful application of our will power. There are no quantum leaps to righteousness, only the slow adding of line to line, precept to precept, grace upon grace. In this remaking of our lives, every improper thought, every bad habit, every evil desire must sooner or later be evaluated against the glory of our Savior. We, not he, must make each painful choice to prove all things, then hold fast to that which is good.

How many experiments and experiences are necessary? Only enough to enable us to give our selves, to yield our hearts unto the Savior; enough experiments to know the voice of the Savior beyond any shadow of doubt; enough experiences of obedience to learn to love with pure love and to continue therein.

3. *Support priesthood authority.* Those who have learned to walk in the Spirit also rejoice in the opportunity to sustain their priesthood-appointed leaders with faith and prayers. They know by the repeated testimony of the Spirit that The Church of Jesus Christ of Latter-day Saints is the kingdom of God on the earth and that those who serve over them in the callings of the priesthood are appointed and sustained by the Savior. As servants of the Savior, they, too, sustain.

Because they sustain, they become the united power and strength that the Church organization brings to the work of righteousness in the world. They sustain in love even as they hope to be sustained. They always sustain in faith and righteousness, receiving instruction from the Savior and obeying him in all things.

4. *Build the kingdom.* Living in righteousness makes possible the establishment of Zion on earth again. What careful priesthood labor there must be to bring the gathered remnants to see eye to eye, having one mind and one heart, dwelling in righteousness with no poor among them! Then the kingdoms of this world will be constrained to admit that this is indeed the kingdom of God and his Christ, for the inhabitants will love one another, even as Christ loves them. Those who support have the joy of seeing the prophecies fulfilled before their very eyes.

He or she who has a shoulder to the wheel, who honors and trusts the driver of the wagon, who knows he is doing the right thing in the right cause, is not taken in by the glitter of apostasy. But what of those not so mature in the work of the Lord? Is there any guaranteed way to prevent apostasy of the newborn or the weak and infirm? The honest answer is no. The love and patience of those who are mature will shelter some of them for a time. But ultimately there is no outside shelter—the only effective shelter is a personal faith, a personal testimony. In every generation Korihor takes his toll of those who will not get themselves founded on the Rock.

Chauncey C. Riddle is a professor of philosophy at Brigham Young University.

Moroni and His Captains

Eugene England

Compared with other portions of the Book of Mormon, the last twenty-one chapters of the book of Alma contain fewer examples of what we usually think of as "scriptural" material—no sermons per se, no visions, almost no prophesying, very little exposition of theological principles. At first it may seem to be one long, detailed record of all-out warfare between the Nephites and the Lamanites, of battles that raged back and forth through a score of cities and destroyed thousands of lives. In this part of the record, Mormon uses the precious space to examine kings and captains with the same care that he elsewhere gives to prophets and teachers. He chronicles treachery and bloodshed with the same exactness that he had earlier used in describing preaching and miracles. However, in this long section—more than a tenth of the total Book of Mormon—Mormon uses hard history to teach us powerful religious lessons: the value of freedom, God's role in preserving it, the moral justifications for waging war to uphold freedom, and the moral limitations on bloodshed, even for freedom's sake.

We can understand this exposition of freedom better if we understand Mormon. He must have been struck by the parallels between Moroni's experiences and his own life of warring against the Lamanites 400 years later. When he read the story of Moroni, Mormon had already been the leader of the Nephite armies through many years of bitter battles. Like that earlier Moroni, he was never identified by the title "general" in the Book of Mormon; nevertheless, both were commanders over the Nephite armies—chief captains over chief captains—and exercised the authority of what we would call the rank of general. (See Alma 43:16-17; 46:11; Mormon 2:1; 5:1.) Mormon's adolescence, from the time he was fifteen, had been given over to military matters. Consequently, he was prepared as few in his nation were to appreciate the consummate skill of Moroni's earlier generalship. Righteous himself, he also must have responded deeply to Moroni's own righteousness. He followed Moroni's example of rigorous, self-sacrificing service both to preserve his people's liberty by combat and also, by teaching and example, to help make his people worthy of God's help. Like Moroni, Mormon refused to let the long, desperate fighting lead him to bloodthirstiness; instead, as the Lord directed him, he resigned his command to stand by "as an idle witness" when their wickedness led them to fight in a spirit of vengeance. (See Mormon 3:9-16.) Surely it tells us much that Mormon named his own son Moroni.

In short, our key to understanding those last twenty-one chapters of Alma lies in Mormon's assessment of Moroni, man and military leader. That assessment is a valuable one for all of us, who, like Mormon, look for models to guide our lives through the conflicts of the present world. Here are Mormon's words for us, as he looked down through time and yearned for us to learn from his people's history: "Now the Nephites were taught to defend themselves against their enemies, even to the shedding of blood if it were necessary; yea, and they were also taught never to give an offense, yea, and never to raise the sword except it were against an enemy, except it were to preserve their lives. And this was their faith, that by so doing God would prosper them in the land, . . . yea, warn them to flee, or to prepare for war, according to their danger; . . . and this was the faith of Moroni, and his heart did glory in it; not in the shedding of blood but in doing good, in preserving his people, yea, in keeping the commandments of God, yea, and resisting iniquity. Yea, verily, verily I say unto you, if all men had been, and were, and ever would be, like unto Moroni, behold, the very powers of hell would have been shaken forever; yea, the devil would never have power over the hearts of the children of men." (Alma 48:14-17.)

Mormon obviously saw Moroni's personal righteousness as a dominant factor in the creation of a national righteousness powerful enough to sustain national freedom against great odds. To drive home his point, he gives us ample detail and ample commentary on those crucial fourteen years from 74 B.C. to 60 B.C. The time divides itself into three periods: a sudden, savage outbreak of war and rebellion that lasted two years, a five-year respite of peace and preparation marred only by a single internal difficulty, then seven exhausting years of siege, insurrection, battle. During the five-year respite, Moroni drove his people urgently to prepare to defend themselves in case of future attacks by the Lamanites—attacks that did indeed come to pass. The social energy resulting from the necessary work of garrisoning cities overflowed into riches, prosperity, and strength (see Alma 50:1-18); and at this break in the action, Mormon took advantage of his role as a teacher of future generations to insert a "thus we see" passage that interprets the whole war, with its causes and effects, in terms of the entire history of God's dealings with the descendants of Lehi: "The people of Nephi did thank the Lord their God, because of his matchless power in delivering them from the hands of their enemies. . . . And there was continual peace among them, and exceedingly great prosperity in the church because of their heed and diligence which they gave unto the word of God. . . . And thus we see how merciful and just are all the dealings of the Lord, to the fulfilling of all his words . . . which he spake unto Lehi. . . . And we see that these promises have been verified to the people of Nephi; for it has been their quarrelings and their contentions, yea, their murderings, and their plunderings, their idolatry, their whoredoms, and their abominations, which were among themselves, which brought upon them their wars and their destructions. And those who were faithful in keeping the commandments of the Lord were delivered at all times, whilst thousands of their wicked brethren have been consigned to bondage, or to perish by the sword, or to dwindle in unbelief, and mingle with the Lamanites." (Alma 49:28, 30; 50:19, 21-22.)

Of course, Mormon is commenting here not only on events 400 years old, but on what continually led to the destruction of the Nephites in the entire course of their history, including his own time. How he must have yearned for that earlier time when Moroni's people humbly thanked God for their victory rather than boasting in their strength as he had seen his own people do. (See Mormon 3:9.) Doubtlessly with longing, he wrote of that brief respite between wars: "But behold there never was a happier time among the people of Nephi, since the days of Nephi, than in the days of Moroni." (Alma 50:23.)

We first meet Moroni in the crisis of the Lamanite attack under Zerahemnah. In a pattern Mormon notices throughout Nephite history, the warfare was instigated not by the Lamanites themselves but by dissenting Nephites. Zerahemnah appointed as his chief captains other former Nephites who were of "a more wicked and murderous disposition than the Lamanites" (Alma 43:6); and then, with traditional resentments and hatreds inflamed, he led his Lamanite armies in an attack against the Nephites in 74 B.C. Moroni, only twenty-five years old, was appointed leader over the Nephites (Alma 43:16-17) and immediately proved his ability by equipping his men with armor, an unexpected innovation, and then by outmanuevering Zerahemnah, whose army was more than double the size of his own (Alma 43:51). His superior tactics included posting spies, but he also sent to Alma, desiring that prophet to "inquire of the Lord whither the armies of the Nephites should go to defend themselves." (Alma 43:23.) It was a perfect combination. Alma told Moroni *where* to march, and his spies told him *when*. The Lamanites ended up surrounded and trapped against the river Sidon. Instead of pressing his advantage, however, Moroni called a truce; he told the Lamanites, "We do not desire to slay you," and then asked Zerahemnah to surrender. (Alma 44:1.)

In the negotiation that followed, Moroni commanded Zerahemnah to surrender "in the name of that all-powerful God, who has strengthened our arms that we have gained power over you." (Alma 44:5.) But Zerahemnah rejected any reality but the obviously materialistic: "We do not believe that it is God that has delivered us into your hands; but we believe that it is your cunning. . . . Behold, it is your breastplates and your shields that have preserved you." (Alma 44:9.)

From points of view so radically different, how could the two men agree? Moroni insisted, on his honor, that the Lamanites could go free, but only if they would covenant never to fight again, while Zerahemnah, with an interesting indication of the seriousness of oaths, declared that he would not swear an oath he knew he would break! (Alma 44:6-8.)

As Moroni returned the Lamanite weapons to recommence the struggle, Zerahemnah suddenly attacked Moroni on the field of truce, but a watchful Nephite soldier intercepted with a blow that took off Zerahemnah's scalp. In a bizarre but effective symbolic action characteristic of the Old Testament and Book of Mormon cultures, the nameless soldier held forth the bleeding scalp on his sword before the Lamanites and threatened: "Even as this scalp has fallen to the earth . . . so shall ye fall . . . except ye will deliver up your weapons of war and depart with a covenant of peace." (Alma 44:14.) This dramatic prophecy struck such fear into the Lamanites that most of them surrendered and made the covenant, though Zerahemnah and a few others still had to be conquered by force.

Moroni's decisive generalship and his faith, which was so

deeply shared with his men that it inspired that nameless Nephite's spontaneous act, had been the Lord's instruments in preserving the people. But Moroni returned from this bloody front-line battle to preserve Nephite liberty only to find that a rebellion had sprung up at home. Amalickiah, proud and rich, had opposed Helaman, the new head of the Church appointed by Alma, and was seeking to become king and to destroy the Church.

Angry at Amalickiah, Moroni "rent his coat; and he took a piece thereof, and wrote upon it—In memory of our God, our religion, and freedom, and our peace, our wives, and our children," fastened it to a pole, and went forth among the people. With this "title of liberty," and the strength of having "poured out his soul to God," he rallied the Nephites with the cry, "Come forth in the strength of the Lord, and enter into a covenant that [ye] will maintain [your] rights, and [your] religion, that the Lord God may bless [you]." (Alma 46:12, 13, 17, 20.) The people, responding to the spiritual power behind this symbolic action, ran to Moroni, "rending their garments in token, or as a covenant, that . . . if they should transgress the commandments of God . . . the Lord should rend them even as they had rent their garments." (Alma 46:21.) Continuing the symbolism, they swore to Moroni, "We covenant with our God, that . . . he may cast us at the feet of our enemies, even as we have cast our garments at thy feet to be trodden under foot, if we shall fall into transgression." (Alma 46:22.)

With a spiritual insight that went much deeper than mere political astuteness, Moroni further welded this new bond that unified his people by linking their action to their great heritage as children of Israel: "We are a remnant of the seed of Joseph, whose coat was rent by his brethren into many pieces; yea, and now behold, let us remember to keep the commandments of God, or our garments shall be rent by our brethren, and we be cast into prison, or be sold, or be slain. Yea, let us preserve our liberty as a remnant of Joseph." (Alma 46:23-24.)

Who among his hearers would not stir to that heroic and

sacred history? But he took the symbolism a step further still and, in the process, gave us a story about our common ancestor Joseph that must have been preserved on the brass plates, though it has not come down to us in our Bible. Before his death, Jacob saw that a fragment of Joseph's coat had not decayed; he then prophesied, "Even as this remnant of garment of my son hath been preserved, so shall a remnant of the seed of my son be preserved by the hand of God, and be taken unto himself, while the remainder of the seed of Joseph shall perish, even as the remnant of his garment." Moroni, revealing that he was a devoted, thoughtful student and teacher of the scriptures as well as a skilled and courageous man of action, spelled out the choice for his people: "And now who knoweth but what the remnant of the seed of Joseph, which shall perish as his garment, are those who have dissented from us? Yea, and even it shall be ourselves if we do not stand fast in the faith of Christ." (Alma 46:24, 27.)

This typically Hebraic form of teaching through physical symbols seems rather unusual to us, but Moroni's people understood it, and they also understood the consequences of their choice. The dissenters were captured, except for Amalickiah and a small group who escaped to the Lamanites. This brought Moroni face to face with a situation that reveals another facet of his character: a humane commitment to the rule of law as deep as his tough and pragmatic devotion to freedom. He was careful to act strictly according to the law in not executing the rebels out of hand. Instead, he gave them the choice between covenanting to support a free government or being put to death. Mormon adds, with what may be regarded as a flash of understated irony, "There were but few who denied the covenant of freedom." (Alma 46:34-35.)

While Moroni was uniting his people in righteous love of freedom, Amalickiah was proving Mormon's repeated observation that former Nephites, who had once known the light, were prone to become the most wicked of all. (See Alma 24:30; 47:36.) "A very subtle man to do evil" (Alma 47:4), Amalickiah stirred up the Lamanites and then played their armies against each other in a clever strategy that enabled him to bring about the murder of the king and take over the throne himself—and even marry the queen—this in a series of betrayals, poisonings, stabbings, and power plays that make the forty-seventh chapter of Alma read like one of Shakespeare's bloodier history plays. But like other villains of history, his evil bravado, successful for a while, led him to overreach himself by seeking to reign over the Nephites, as well as the Lamanites. Moroni's fortified cities repelled the attack of his armies, and the Lamanites, cowed by their second military disaster in two years due to superior Nephite armaments and tactics, retreated in such psychological and physical exhaustion that not even Amalickiah's wrath could stir them up again at that time.

Thus came the five-year period of freedom from Lamanite attack. But even during that breathing space not all was well all of the time, for in the fifth year of peace another Nephite dissenter, Morianton, appealed to a group of land-hungry Nephites to flee into the land northward and there set up a separate kingdom. Acting under Moroni's order, an army led by a chief captain named Teancum headed them off at a strategic location, killed Morianton, hauled the dissenters back, and presided over their covenanting to keep the peace. (See Alma 50:25-36.)

In many ways, Teancum was a heroic extension of Moroni's own quickness, decisiveness, and boldness. Teancum's personal courage went almost to the point of recklessness, in a way that appeals to our sense of adventure even while we recognize the dangers. When Amalickiah again stirred up his Lamanites to attack, in the midst of another internal dissension among the Nephites, it was Teancum's army that intercepted and repulsed him. (See Alma 51:29-31.) We do not know whether Teancum soberly calculated the cost in lives of another battle or was inflamed with fury against the renegade Nephite who had caused so much bloodshed. At any rate, while the armies slept in exhaustion, he crept through the Lamanite camp to Amalickiah's tent, killed him silently, and then withdrew. When the Lamanites awoke on the first day of the new year (in 66 B.C.) to find their king dead and the Nephites poised for battle again, they fled in terror to regroup behind Ammoron, Amalickiah's brother. (See Alma 51:33-37; 52:1-3.) Moroni then joined Teancum for a decoy-attack that completely routed the already demoralized Lamanites. And again Moroni, though wounded and sore pressed in the heat of battle, still gave the confused Lamanites every opportunity to surrender, promising, "We will forbear shedding your blood." (Alma 52:37.)

Teancum was not Moroni's only chief captain; the record also mentions Antipus, Gid, Helaman, and Lehi and refers to numerous others. (See, for example, Alma 52:19.) But Teancum, Helaman, and Lehi are singled out for special mention. Mormon, who knew what loyalty tested in battle meant, reveals a great deal in what he tells us of Moroni's relationships with his chief captains. In any military society, the brutalities of war can unite men in a kind of competition of escalating toughness, competency in killing, and callousness to sensitive feelings. Instead, we see in Moroni and his chief captains an exceptional and exemplary masculine relationship based partly on shared skills and shared dangers but also on a loving friendship and a righteous desire for liberty and peace. All of these men were courageous in defense of liberty.

Lehi's reputation as a warrior was such that the Lamanites were afraid to attack a city he held because they "feared [him] exceedingly." (Alma 49:17.) Mormon goes on to say, "This Lehi was a man who had been with Moroni in the more part of all his battles"; and then he adds this high praise: "He was a man like unto Moroni, and they rejoiced in each other's safety, yea, they were beloved by each other, and also beloved by all the people of Nephi." (Alma 53:2.)

Teancum's personal valor—possibly modeled on Moroni's personal involvement in battle—led him not only to kill Amalickiah but also into fatal danger when he penetrated Ammoron's camp and killed him. We know his motivation this time. He was "exceedingly angry . . . , insomuch that he considered that Ammoron . . . had been the cause of so much war and bloodshed, yea, and so much famine." (Alma 62:35.) Teancum must have known the odds against his success. Ammoron was in a fortified city, not a tent on the other side of a battlefield. He had to scale the wall and then search for the king "from place to place." Apparently he could not get close enough to kill the king quietly, for he had to "cast a javelin at him." And thus the king was able to awaken his servants before he died, and they pursued and killed Teancum. (Alma 62:36.)

Epitaphs are not common in the Book of Mormon, but Mormon records that Lehi and Moroni were "exceedingly sorrowful," and he gives the reasons: Teancum "had been a man who had fought valiantly for his country, yea, a true friend to liberty; and he had suffered very many exceedingly sore afflictions." (Alma 62:37.)

Helaman was an unusual general—and Mormon lets us know that by including some of Helaman's correspondence with Moroni, written while each was fighting on a different front. Helaman was a son of the prophet Alma, and one of the "high priests over the church." (Alma 46:6.) Yet in this time of his people's need, he took up arms and went into battle, still retaining his own gentleness and righteous aversion to bloodshed.

While Moroni, Teancum, and Lehi were fighting the Lamanites in an attempt to retake the city of Mulek, which was "on the east borders by the seashore" (Alma 51:26), other Lamanite armies had penetrated the Nephite lands "on the west sea, south" (Alma 53:8). It was Helaman who filled the breach by undertaking a lengthy march at the head of a hastily recruited army of two thousand young men, the sons of the "people of Ammon," from their land "to the support of the people in the borders of the land on the south by the west sea." (Alma 53:22.)

The "people of Ammon" were a group of former Lamanites that Ammon had converted about twenty-five years before. These people had been settled in Nephite territory, with Nephite armies set between them and the Lamanites for their protection, for at the time of their conversion they had sworn never to take up arms again, even in defense. Part of that covenant was a willingness to die rather than break that oath (see Alma 24:18), and their willingness had been tested almost immediately when bloodthirsty Lamanites (stirred up by dissident Nephites) slaughtered them, without resistance, until the power of such sacrificial love moved them to "forbear from slaying them" (Alma 24:24). At that point more than a thousand of the Lamanites were converted, moving Mormon to comment, "Thus we see that the Lord worketh in many ways to the salvation of his people." (Alma 24:27.)

Now a generation later, these Ammonites were "moved with compassion" (Alma 53:13) when they saw their beleaguered Nephite brethren struggling against the Lamanites on so many fronts, and they considered breaking their oath and going to the aid of those who had been protecting them for so many years. But Helaman "feared lest by so doing they should lose their souls" (Alma 53:15), and he persuaded them not to take up their weapons again. However, two thousand of their young sons, who had not sworn the oath, volunteered as warriors and asked Helaman to lead them in the southern campaign. (See Alma 53:16-19.)

This was an unlikely army, young men raised by parents whose resolute pacifism was part of their most sacred commitments, led by a Church leader turned military captain. But their story proves that, contrary to the wisdom of men, they are the very type of army the Lord can best accept and make effective in battle—while still protecting them from the soul-destroying evil of bloodlust. Helaman, whatever his doubts may have been about their fighting ability, had no qualms about the character of his "stripling soldiers." They were "exceedingly valiant for courage, and also for strength and activity," he reported to Moroni, but also they were "men who were true at all times in whatsoever thing they were entrusted. Yea, they were men of truth and soberness, for they had been taught to keep the commandments of God and to walk uprightly before him." (See Alma 53:20-22.)

In an exciting story of march and countermarch, they decoyed the Lamanite defenders out of the city of Antiparah so that Antipus could occupy it and in turn pursue the Lamanite army. After fleeing for two days, Helaman saw that the Lamanites, who had been hot on their heels, were no longer in sight and suspected that they had stopped to lure them back into a trap. He knew he did not have the numbers to stand against the Lamanites, but he was also aware that they might have turned back to attack Antipus. And so he asked his two thousand young men, "What say ye, my sons, will ye go against them to battle?" There followed one of the great scenes of the Book of Mormon—and one of the great lessons Mormon was using this space to teach. This citizen army, not professionally trained, not indoctrinated in hatred of their enemies, responded in a way that moved Helaman to write, "And now I say unto you, my beloved brother Moroni, that never had I seen so great courage, nay, not amongst all the Nephites."

What is the source and spirit of their courage? Hear Helaman's report: "For as I had ever called them my sons (for they were all of them very young) even so they said unto me: Father, behold our God is with us, and he will not suffer that we should fall; . . . we would not slay our brethren if they would let us alone; therefore let us go, lest they should overpower the army of Antipus. Now they never had fought, yet they did not fear death; and they did think more upon the liberty of their fathers than they did upon their lives; yea, they had been taught by their mothers, that if they did not doubt, God would deliver them. And they rehearsed unto me the words of their mothers, saying: We do not doubt our mothers knew it." (Alma 56:44-48.)

Helaman thus paid one of the greatest compliments in all scripture to those courageous women who had once faced death in *passive acceptance* in order to stop bloodshed, but had given their sons the valiant faith to face death as well in *active resistance* to bloodshed. That faith was rewarded, for they "fought as if with the strength of God . . . with such miraculous strength, and with such mighty power . . . that they did frighten [the Lamanites]," Helaman exulted, "but behold, to my great joy, there had not one soul of them fallen to the earth." (Alma 56:56.)

In two additional engagements, Helaman's stripling warriors did not fall below the high standard they had set in that first battle. They stood "firm and undaunted" (Alma 57:20), even when they stood nearly alone; they continued to vindicate their noble mothers' faith that they would not be slain, because they were "strict to remember the Lord their God from day to day" (Alma 58:40).

But meanwhile, needed and expected supplies and reinforcements had not been forthcoming from Zarahemla. Moroni, unaware that a new group of dissenting monarchists had risen against Pahoran, the chief judge, and driven him from Zarahemla, wrote a stinging rebuke and threat for the seeming laxity of the central government. Characteristically, his terms were scriptural: "Ye should remember that God has said that the inward vessel shall be cleansed first, and then shall the outer vessel be cleansed also. . . . Except ye do repent . . . and begin to be up and doing, . . . behold it will be expedient that we contend no more with the Lamanites until we have first cleansed our inward vessel, yea, even the great head of our government." (Alma 60:23-24.)

Touched by Moroni's spirit, Pahoran replied with remarkable mildness for a ruler who had been wrongly blamed, "You have censured me, but it mattereth not; I am not angry, but do rejoice in the greatness of your heart." (Alma 61:9.)

The greatness of Pahoran's own heart is further demonstrated by his chief concern, which was not to retain the *power* of his office, but "whether it should be just in us to go against our brethren"—that is, the "king-men" under Pachus who had rebelled. Moroni's own righteous pleas to the Lord were the answer to Pahoran's aversion to shedding the blood even of enemies; thus, the judge quoted the general's words in affirming their joint policy: "But ye have said, except they repent the Lord hath commanded you that ye should go against them." (Alma 61:19-20.) Together they summoned soldiers, not to their personal cause, but to preserve freedom. After they put down the rebellion, their behavior again testified to their respect for law. The rebels were not summarily dispatched, but "received their trial, according to the law," and either enlisted in freedom's cause or were executed. (Alma 62:9.)

Again, attention undivided, Moroni focused his efforts on winning the war, personally scaling the wall of a Lamanite-held city and directing his men over the wall in secret. When the morning came, the astonished and frightened Lamanite defenders found themselves helpless. (See Alma 62:20-23.) This coup must have been doubly satisfying to Moroni's righteous heart, for they took the city "without the loss of one [Nephite] soul" and "many of the Lamanites . . . were desirous to join the people of Ammon and become a free people." (Alma 62:26-27.)

Final battles took about another year, then both Helaman and Moroni turned to a work that showed the spiritual depth in both men. Helaman, sensitive to the spiritual needs of a people harrowed by long war, established the Church again so successfully that "notwithstanding their riches, or their strength, or their prosperity, they were not lifted up in the pride of their eyes; neither were they slow to remember the Lord their God." (Alma 62:49.) This rare humility is Helaman's monument. Moroni's was in the garrisoned cities, carefully fortified and rebuilt for the future needs of the people. But after doing this, he gave the command of the armies to his son, Moronihah, and "retired to his own house that he might spend the remainder of his days in peace." (Alma 62:43.) He was only about thirty-nine years old, a man of personal power, honored prowess, and commanding presence. We wonder about the rest of his life (he died at about age forty-three—see Alma 63:3) and the continuing contribution he may have honorably made to his society; but Mormon tells us nothing. The lesson Mormon wanted us to learn from Moroni's life is centered in those years of terrible conflict, when both body and spirit were tried by combat, treachery, and the loneliness of command relieved by the fidelity of friendship.

Let me suggest some of the lessons Mormon wanted us to learn from this tale of carnage and villainy, of fighting prophets and peace-loving captains:

1. *War most often comes to a people because of their unrighteousness and internal dissensions.*

2. *No matter how it comes, there is no single morally right response to the threat of violence.*

God directs different people, with different backgrounds in different situations, according to his purpose in each situation. The Nephites were preserving the only scriptures that we know of in the New World, the only knowledge of the coming Savior; and God commanded them, "Inasmuch as ye are not guilty of the first offense, neither the second, ye shall not suffer yourselves to be slain by the hands of your enemies." On the contrary, they were "to defend themselves, and their families, and their lands, their country, and their rights, and their religion." (Alma 43:46-47.)

In contrast, the people of Ammon had been steeped in the bloodthirsty tradition of the Lamanites before their conversion and were in danger of slipping back into bloodthirstiness if they again took up arms—even in a good cause. "It has been all that we could do . . . to repent of all our sins and the many murders which we have committed, and to get God to take them away from our hearts," their inspired leader, Anti-Nephi-Lehi, said. (Alma 24:11.) Thus they pledged the sacrifice of their own lives rather than take such a soul-destroying risk, and the Lord blessed them and preserved them by the hand of their Nephite brethren. But then those remarkable people's own children took up arms in the Nephite cause and, led by the priest-captain, fought valiantly and triumphed in bloody, desperate battle without losing their own gentle righteousness and worthiness before the Lord.

And that seems to be the Lord's chief concern: He, the giver of life and the one who can restore it, can guarantee that life will continue in the next world. He alone can take life or direct when it should be taken in order to preserve greater values. Laban's life was weighed against a nation that might "dwindle and perish in unbelief." (1 Nephi 4:13.) Many of the Nephites' battles were to preserve a righteous remnant in the land of promise.

3. *Even when we take the awesome step of going to war, there are righteous limitations that must be observed:* "The Nephites were inspired by a better cause, for they were not fighting for monarchy nor power but they were fighting for their homes and their liberties, their wives and their children, and their all, yea, for their rites of worship and their church." (Alma 43:45.)

And when we fight in what society has judged a better cause, or even if it were that God directed a people to wage war, it seems apparent that the Lord is still deeply concerned that we not succumb to the common results of violence—carnal insensitivity, rage, vengeance—becoming what the Nephites called "blood-thirsty."

The prophet-general Mormon emphasizes again and again the proper Nephite reticence about fighting, their lack of desire for vengeance, their quickness to let Lamanites surrender—especially calling attention to the moral leadership of Moroni in these things: "He did not delight in murder or bloodshed, but he delighted in the saving of his people from destruction." (Alma 55:19.)

At the end of this long period of warfare Mormon reminds us that it is not war—even loss of physical life—that is most crucial, but rather the spiritual effect of an action on people's character and salvation: "Behold, because of the exceedingly great length of the war . . . many had become hardened; . . . and many [others] were softened because of their afflictions, insomuch that they did humble themselves before God, even in the depth of humility." (Alma 62:41.) As we face the conflicts of this present world, may we be like Moroni and those humble Nephites who learned righteousness from his example.

Eugene England is an associate professor of English at Brigham Young University.

Six Nephite Judges

James R. Moss

In A.D. 30, the last chief judge of the once-great Nephite nation was assassinated by a secret combination of judges, lawyers, and apostate high priests. That murder ended the sole republic of the Nephite record and continued a process of social disintegration halted only by the coming of the resurrected Christ. In that process, the unrighteous Nephites destroyed what remained of governmental regulation and divided their society into tribal units. One large band selected "one of the chiefest who had given his voice against the prophets who testified of Jesus" to be their king. (3 Nephi 7:10.) The reign of the judges had lasted only 120 years.

It may initially seem difficult for us, nearly two thousand years later, to become interested in the men who served as chief judge of the Nephites. The resurrected Savior; powerful prophets like Nephi, the elder Alma, and the brother of Jared; or impressive missionaries like the sons of Mosiah naturally draw our attention. The great captain Moroni, his namesake chronicler, and many other prominent spiritual and military leaders are magnetically attractive and seem to push such names as Nephihah, Pahoran, and Lachoneus down into the footnotes of our scriptural memory. But woven through the rich tapestry of Nephite history are golden threads of spiritual strength and active righteousness—lessons for our day from the lives of these Nephite judges.

A brief review of the scriptural record from Alma to 3 Nephi identifies twelve men who served as chief judge. (There may have been others during a period of anarchy from about 26 B.C. to about A.D. 1.) The longest term of office lasted twenty-nine years, the shortest less than a year. Their average tenure was about eight years (counting only the judges and tenures we have record of). Of the twelve, six were killed in office, and little more than their names and violent deaths remain in the record. Three others also died in office, but of natural causes; two resigned in times of unrighteousness to pursue urgent missionary callings. One (Lachoneus I) likely also died in office, but the record does not say. It is to these last six men that we can look for models of personal and political Christianity in action. It is *only* these six men we will consider here, and references to "the judges" herein will be to them. Who were they? What was their function in the Nephite society? Against what problems did they struggle in discharging their responsibilities? What qualities and characteristics did they exemplify? What impact did they have on their own time—and what impact can they have on ours?

To answer these questions, it is necessary to begin with the last Nephite king, Mosiah, and his message to his people in Mosiah 29. Each of the aged king's four sons refused to accept the heirship to inherit Mosiah's crown, preferring instead to fulfill their divinely approved mission to the Lamanites. Mosiah used this opportunity to evaluate the monarchy itself; and he launched a powerful political and spiritual campaign to abolish it and replace it with a republic governed by judges. The people responded positively; in 91 B.C. they selected the younger Alma as their first chief judge.

Mosiah's reasons for advancing the cause of democracy also provide a charter under which the chief judges functioned. Understanding the charter is crucial to understanding the judges and their lessons for us today. After reviewing the undesirable characteristics of an absolute monarchy, Mosiah charged his people: "Therefore, choose you by the voice of this people, judges, that ye may be judged according to the laws which have been given you by our fathers, which are correct, and which were given them by the hand of the Lord. Now it is not common that the voice of the people desireth anything contrary to that which is right; but it is common for the lesser part of the people to desire that which is not right; therefore this shall ye observe and make it your law—to do your business by the voice of the people. And if the time comes that the voice of the people doth choose iniquity, then is the time that the judgments of God will come upon you; yea, then is the time he will visit you with great destruction even as he has hitherto visited this land." (Mosiah 29:25-27.)

Four great governmental principles that guided the reign of the judges are identified in this charter: (1) The concept that law, not force, authority, or personality, rules in society; (2) the procedure that law will be determined by the voice of the people, supporting and preserving their free agency; (3) the recognition that correct principles of law are given to man by God through the prophets; and (4) a commitment to the necessity for a spiritual foundation of that law in society.

The judges' devotion to the rule of law in society shows in the decisive action they took in cases of deliberate rebellion. When Nehor practiced priestcraft and then murdered the old warrior Gideon, he was tried and executed quickly, for as Alma said in pronouncing the death sentence, "This people must abide by the law." (Alma 1:14.) When Pahoran was appointed to fill the vacancy in the judgment seat created by the death of his father Nephihah in 67 B.C., the "oath and sacred ordinance" he took upon himself included the charge "to bring the wicked to justice according to their crime." (Alma 50:39.) He had that oath tested by kingmen desiring to reestablish a monarchy among the Nephites. Alma had faced the same challenge from Amlici in his first years as chief judge; twice in his fifteen-year reign Pahoran imposed legal sanctions against monarchists. (Alma 2:1-13; 51:1-7; 62:7-11.) And when the Gadianton chief Giddianhi tried to win Lachoneus over to another form of monarchy with subtle bribery, threats, and a web of half-truths, that great judge rallied his people swiftly to preserve the rule of law in their democracy. (See 3 Nephi 3:1-17.)

But criminals and revolutionaries were not the only Nephites to feel the judges' commitment to this principle. The judges' judicial actions were characterized by the strictest adherence to principles of equity and justice. The record says of Nephihah, who served as chief judge for sixteen years, that he died "having filled the judgment-seat with perfect uprightness before God." (Alma 50:37.) And the scriptural eulogies of Helaman II, his son Nephi, and Lachoneus all stress "justice and equity" as the dominant themes of their righteous administrations. (Helaman 3:20, 37; 3 Nephi 6:4.) In stark contrast to the infamous lawless lawyers who scourged the Nephites with their litigious greed and professorial priestcraft (Alma 10:14-15; 3 Nephi 6:19-30), the judges believed in the law, lived by the law, and wielded it as a powerful weapon to preserve social righteousness and civic morality in their society. (See 3 Nephi 6.)

The Nephite judges with equal loyalty supported the second principle in the charter: that of free agency in political life, preserving the right of the people to determine their own laws. Despite great pressure during national emergencies, with monarchists and secret combinations within and hostile Lamanite armies without, they resisted and rejected a double temptation: to become tyrants themselves and to abdicate their stewardships to ensure their personal security. But the risk involved did not prevent the judges from serving: the judgeship cost the six judges mentioned earlier their lives; a seventh was saved only because Helaman II's loyal servant thwarted Kishkumen's assassination attempt. (Helaman 2:2-9.)

Probably the greatest and most agonizing test for the chief judges came when they had to let the people decide issues where their own free agency was at stake. When Amlici campaigned to become king, Alma let the matter come to a vote; the voice of the people rejected Amlici, and it was only for his refusal to abide by that decision that he was punished. (Alma 2:5-7, 31.) Pahoran likewise allowed the monarchists their day in the court of public opinion; only when the king-men began a rebellion against the people's will did he move against them. (See Alma 51.)

This confidence in the ability of the people to govern themselves reveals a refreshing governmental humility in the Nephite judges. They trusted the people, and realized that their own stewardship was that of a servant and not of a master. They recognized the limits of their own rights and responsibilities as well as those of the people they governed. We see this quality in Nephihah's humble refusal to accept the guardianship of the sacred records when Alma offered them to him. (Alma 50:38.) It is even more apparent in the relationship between Nephihah's son Pahoran and the charismatic captain Moroni. Who today can fail to be aroused by Moroni's stinging rebuke to Pahoran in Alma 60, and at the same time not marvel at the prudent patience with which the chief judge replied in Alma 61?

When Pahoran wrote Moroni as his "beloved brother," rejoicing in his "greatness of . . . heart," and speaking of his joy in receiving the captain's letter, he not only set for us a glowing standard in refusing to be offended by an associate, but also emphasized in unmistakable terms the principle of *shared* governmental power in a republic. Well could the chief judge say without boasting, "I, Pahoran, do not seek for power, save only to retain my judgment-seat that I may preserve the rights and the liberty of my people. My soul standeth fast in that liberty in the which God hath made us free." (Alma 61:9.)

In implementing the third principle of Mosiah's charter, that of divine direction for their laws, the Nephite judges moved beyond the artificial confines traditionally separating religion and politics in our own day. To the judges, there was no dividing line between the spiritual and the temporal. They seemed to accept prophetic direction as readily in legal matters as they did in the ecclesiastical. In fact, four of the judges were themselves prophets, while a fifth was an elder. (The term *elder* may have had different connotations in the Nephite church, of course.) And although the record is silent regarding any priesthood office held by the remaining judge, it consistently witnesses that gospel priorities and prophetic guidance upheld the law throughout most of the reign of the judges. Thus Pahoran relied upon the inspiration of captain Moroni in the justice of opposing the king-men with force. (Alma 61:19-20.) Lachoneus caused his people to "cry unto the Lord" in a time of governmental crisis. (3 Nephi 3:12.) And no more vivid example of harmony between religious and judicial functions can be found than in the oath of Pahoran to "judge righteously, and to keep the peace and the freedom of the people, and to grant unto them their sacred privileges to worship the Lord their God, yea, to support and maintain the cause of God all his days." (Alma 50:39.)

By sometimes installing their prophet as judicial leader, the Nephites followed the patriarchal pattern of government first instituted by Adam and imitated with varying degrees of success by later generations. (Abraham 1:26.) Although resignations and assassinations broke the patriarchal chain of judges five times, no less than seven of the judges were descendants of their judicial predecessors.

But the fourth principle of Mosiah's charter is the most important one. Beyond the judges' adherence to the rule of law, their defense of free agency, and their use of gospel principles in directing the law, their recognizing the need for a spiritual foundation for law and their efforts to develop a social commitment to it stand out as a warning testament to our own time. They doubtless remembered Mosiah's stern warning that if the people ceased to be righteous, the law would work against civic happiness. To keep public standards of morality high, the judges did two things: (1) They began with themselves by striving to conform their personal and professional lives to gospel standards. (2) When necessary, they resigned the judgment seat to devote their full energies to preaching repentance and, consequently, to strengthening the spiritual foundation of the law.

The scriptures are clear that these were righteous men. Nephihah's "perfect uprightness," Pahoran's sacred oath of office, and Lachoneus's encouraging example among his people all demonstrate their personal spirituality. (Alma 50:37, 39; 3 Nephi 3:12, 15-16, 25.) Helaman II "did do that which was right in the sight of God continually," and his son Nephi "began to grow up unto the Lord" in his youth, and "did keep the commandments of God" as an adult. (Helaman 3:20-21, 37.)

That seven of the judges descended from other judges also indicates they did not neglect their family responsibilities, but taught their children the ways of the Lord by precept as well as example. It was no mere coincidence or the result of haphazard teaching that Nephi was able to recall in detail a sermon his father, Helaman II, had taught him over nine years before—recall so well that he was able to share it with the Nephite nation when he resigned from the judgment seat in A.D. 30. (Helaman 5:5-12.) The record dramatically shows the impact of a strong father-son relationship, for "these were the words which Helaman taught to his sons; yea, he did teach them many things which are not written, and also many things which are written. And they did remember his words; and therefore they went forth, keeping the commandments of God." (Helaman 5:13-14.)

Not only were these judges exemplary fathers, but they were fine sons as well. As Helaman "did walk after the ways of his father," so Nephi "did walk in the ways of his father." (Helaman 3:20, 37.) Both realized the responsibility they shared as student-son and teacher-father in the learning process. Neither abdicated his stewardship within the family for personal or professional responsibilities elsewhere.

When personal righteousness and example were not sufficient to stem the tide of moral deterioration, two judges, both also prophets, resigned the judgment seat and spent the remainder of their lives preaching the gospel. Both did so under conditions of great spiritual apostasy and economic and political breakdown, when personal pride and spiritual corruption had combined to lead the people to choose iniquity. (Alma 4; Helaman 5.)

Alma delivered up the judgment seat to righteous Nephihah after only eight years, "that he himself might go forth among his people, . . . to stir them up in remembrance of their duty, . . . and that he might pull down, by the word of God, all the pride and craftiness and all the contentions which were among his people, seeing no way that he might reclaim them save it were in bearing down in pure testimony against them." (Alma 4:19.) Alma concentrated on spiritual reform as the basis for social reform because "the preaching of the word had a great tendency to lead the people to do that which was just—yea, it had had more powerful effect upon the minds of the people than the sword, or anything else, which had happened unto them." (Alma 31:5.)

Fifty-three years after Alma, Nephi also resigned the judgment seat, for he saw that the Nephites "had altered and trampled under their feet the laws of Mosiah, or that which the Lord commanded him to give unto the people; and they saw that their laws had become corrupted, and that they had become a wicked people." (Helaman 4:22.) Social conditions then graphically fulfilled Mosiah's prophecy of sixty years before (see Mosiah 29): "For as their laws and their governments were established by the voice of the people, and they who chose evil were more numerous than they who chose good, therefore they were ripening for destruction, for the laws had become corrupted. Yea, and this was not all; they were a stiffnecked people, insomuch that they could not be governed by the law nor justice, save it were to their destruction. And it came to pass that Nephi had become weary because of their iniquity; and he yielded up the judgment-seat, and took it upon him to preach the word of God all the remainder of his days." (Helaman 5:2-4.)

The Nephite Judges

Judge	Relation to Predecessors	Church Role	Approx. Tenure	Cause of Termination
Alma II	None	Prophet	91-83 B.C.	Resigned
Nephihah	Nominated by Alma II	Elder	83-68 B.C.	Died
Pahoran I	Son of Nephihah	(?)	68-53 B.C.	Died
Pahoran II	Son of Pahoran I	(?)	52 B.C.	Assassinated
Pacumeni	Son of Pahoran II	(?)	52-51 B.C.	Killed by invaders
Helaman II	Grandson of Alma II	Prophet*	50-39 B.C.	Died
Nephi	Son of Helaman II	Prophet	39-30 B.C.	Resigned
Cezoram	Nominated by Nephi	(?)	30-26 B.C.	Assassinated
Son of Cezoram	Son of Cezoram	(?)	26 B.C.	Assassinated
(Gadianton Robbers in the Judgment Seat, 26 B.C.–A.D. 1)				
Seezoram	(?)	(?)	26-20 B.C. (?)	Assassinated
Lachoneus I	(?)	Prophet	A.D. 1-30	(?)
Lachoneus II	Son of Lachoneus I	(?)	A.D. 30	Assassinated

*We do not know for sure that Helaman II was a prophet. We do know, however, that he was the keeper of the sacred records (see Alma 63:11-13), which almost invariably were in the hands of the prophet, that the book of Helaman was named after him, and that he was a righteous and godly man (see Helaman 3:20). Given his background, character, and responsibility, it is probably safe for us to assume that he was indeed a prophet.

With both Alma and Nephi, the reformation resulting from their preaching provided the spiritual foundation necessary for the rule of law to once again function in Nephite society. Economic equality replaced class persecution, political freedom replaced oppression, chastity replaced immorality, and peace and joy abounded in the land. Such was the legacy of two great prophet-judges who well understood the attributes essential in a free people under law.

And so we have the exemplary Nephite judges. Obviously, but little can be told of them from the abridged record Mormon has given to us. But surely he made his selection for a reason. As Moroni completed his father's compilation, he addressed himself to us when he said, "Behold, I speak unto you as if ye were present, and yet ye are not. But behold, Jesus Christ hath shown you unto me, and I know your doing." (Mormon 8:35.) The Book of Mormon is a message for our day. Both Mormon and Moroni saw it clearly, and wrote accordingly. What, then, would they have us learn from the Nephite judges?

There are personal lessons, of course. As individuals, the judges were whole men, balanced in their mortal activities, capable of constructive contribution in a variety of social concerns, and actively engaged in the pursuit of personal progress. As fathers, they honored their patriarchal stewardships. As citizens, they influenced for good the lives of those around them by example, by precept, and by action. They are worthy of emulation for these qualities alone.

But the greatest lesson the judges have left for us is their example of how we can preserve and protect our personal and political free agency in an age of increasing social and governmental uncertainty. It is a lesson of vital importance to all mankind.

The Nephite republic lasted only 120 years. The history of its life and death is an inspired guide to judging the progress of our own civilization. Understanding why it lived and why it died is imperative if we today are to retain our own freedom. It lived because four dedicated missionaries were willing to sacrifice fourteen years of their lives and their right to royalty to preach the gospel of Jesus Christ to their bitterest enemies. It died through temporal greed and the loss of brotherly love and concern. It lived because a wise monarch envisioned the sacred foundations of proper government and wrote an inspired charter of liberty for his nation. It died through the accumulated unrighteousness of internal secret combinations and monarchial conspiracies, drained by the wounds of its own political divisiveness. It lived because men such as Helaman and Lachoneus were so committed to principles of the law and the gospel that they served their fellowmen at great risk and personal danger. It died through those who, rather than face social ostracism and threatened violence, chose the false security of subservience by giving up the proper procedures and practices of this government.

It lived because men such as Nephihah and Pahoran were resolute in their defense of freedom under law, and remained humble in the possession of great governmental power. It died in official arrogance and political tyranny. It lived because of Alma and Nephi, "men that had understanding of the times, to know what Israel ought to do" (1 Chronicles 12:32), and who were actively in but "not of the world" (John 17:14). It died when good men did too little, when a confused and troubled nation failed to turn to the light of the gospel and chose instead to walk in the darkness of its own worldly learning and criminal conceit.

There is a critical time in the lives of men and nations when they must make an ultimate decision: to exercise their free agency righteously, or set in motion a spiraling sequence of spiritual suicide. For 120 years under the Nephite judges, national allegiance wavered between a bright hope of prophetic progress and the stagnation of compounded apostasy. In the end, the Nephites chose the "other gospel" (Galatians 1:8) and reaped the judgments Mosiah had prophesied.

And what of the judges? They went down with the ship of state, but they never stopped bailing. When the tides of national adversity were running the highest, they met them head on, "idealists without illusions" who counted the costs and were content with the contest. The lesson is clear. The choice is ours.

James R. Moss is an associate professor of Church history at Brigham Young University.

Nephi, Lehi, and Samuel the Lamanite

Brian Best

Most of us are incurably romantic in our attitudes toward life. We like to mentally entertain happy endings, lucky breaks, effortless successes, and sudden character transformations. Some among us even seem to regard salvation as a matter of good fortune and hope God will be particularly merciful on that great and final judgment day.

Yet, over and over, the scriptures demonstrate that life is not a romantic fairy tale, but a law-abiding and largely predictable reality. Mercy is not something to be bestowed upon us gratuitously at the day of judgment, but something that has already been offered through the atonement of Christ, and we are able to receive that mercy only upon conditions of repentance and obedience.

In its unwavering insistence on the conditions that govern justice and mercy, the Book of Mormon is perhaps the most emphatically anti-romantic book ever written. On nearly every page it drives home the all-important lesson that the choices we make operate unerringly in a universe of law to bring about predictable consequences. To the writers of the Book of Mormon, nothing is more insidiously false than the notion that God dispenses mercy freely no matter what we do and that our salvation depends chiefly upon his tenderheartedness. Prophet after prophet emphasizes the contrary; that justice cannot be robbed and that mercy can be granted only according to laws and conditions. Alma speaks for them all when he explains: "According to justice, the plan of redemption could not be brought about, only on conditions of repentance of men in this probationary state, yea, this preparatory state; for except it were for these conditions, mercy could not take effect except it should destroy the work of justice. Now the work of justice could not be destroyed; if so, God would cease to be God." (Alma 42:13.)

The book of Helaman vigorously illustrates this same teaching: that man must use his agency to choose the way of salvation according to the conditions upon which mercy is based; otherwise, he will forfeit the proffered blessings according to the laws and judgments of a just God. As Nephi and Lehi, the sons of Helaman, pursue the duties of their ministry, and as Samuel the Lamanite joins with them later in their largely futile efforts to prepare a rebellious people to accept the coming of Christ, we see that even God is unable to reclaim those who refuse to accept the conditions that would allow them a place in the merciful plan of redemption.

But if the teetering of man between the claims of justice and the claims of mercy were all the scriptures offered for our edification, the reading might have very little human appeal. It is often difficult to get excited about abstract principles, even when they affect our eternal destiny. Fortunately, the Book of Mormon, like all the scriptures, has another dimension that makes it possible for us to share feelingly in the conflict. When we read the book of Helaman, for instance, we do not just read of the conflict of good and evil; we read of people involved in that conflict, people who feel strongly about what is happening to themselves and to others.

Nephi, the son of Helaman, through whose eyes (though at times with Mormon's editorial comment) we see most of the events, is not just a recorder, not a computerized robot collecting and storing up evidence for and against the children of men; he is a dedicated and caring human being. When we read his words or those which he quotes from the teachings of Samuel the Lamanite, we are permitted to share in more than just historical or doctrinal observations and judgments; through these words we also experience the proper and powerful feelings of a servant of God and come to know more fully how it feels to be righteous and obedient. Through sharing vicariously the aspirations and disappointments, the joys and sorrows of Nephi or Samuel, we discover more fully the love of virtue that we ourselves possess and come to recognize more expertly and cherish more earnestly the behavior and feelings that constitute that virtue.

In order to relate more completely to the problems of Nephi, Lehi, and Samuel as recorded in the book of Helaman, let us become familiar with the historical setting of the book. It begins about 52 B.C. with a brief summary of the events that precede Helaman's becoming chief judge over the Nephites and introduces us to the newly organized band of robbers begun by the assassin Kishkumen and continued after his death by Gadianton. In a parenthetical note, Mormon tells us that as we read on through the Book of Mormon, we will see that this band of robbers finally causes the entire destruction of the Nephite nation. (Helaman 2:12-14.) But in Helaman's day the band is small, only a minor threat to political stability.

At the death of Helaman, about 39 B.C., Nephi, his eldest son, becomes the chief judge. (Helaman 3:37.) Nine years later, recognizing the inability of law to govern an overwhelmingly lawless society, and realizing also his inability to be fully effective as both judge and prophet, Nephi yields up the judgment seat to Cezoram and, with his brother Lehi, begins an untiring thirty-year ministry to try to convert his people from their sinful ways. (Helaman 5:1-4.) The difficulty of their task is overwhelming—much like trying to eliminate crime, governmental corruption, immorality, and unbelief from a modern nation.

In fact, the Nephite nation was very much like those we

are familiar with. Its representative form of government depended for its stability on its laws and on the integrity of its citizens and public officials. (Helaman 5:2.) Moreover, the Nephites were in a time of great prosperity and, except for a few minor conflicts, were enjoying peace following a devastating war that had occurred about twenty years earlier. (See Alma 48-62.) Crime, in the form of the Gadianton robbers, was making rapid advances, even among members of the Church. And finally, because of their wealth and prosperity, the people were becoming increasingly proud, worldly, rebellious, and contemptuous of the poor and the humble believers in Christ. Add to these circumstances the fact that prophets were foretelling the imminent coming of Christ—within about forty years, as it turned out—and we see how similar their day was to our own.

One other note should perhaps be added. The Nephites were becoming increasingly wicked; yet, like people nowadays, they seem not to have recognized how far they had degenerated from the truths they had once known. Even at the height of their wickedness, shortly before the birth of Christ when Samuel the Lamanite was preaching of their impending destruction, they still seem to have retained some semblance of religious belief. According to Samuel, they said among themselves, "If our days had been in the days of our fathers of old, we would not have slain the prophets; we would not have stoned them, and cast them out." (Helaman 13:25.)

To hear them talk, one would surmise that they thought of themselves as enlightened, civilized, and properly religious. As in our day, pride, worldliness, and sin seem to have captured them unawares. Thus, to them, the prophets who called attention to their sins seemed to be madmen or schemers deserving of persecution (see Helaman 13:26); to them, those who taught of the birth of one to be called Christ, the Son of God, seemed to be teaching unreasonable doctrines or attempting to impose a fable upon the people in order to keep them in subjection through superstition. Their criticism of Samuel's teachings about the coming of Christ and the marvelous signs that would attend his birth illustrates well how their faulty religious attitudes and beliefs kept them from comprehending the truth of Samuel's message: "We know that this is a wicked tradition, which has been handed down unto us by our fathers, to cause us that we should believe in some great and marvelous thing which should come to pass, but not among us, but in a land which is far distant, a land which we know not; therefore they can keep us in ignorance, for we cannot witness with our own eyes that they are true. And they will, by the cunning and the mysterious arts of the evil one, work some great mystery which we cannot understand, which will keep us down to be servants to their words, and also servants unto them, for we depend upon them to teach us the word; and thus will they keep us in ignorance if we will yield ourselves unto them, all the days of our lives." (Helaman 16:20-21.)

This is not the speech of persons who admit they have abandoned religion and are rebelling willfully against God. It seems very likely that the great wickedness of these people was not very different from what the world today accepts as normal. And in that world, where the pursuit of wealth, power, and pleasure is the norm and where religion is mostly a formal ritual, it is usually the true prophet, not the sinner, who is made to appear abnormal.

Therefore, Nephi, Lehi, and Samuel were neither popular nor very successful in the long run in their efforts to save their society, although the power of the miracles that attended their ministry did result temporarily in great conversions among both the Nephites and the Lamanites.

In contrast to the shifting, unstable, materialistic ways of the people generally are the steadfastness and stability of these three prophets and the few who faithfully follow them. They seem to be a race apart—a different kind of being altogether from the other souls they walk among. They are spiritual men, sons of God; those who reject them are natural men, or enemies of God. Walking in obedience to divine law, these prophets participate more and more fully in the mysteries of God, "having many revelations daily" (Helaman 11:23), while the foolish masses lose even the knowledge they once possessed, until, as Alma warned, they "know nothing concerning the mysteries; and . . . are taken captive by the devil, and led by his will down to destruction. Now this is what is meant by the chains of hell" (Alma 12:11). In fact, so far did these people go in their rejection of the word of God that they were about to place themselves outside the saving power of either justice or mercy. Samuel prophesied that were they to continue in their sins and not repent, they would soon find it said of them: "Your days of probation are past; ye have procrastinated the day of your salvation until it is everlastingly too late, and your destruction is made sure; yea, for ye have sought all the days of your lives for that which ye could not obtain; and ye have sought for happiness in doing iniquity, which thing is contrary to the nature of that righteousness which is in our great and Eternal Head." (Helaman 13:38.)

Notice that Samuel did not tell them they had offended God and were about to be cut off from his love; rather, he told them that their behavior was contrary to the nature of happiness and righteousness, or that they had gone contrary to eternal law and were separating themselves from that which is the nature of God.

Not only did these people reject divine law; they also rejected the witness of many signs and miracles. And Samuel explained to them that even greater signs would be given as the birth of Christ drew nearer, "to the intent that there should be no cause for unbelief among the children of men." (Helaman 14:28.) Then, stressing once more the laws by which the destiny of men is governed, Samuel explained that these many signs and wonders would be given so "that whosoever will believe might be saved, and that whosoever will not believe, a righteous judgment may come upon them." (Helaman 14:29.) Finally, detailing the laws according to which salvation or damnation is administered to mankind, he admonished: "Remember, remember, my brethren, that whosoever perisheth, perisheth unto himself; and whosoever doeth iniquity, doeth it unto himself; for behold, ye are free; ye are permitted to act for yourselves; for behold, God hath given unto you a knowledge and he hath made you free. He hath given unto you that ye might know good from evil, and he hath given unto you that ye might choose life or death; and ye can do good and be restored unto that which is good, or have that which is good restored unto you; or ye can do evil, and have that which is evil restored unto you." (Helaman 14:30-31.)

In Samuel's pleading tone, we see again that the power of the book of Helaman lies in its concern for real human souls, not just in its concern with abstract principles of good and evil. We see it unfolding through the eyes, minds, and hearts of righteous men who, fired by the vision and power of God, are doing all they can to avert catastrophe and are being frustrated every step of the way by the very persons they are laboring so diligently to save. The pain of the irony alone is at times almost overwhelming.

Because the book of Helaman is taken largely from the record of Nephi, we know more of his personal battle against the evils of his day than we do of his brother Lehi. Although Lehi undoubtedly labored and suffered in much the same way that Nephi did, we know nothing of his personal feelings but are told only generally of his diligence and righteousness. Along with Nephi, he determined to "preach the word of God all the remainder of his days" (Helaman 5:4); he accompanied Nephi in his preaching in the land Bountiful and the land southward; he assisted in the conversion of many dissenting Nephites and eight thousand Lamanites in and around the land of Zarahemla; and he shared with Nephi a remarkable spiritual experience in a Lamanite prison. He also accompanied Nephi on the futile mission to the land northward and continued with Nephi in the ministry around Zarahemla, experiencing many revelations and doing much preaching among the people. We are told that he "was not a whit behind [Nephi] as to things pertaining to righteousness." (Helaman 11:19.)

An even greater lack of information hampers our efforts to come to know Samuel's personality. We know little of the man except what we can glean from the brief summary of his activities and the extensive quotations from his preaching. We know that he was a man of courage and determination and that he was obedient to the Lord's commands. After he had preached to the Nephites for many days, "they did cast him out, and he was about to return to his own land" (Helaman 13:2); but when the voice of the Lord came to him, commanding him to return and continue his prophesying, he immediately obeyed (Helaman 13:3). A lesser man might have been daunted by the refusal of the populace to let him enter the city, but Samuel, determined to obey the Lord, climbed upon the city wall and "cried with a loud voice, and prophesied." (Helaman 13:4.)

We discover that Samuel was close to the Spirit and sensitive to its promptings: he preached and prophesied "whatsoever things the Lord put into his heart." (Helaman 13:4.) We know, too, that he was commanded and instructed by an angel of the Lord (Helaman 14:9, 28), and that the power of the Lord protected him from physical harm: when the rebellious Nephites tried to kill him, "the Spirit of the Lord was with him, insomuch that they could not hit him with their stones neither with their arrows" (Helaman 16:2).

The portion of Samuel's prophecies contained in Helaman 15 is a sobering warning to those who have been called the people of God. Samuel reminds the Nephites that they "have been a chosen people of the Lord" (Helaman 15:3) in contrast to the Lamanites, whom the Lord has not favored "because their deeds have been evil continually . . . because of the iniquity of the tradition of their fathers" (Helaman 15:4). The Nephites have no cause for pride, however, because the Lamanites are steadfast and firm "when they are once enlightened" (Helaman 15:10), and Samuel declares that "it shall be better for them than for you except ye repent" (Helaman 15:14).

Samuel's exhortation and warning do not come from any cultural smugness, however, but from love for the Nephites—his "beloved brethren." (Helaman 15:1.) Only when the Lord no longer restrains him and when the Nephites make an attempt on his life does he return to his own country—where he begins "to preach and to prophesy among his own people." (Helaman 16:7.)

Thus, through Nephi's quotations from the preaching of Samuel, we are able to perceive the tenacity and depth of devotion and feeling of that great prophet; but our insight into his personality is necessarily limited because we are seeing him through the eyes of another. Nephi himself remains central throughout the book of Helaman; it is his personality that dominates. If we are to share the feelings of a prophet, if we are to taste personally the joy of seemingly great missionary successes and then the pain of watching all those successes disintegrate as a society plummets toward destruction, we must do so through him.

When the account of this Nephi begins, we learn of the riches and pride within the church and the wickedness of the people generally—and we learn of Nephi's choice to yield up the judgment seat and turn to preaching, since he had become "weary" because of the iniquity of the people. (Helaman 5:4.) We can see at once the human element in Nephi's choice: we see that his turning to full-time preaching is not only the right or reasonable thing to do, it is the thing he *must* do because of his feelings about extremely distressing circumstances. The record then tells us more about this man whose emotions are involved in his decisions. He and his brother recall the words of Helaman, their father. We notice that these words are urgent and tender. Over and over we hear a loving, dedicated parent entreating: "My sons . . . my sons . . . my sons" (see Helaman 5:6-8); "O remember, remember, my sons" (Helaman 5:9); "and now, my sons, remember, remember that it is upon the rock of our Redeemer, who is Christ, the Son of God, that ye must build your foundation" (Helaman 5:12). Is it surprising that sons of such a father would also feel deeply and urgently the need to preach repentance to a society falling into unbelief?

Moreover, these men were not merely preaching doctrine learned by rote; they, like their father, had experienced personally the power and wisdom of God. Nephi tells us that he and his brother preached with "great power and authority, for they had power and authority given unto them that they might speak, and they also had what they should speak given unto them." (Helaman 5:18.)

A particularly impressive witness of the power of God occurred when they found themselves in a Lamanite prison, kept "many days without food." (Helaman 5:22.) When the Lamanites and the Nephite dissenters came to the prison to put them to death, suddenly they found themselves "encircled about as if by fire." (Helaman 5:23.) In the way the following sentence repeats certain words, notice traces of the amazement they must have felt: "Nephi and Lehi were not burned; and they were as standing in the midst of fire and were not burned." (Helaman 5:23.) These men were human. In the prison they experienced hunger, fear, apprehension, then amazement and hope as they participated in this mighty miracle. "When they saw that they were encircled about with a pillar of fire, and that it burned them not, their hearts did take courage." (Helaman 5:24.)

Recognizing that "God [had] shown . . . this marvelous thing" (Helaman 5:26), they began to preach with boldness. Suddenly the earth trembled, the walls of the prison shook, and a cloud of darkness overshadowed the prison. (Helaman 5:27-28.) Through this cloud a voice was heard: "Repent ye, repent ye, and seek no more to destroy my servants whom I have sent unto you to declare good tidings." (Helaman 5:29.) The voice spoke again. Nephi tries to share with us the unusual nature of this voice and the power with which it affected him. This voice, he says, was "not a voice of thunder, neither . . . a voice of a great tumultuous noise, but . . . a still voice of perfect mildness, as if it had been a whisper, and it did pierce even to the very soul." (Helaman 5:30.) Yet each time the voice spoke, the walls of the prison trembled as if they were about to fall. The voice came a third time, speaking "marvelous words which cannot be uttered by man; and the walls [of the prison] did tremble . . . and the earth shook as if it were about to divide asunder." (Helaman 5:33.) Through all this, the people in the prison were so awestruck and fearful that they could not move. Then through the cloud of darkness they saw the faces of Nephi and Lehi, and "they did shine exceedingly, even as the faces of angels." (Helaman 5:36.)

Who can read of this experience, allowing his mind's eye to picture it, without feeling more deeply about the reality of God, about Nephi and Lehi, and about the significance of his own life. Vicariously, we experience something of what Nephi and Lehi experienced. We participate in a real-life drama with living prophets, and like them we are amazed, overjoyed, exalted in our feelings. In brief, we learn more than just doctrine.

With this miraculous event, the great work of conversion among the Lamanites commenced. The three hundred persons who witnessed these miracles in the prison were converted and began to testify among their brethren. Before long the entire Lamanite nation was filled with believers. (Helaman 5:49-50.) Their hearts changed, they laid down their weapons, yielded up the lands they had won by conquest from the Nephites, and returned to their own lands. (Helaman 5:51-52.) Lamanite missionaries then began to testify to the Nephites. (Helaman 6:4-5.) Surely Nephi is reflecting his own intense feelings of joy when he writes: "The people of the church did have great joy because of the conversion of the Lamanites, yea, because of the church of God, which had been established among them. And they did fellowship one with another, . . . and did have great joy." (Helaman 6:3.)

Imagine the happiness of Nephi and Lehi about 29 B.C. as

they beheld the results of their labors: "peace in all the land, insomuch that the Nephites did go into whatsoever part of the land they would, whether among the Nephites or the Lamanites." (Helaman 6:7.)

Then Nephi, accompanied by Lehi, began a six-year missionary journey in the land northward (Helaman 6:6; 7:1), during which the people there "did reject all his words" (Helaman 7:3). Undoubtedly discouraged, Nephi returned to Zarahemla, only to find that the peaceful situation he had left such a short time before had degenerated considerably. He found "the people in a state of . . . awful wickedness, and those Gadianton robbers filling the judgment-seats—having usurped the power and authority of the land; laying aside the commandments of God." (Helaman 7:4.) Here we get one of our most intimate glimpses of the man Nephi. The record states: "Now this great iniquity had come upon the Nephites, in the space of not many years; and when Nephi saw it, his heart was swollen with sorrow within his breast; and he did exclaim in the agony of his soul: Oh, that I could have had my days in the days when my father Nephi first came out of the land of Jerusalem, that I could have joyed with him in the promised land; then were his people easy to be entreated, firm to keep the commandments of God, and slow to be led to do iniquity; and they were quick to hearken unto the words of the Lord—yea, if my days could have been in those days, then would my soul have had joy in the righteousness of my brethren. But behold, I am consigned that these are my days, and that my soul shall be filled with sorrow because of this the wickedness of my brethren." (Helaman 7:6-9.)

Recall that Nephi uttered this lament upon a tower in his garden, pouring out his soul to the Lord in his agony. People passing by happened to overhear him and marveled at the depth of his mourning. Hurriedly, a multitude gathered to discover the cause of such great grief. (See Helaman 7:10-11.) Read Nephi's words (see Helaman 7:13-29) as he chides these people for their unbelief and wickedness. The words are not just "doctrine" to be learned by chapter and verse; they are the passionate overflowing of a man's sorrow, and they range from desperate pleading ("O repent ye, repent ye! Why will ye die?") to amazement and exasperation ("O, how could you have forgotten your God in the very day that he has delivered you?").

Picture Nephi's frustration as he tried to convince the people that he was indeed the Lord's messenger by prophesying the murder of the chief judge (Helaman 8:27-28), only to find himself accused of being an accomplice and cast into prison (Helaman 9:16-20). Picture then the results of his second prophecy regarding the man who had committed the murder. (See Helaman 9:25-36.) When the prophecy turned out to be true, Nephi was hailed as a great prophet; some even called him a god. (Helaman 9:40-41.) But in their controversy over exactly what Nephi was, the people became angry with one another, divided into disputing parties, and went their ways, "leaving Nephi alone, as he was standing in the midst of them." (Helaman 10:1.) Left alone, isolated from his fellow beings, Nephi perhaps felt very lonely and discouraged.

Yet notice how the command of God prevailed over all Nephi's moods and disappointments. Nephi started toward his home, "pondering upon the things which the Lord had shown unto him." (Helaman 10:2.) Suddenly a voice spoke to him, saying: "Blessed art thou, Nephi, for those things which thou hast done; for I have beheld how thou hast with unwearyingness declared the word, which I have given unto thee, unto this people." (Helaman 10:4.) Certainly the Lord knew of Nephi's personal grief and chose this moment to buoy him up. But more! This time it is obvious that the Lord was regarding his servant in a new and very special way: "Because thou hast done this with such unwearyingness, behold, I will bless thee forever; and I will make thee mighty in word and in deed, in faith and in works; yea, even that all things shall be done unto thee according to thy word, for thou shalt not ask that which is contrary to my will. Behold, thou art Nephi, and I am God. Behold, I declare it unto thee in the presence of mine angels, that ye shall have power over this people, and shall smite the earth with famine, and with pestilence, and destruction, according to the wickedness of this people." (Helaman 10:5-6.)

One is reminded of the Prophet Joseph Smith's comment: "When the Lord has thoroughly proved him, and finds that the man is determined to serve Him at all hazards, then the man will find his calling and his election made sure." (*Teachings of the Prophet Joseph Smith,* p. 150.) And then, obedient to the Lord's command, Nephi turned around, without even returning to his home, and began again to preach repentance to the people.

With only intermittent successes, this mighty prophet continued to serve faithfully, once asking the Lord to bring a famine upon the people in order to bring a halt to their wickedness and warfare, rather than destroy them. (Helaman 11:4-5.) Yet, never one to give up hope, Nephi readily consented to plead with the Lord to end the famine when, three years later, the people showed some evidence of repentance. (Helaman 11:7-9.) His prayer for them shows how deeply he could love his people even in their iniquity: "O Lord, thou didst hearken unto my words when I said, Let there be a famine, that the pestilence of the sword might cease; and I know that thou wilt, even at this time, hearken unto my words, for thou saidst that: If this people repent I will spare them. Yea, O Lord, and thou seest that they have repented, because of the famine and the pestilence and destruction which has come unto them. And now, O Lord, wilt thou turn away thine anger, and try again if they will serve thee? And if so, O Lord, thou canst bless them according to thy words which thou hast said." (Helaman 11:14-16.)

But within ten years all was corrupt again, and the whole of chapter twelve of Helaman records a powerful lamentation that contrasts human frailty with God's goodness. There is some question as to whether this chapter is a quotation of Nephi's words or a commentary by the abridger, Mormon. But even if the passage is not Nephi's work, it seems to reflect the attitudes and philosophy that must undergird the kind of life he lived. Beginning with a general comment on the "unsteadiness of the hearts of the children of men," the author seems to offer an apology for the human race; nevertheless, he goes on hopefully to assert his faith that "the Lord in his great infinite goodness doth bless and prosper those who put their trust in him." (Helaman 12:1.) This law he regards as a certainty, and though most of the rest of his lamentation bemoans man's foolishness, pride, and disobedience, he concludes by praising "our great and everlasting God" (v. 8) and reasserting his faith in the everlasting nature of God's eternal law and the absoluteness of his word: "And behold, if the Lord shall say unto a man—Because of thine iniquities, thou shalt be accursed forever—it shall be done. And if the Lord shall say [unto a man]—Because of thine iniquities thou shalt be cut off from my presence—he will cause that it shall be so. And wo unto him to whom he shall say this, for it shall be unto him that will do iniquity, and he cannot be saved; therefore, for this cause, that men might be saved, hath repentance been declared. Therefore, blessed are they who will repent and hearken unto the voice of the Lord their God; for these are they that shall be saved. . . . And I would that all men might be saved. But we read that in the great and last day there are some who shall be cast out, yea, who shall be cast off from the presence of the Lord; yea, who shall be consigned to a state of endless misery, fulfilling the words which say: They that have done good shall have everlasting life; and they that have done evil shall have everlasting damnation. And thus it is. Amen." (Helaman 12:21-23, 25-26.)

It is sobering that the narrative of Nephi's loving and untiring service in behalf of his people must end with this passage reaffirming the immutability of God's laws and man's inability to be saved except through obedience to those laws.

While the signs and wonders increased as the time of the birth of Christ drew near, Nephi continued to preach and baptize whatever converts had responded to the teaching of Samuel and himself. (It is interesting that there is no record of Samuel's ever having baptized any of the people who were converted through his preaching: "As many as believed on [Samuel's] word went forth and sought for Nephi . . . desiring that they might be baptized." [Helaman 16:1; see also Helaman 16:3-5.]) Lehi may have died, since he is not mentioned toward the end of the book of Helaman. Yet "notwithstanding the signs and the wonders which were wrought among the people of the Lord, and the many miracles which they did, Satan did get great hold upon the hearts of the people upon all the face of the land." (Helaman 16:23.)

Nephi's mission ended sometime during the year before Christ's birth. After "giving charge unto his son Nephi, who was his eldest son, concerning the plates, . . . he departed out of the land, and whither he went, no man knoweth." (3 Nephi 1:2-3.) Like Moses, this special servant of God seems to have been taken by the Lord for special purposes.

It would be difficult to find in all of scripture a more devoted and powerful prophet than Nephi, the son of Helaman. As we read his account of his own labors, as well as the labors of Lehi and Samuel the Lamanite, our hearts are touched by the intensely human concern of these prophets for the people to whom they are sent to minister. Yet, with all their humanity, they stand as unfaltering witnesses of the irrevocability of eternal law—not only of the just law that judges and condemns the unrepentant, but of the law of mercy by which glory enters and transforms the lives of all those who choose to obey the commandments of God.

Brian S. Best is an associate professor of English at Brigham Young University.

The Nephi We Tend to Forget

Marilyn Arnold

There are some Book of Mormon figures whom we glimpse only briefly, whom we can never know well, but who intrigue us immensely because that brief glimpse seems to show us the tip of a remarkable iceberg. Nephi, the grandson of Helaman, is such a figure for me. He moves very quietly onto the scene and backs very quietly out of it, but he is no ordinary record-keeper. This is the man who was the spiritual leader of the Nephites at the time of the birth of the Savior and during the Savior's ministry on the American continent. This is the man who wrote the account that Mormon abridged as Third Nephi, one of the most powerful sections of the Book of Mormon. So great was his faith and so vigorous his spiritual power that he raised his brother from the dead and communed regularly with angels.

Rereading Third Nephi, I have become more and more aware that perhaps our only real access to Nephi's character is through Mormon's perception of him as Mormon reads and abridges Nephi's record. I think Mormon must have been impressed with Nephi because he keeps interrupting his narrative to pay respect, either directly or indirectly, to the earlier prophet. (See, for example, 3 Nephi 7:15-16 and 3

Nephi 8:1.) Since we can, in effect, know Nephi only secondhand, it seems important that we try to look through Mormon's eyes, try to see Nephi as Mormon saw him. Careful study of Mormon's abridgement confirms in both subtle and obvious ways that Mormon knew he had encountered a remarkable human being.

I have often wondered, in reading between the lines, if Mormon might have been a little reluctant to cut and summarize Nephi's account. It appears that at times he prefers to omit parts of the account rather than attempt to shorten it. Speaking of Nephi's ministerings, for instance, he says, "And all of them cannot be written, and a part of them would not suffice, therefore they are not written in this book. And Nephi did minister with power and with great authority." (3 Nephi 7:17.)

Even in making rather casual references to the record, Mormon adds extra praise for Nephi: "And now it came to pass that according to our record, and we know our record to be true, for behold, it was a just man who did keep the record—for he truly did many miracles in the name of Jesus; and there was not any man who could do a miracle in the name of Jesus save he were cleansed every whit from his iniquity." (3 Nephi 8:1.)

As an English teacher, I am perhaps doubly sensitive to language, and I cannot help feeling that Nephi was a gifted writer. Whether Third Nephi is largely composed of Mormon's words as inspired by Nephi's record or consists of direct quotations from that record, the language is often eloquent and vivid. One of the most moving passages in all scripture is the description in Third Nephi of the multitude's response to the prayer Jesus offered in their behalf: "And after this manner do they bear record: The eye hath never seen, neither hath the ear heard, before, so great and marvelous things as we saw and heard Jesus speak unto the Father; and no tongue can speak, neither can there be written by any man, neither can the hearts of men conceive so great and marvelous things as we both saw and heard Jesus speak; and no one can conceive of the joy which filled our souls at the time we heard him pray for us unto the Father." (3 Nephi 17:16-17.)

Interesting as these kinds of observations are, it is nevertheless Mormon's perception of Nephi's great spiritual stature that really stirs our minds and hearts. More concerned about the well-being of his people than about himself, strong in spirit and will, Nephi kept a record chiefly to bear witness to the divine ministry of Jesus among the Nephites. Moving chronologically through Third Nephi, we become more and more aware of Nephi's spiritual magnitude, largely, I think, because Mormon was keenly aware of that magnitude. It is somewhat difficult to get even a limited understanding of Nephi's character because there is so little direct description of him and there are so few explicit references to his activities. I find, however, that as I read Mormon's account, a picture of a dynamic spiritual leader takes shape because the few statements Mormon does make resound through my mind as I read the book of Third Nephi.

We first hear of Nephi when we are told, simply, that his father (also named Nephi) "had departed out of the land of Zarahemla, giving charge unto his son Nephi, who was his eldest son, concerning the plates of brass, and all the records which had been kept, and all those things which had been kept sacred from the departure of Lehi out of Jerusalem." (3 Nephi 1:2.) Apparently the elder Nephi just disappeared—no one knew where (see verse 3)—and the younger Nephi was instructed to keep the Nephite records. This was at the time when the faithful were watching for the prophetic signs that would signal the birth of the Savior into the world. The believers were getting a bit anxious, and the unbelievers were happily insisting that the time had passed when the prophecies were to have been fulfilled. The unbelievers even set a day by which time the chief sign, a night without darkness, had to come or the believers would be executed. It is at this point that Mormon gives us our first indication of Nephi's spiritual strength. In great sorrow over the wickedness of his people, Nephi went to the Lord in prayer. We often cite the example of Enos, who prayed long and earnestly, but we might point to Nephi as well. He "bowed himself down upon the earth, and cried mightily to his God in behalf of his people. . . . And it came to pass that he cried mightily unto the Lord all that day; and behold, the voice of the Lord came unto him." (3 Nephi 1:11-12.)

After praying fervently all day long, Nephi heard this beautiful and loving reply: "Lift up your head and be of good cheer; for behold, the time is at hand, and on this night shall the sign be given, and on the morrow come I into the world, to show unto the world that I will fulfil all that which I have caused to be spoken by the mouth of my holy prophets." (3 Nephi 1:13.) The signs were indeed manifest, and Nephi was blessed thereafter with abundant success, baptizing and performing works of righteousness, in spite of Satan's increased efforts. (See 3 Nephi 1:22-23.)

The next several chapters in Third Nephi deal principally with political and social events and problems, and it is not until chapter seven that we get further confirmation of Nephi's powerful ministry. The people had divided into tribes and grown wicked, stoning the prophets and casting them out. In spite of what must have been immense personal danger, Nephi "went forth among them in that same year, and began to testify, boldly, repentance and remission of sins through faith on the Lord Jesus Christ." (3 Nephi 7:16.) Mormon reports that when Nephi did this the people "were angry with him, even because he had greater power than they," power so great, says Mormon, that it was not possible for his hearers to disbelieve his words. (3 Nephi 7:18.) Even his enemies were affected by his spiritual might and were forced, in spite of themselves, to acknowledge in their hearts that he spoke the truth.

At the beginning of his brief account of Nephi's ministry in chapter seven, Mormon gives a quick summary of Nephi's spiritual experiences—a list impressive not only for the deeds themselves but for the matter-of-fact, simple way the acts are described. Mormon speaks of Nephi as "having been visited by angels and also the voice of the Lord, . . . having seen angels, and being eye-witness, and having had power given unto him that he might know concerning the ministry of Christ." (3 Nephi 7:15.) One line of Mormon's description of Nephi is particularly moving: "So great was his faith on the Lord Jesus Christ that angels did minister unto him daily." (3 Nephi 7:18.) We can scarcely imagine what it would be like to receive daily ministerings from angels; to have that kind of faith and to be that close to the Lord is almost incomprehensible to most of us. Yet through Nephi's example we come to understand that such a life pattern is indeed possible for human beings.

The performing of miracles in the Savior's name seems not to have been uncommon for this mighty prophet. Mormon's sketchy list in verses 19 and 20 of chapter seven probably gives only a bare suggestion of the nature of Nephi's spiritual power: "And in the name of Jesus did he cast out devils and unclean spirits; and even his brother did he raise from the dead, after he had been stoned and suffered death by the people. And the people saw it, and did witness of it, and were angry with him because of his power; and he did also do many more miracles, in the sight of the people, in the name of Jesus."

This passage is highly significant, revealing so much more than it actually says. We sense a gripping drama behind the rather matter-of-fact note that Nephi raised his brother after the brother suffered death by stoning. We sense the mood of the times, the great cloud of danger under which Nephi and his family must have lived constantly. The wicked could not tolerate a man among them who was so strong in faith that he could, through the power of the priesthood, restore the dead to life. So courageous was Nephi that, knowing of the people's great anger, he still moved among them openly performing miracles and preaching the gospel. And in spite of fierce opposition, he made such an impression on some that they repented and were baptized. (See 3 Nephi

7:21-22.) He also ordained a number of men to the ministry, and they, too, went about baptizing the repentant. (See 3 Nephi 7:25-26.) Thus, it would appear that Nephi faithfully directed the work of the church, helping to keep faith in the Savior alive in the New World during the Savior's earth life in the Old World.

It is significant, too, that when the Savior appeared to the people of Nephi, the more righteous of whom were spared in the great destruction that followed the crucifixion, he singled out Nephi and called him to come forth. Clearly, the Lord knew his servant. It was to Nephi that Jesus gave the first responsibility for bringing souls to their Savior. Before calling any others to the ministry, Jesus called Nephi and set him apart. Four verses describe that event: "And it came to pass that he spake unto Nephi (for Nephi was among the multitude) and he commanded him that he should come forth. And Nephi arose and went forth, and bowed himself before the Lord and did kiss his feet. And the Lord commanded him that he should arise. And he arose and stood before him. And the Lord said unto him: I give unto you power that ye shall baptize this people when I am again ascended into heaven." (3 Nephi 11:18-21.)

Of the twelve then called by the Savior, only Nephi is named in Mormon's account at this point in the record: "And it came to pass that when Jesus had spoken these words unto Nephi, and to those who had been called, (now the number of them who had been called, and received power and authority to baptize, was twelve) . . ." (3 Nephi 12:1.)

Significantly, Nephi was also the first among the group to be baptized, and it was he who baptized the other disciples whom Jesus had chosen. (3 Nephi 19:11-12.)

Those baptisms marked a glorious event, for after the ordinances had been performed, Nephi and the others were so filled with the Spirit that they seemed to be encircled by fire. Angels came, and then the Savior himself, in what must have been one of the most thrilling spiritual events ever experienced by mortals. At the climax of that event, Mormon reports that the Lord's "countenance did shine upon them, and behold they were as white as the countenance and also the garments of Jesus; and behold the whiteness thereof did exceed all the whiteness, yea, even there could be nothing upon earth so white as the whiteness thereof." (3 Nephi 19:25.) Clearly only a man of great spiritual strength could have presided over the Church at such a time.

The Savior's appearance in the New World initiated a period of peace and righteousness that must have brought great joy to a person like Nephi. And it is with the Savior's final departure that the Book of Mormon account of Nephi concludes. We learn further only that he passed on the records to his son, also named Nephi. (See 4 Nephi, heading.)

And so ends our brief acquaintance with this Nephi. I believe that certain men are indeed chosen to lead the Lord's church at particular times in history. The fact that Nephi, grandson of Helaman, was chosen to be its head during the time when the Lord himself came to earth and selected his prophet gives a strong indication of where that man should stand in our esteem. And even though our knowledge of Nephi is somewhat tentative, gathered as it is from a few clues Mormon gives us about him, we can scarcely doubt the quality of his leadership or the immensity of his faith.

Marilyn Arnold is a professor of English at Brigham Young University.

The Shepherd and His Other Sheep

Arthur R. Bassett

In his last major discourse, the King Follett Sermon, the Prophet Joseph Smith made some extremely significant comments concerning our relationship with the Master. The Prophet quoted the words the Savior uttered before he entered Gethsemane: "This is life eternal, that they might know thee the only true God, and Jesus Christ, whom thou hast sent." (John 17:3.) Then the Prophet commented: "If any man does not know God, and inquires what kind of a being He is,—if he will search diligently his own heart—if the declaration of Jesus and the apostles be true, he will realize that he has not eternal life; for there can be eternal life on no other principle." *(History of the Church* 6:304.)

The significant relationship between knowing God and eternal life is clarified by the Lord's explanation to Joseph in 1830 that "Endless" is another name properly applied to Him, and, consequently, that *Eternal* punishment or *Endless* punishment is *God's* punishment. (See D&C 19:10-12.) It seems to follow then that eternal life is God's life. Therefore, the Prophet's statement can be taken to mean, in part, that eternal life, being God's life, is understood only as one comes to know God and Christ. Knowing the Master ultimately seems to mean becoming like the Master.

Joseph Smith stressed the same point in the sermon: "If men do not comprehend the character of God, they do not comprehend themselves." *(History of the Church* 6:303.) More pointedly, a little later he adds: "Here, then, is eternal life—to know the only wise and true God; and you have got to learn how to be gods yourselves, and to be kings and priests to God, . . . by going from one small degree to another, and from a small capacity to a great one; from grace to grace, from exaltation to exaltation." *(History of the Church* 6:306.)

From these statements it is evident that our knowledge—in the deeper sense of that word—of Christ will measure whether we obtain eternal life or not. In light of this understanding, we as disciples today should be extremely grateful for the additional insights about the resurrected Lord that were recorded in the Book of Mormon. They lead us further toward an understanding of the Master. This account shows us, as possibly nothing else, how concerned he was that we understand his doctrine, the scriptures that teach of him, and the ordinances of his kingdom.

Two additional contributions found in this account are the opportunity to see the Lord at prayer and, perhaps most importantly, interacting with his chosen disciples and with the multitude gathered near the temple at Bountiful. I am moved by his complete compassion, poured out upon those afflicted by illness and upon the children.

Let us begin with what we learn about him as a teacher of doctrine. We clearly see that he met the student at the student's level of understanding, dealing with several different levels of comprehension simultaneously. This beautiful clarity was not exactly the same thing as simplicity. Although simplicity was paramount, the Master was not one to oversimplify life. He seemed deeply concerned that his disciples understand clearly the general principle before dealing with the particulars, and his apparently simple general statements are summaries that accommodate the particulars.

For example, consider his brief teaching moment with the disciples before addressing the entire multitude. (See 3

Nephi 11.) This moment comes just after that electrifying experience during which the multitude heard the quiet, penetrating voice of the Father, witnessed the bodily descent of the Master from the heavens, and individually saw and touched his wounds.

Jesus repeatedly warns the Twelve he has just chosen against any form of disputations, particularly disputations concerning his doctrine. For, he warned, "he that hath the spirit of contention is not of me, but is of the devil, who is the father of contention, and he stirreth up the hearts of men to contend with anger, one with another." Rather, the Lord instructed, "This is my doctrine, that such things should be done away." (3 Nephi 11:29-30.)

As the Prince of Peace, his goal is to abolish hatred and strife in the world. What he told the Nephite Twelve was a general principle that contains many specific applications.

Christ wanted the Nephites to understand his essential doctrine, and he explained it as simply as possible to the Twelve: Men were to believe in him and repent; then they were to enter into a covenant with him through baptism; lastly, they were to be aided by the Holy Ghost. That, to Christ, was the essence of his doctrine, which he amplifies into more precise specifics in the Nephite counterpart of the Sermon on the Mount. First the general framework, then the details—his method involved beginning with first principles.

Jesus was also patiently careful to make certain the Nephites understood their role in history as "other sheep" of his fold, and also their time in history—he carefully explained the scattering and gathering of Israel and the gospel's restoration. (See especially 3 Nephi 20–22.)

Obviously, the Master felt that the key to understanding lay in the scriptures, for he spent much of that precious time explaining scriptures. Especially was he concerned that the Nephites understand Isaiah. Nephi, the son of Lehi, had quoted extensively from Isaiah at the beginning of the book, remarking that his soul "delighteth in the words of Isaiah." (2 Nephi 25:5.) Moroni concluded the Book of Mormon record in much the same way, instructing his people to "search the prophecies of Isaiah." (Mormon 8:23.) Christ told the Nephites, "A commandment I give unto you that ye search these things diligently; for great are the words of Isaiah." (3 Nephi 23:1.)

In addition to this commandment, Jesus carefully went through some relevant prophecies and explained them. He also asked to see the Nephite scriptures, examined them carefully, and told the Nephites to include a record of the fulfillment of a prophecy of Samuel the Lamanite about the resurrection of others besides Jesus. (See 3 Nephi 23.) Christ also added some prophecies of Malachi, which included a prophecy about Elijah's coming in the last days to prepare the way for eternal family unity. (See 3 Nephi 24–25.)

After this scriptural instruction, the Master carefully explained "all things, even from the beginning until the time that he should come in his glory," so the Nephites might understand the total outline of the Father's plans. (3 Nephi 26:3.) Apparently Nephi recorded "the more part" of the Savior's words (3 Nephi 26:7), but the Lord later instructed Mormon not to copy all of it, saying, "I will try the faith of my people" (3 Nephi 26:11). Apparently our use of the scriptures will measure our faith. If we do not read and use that which has been given to us, the Lord will not give us more.

This seems just. Besides the scriptures, there are two other sources of knowledge concerning God—one's own personal experience with him and the experience of others; indeed, much of the scriptures is devoted to accounts of personal experiences of prophets with God. If we neglect reading scripture because we lack the interest to make the effort, it seems unlikely that God will do more to give us further information. Thus, one of the vital sources of knowing eternal life may be shut off if we neglect the scriptures.

In addition to the Lord's concern about the scriptures was his concern for ordinances. His instructions about baptism and the sacrament reveal how these ordinances signify forgiveness, rebirth, and spiritual nourishment in a covenant of love. Again the Prince of Peace expressed his concern for unity and the avoidance of disputations among his disciples: "On this wise shall ye baptize; and there shall be no disputations among you." (3 Nephi 11:22.)

Perhaps it is not without significance that one of the Master's first acts after appearing to the Nephites was to reemphasize the ordinance of baptism, through which his people might bind themselves in a covenant with him. He spent much of that first day instructing the disciples in what the baptismal covenant comprises, what the Master expected of the disciple, what the disciple might, in turn, expect of the Master, and how it was to be administered. At the waters of Mormon, Alma had earlier explained the baptismal covenant under the Mosaic law (see Mosiah 18:8-10); in Bountiful, Christ explained the significance of the new covenant.

He also spent time that first day explaining the sacramental ordinance and its significance.

As it was, no more fitting setting could have existed for the first recorded administration of the sacrament to the Nephites, following as it did one of the greatest spiritual outpourings recorded—healing the sick and blessing the children. Part of the sacramental instructions are to partake in memory of him. A people could hardly have had more significant memories of their Savior's love than the Nephites had of that first day—unless it was on the second day, after they had experienced the rich outpouring of the Spirit as they entered into prayer with the Master. Significantly, the sacrament was again administered that day by the Master, who miraculously provided it for them.

How could those present ever partake of the sacrament again without remembering both occasions? And part of what they would remember was life, not death, the resurrected life of their Lord, the words and emblems of eternal life that he had given them.

After the initial administering of the sacrament, the Master specified that it was to be given only to those worthy to partake of it; however, he was very clear that members should not cast out the unworthy. (3 Nephi 18:28-30.) Besides referring to current members who are temporarily unworthy, his instructions seem appropriate for situations of excommunication and disfellowshipping: "Ye shall not cast him out from among you, but ye shall minister unto him and shall pray for him unto the Father, in my name.... For ye know not but what they will return and repent, and come unto me with full purpose of heart, and I shall heal them; and ye shall be the means of bringing salvation unto them." (3 Nephi 18:30, 32.)

It is in his prayer, however, that we sense the spiritual profundities of the Master in his visit to the Nephites. No counterpart of these experiences can be found in his New Testament ministry, unless it might be in the prayer offered by Christ before entering Gethsemane. (See John 17.)

He had taught the Nephites about prayer, including the Lord's Prayer, in the course of the great sermon. (3 Nephi 13:5-15.) He had warned them against hypocrisy, given them a model prayer, taught them to pray always in his name, believing and asking what was right (two important qualifications for any prayer), and counseled them to pray in their families. (3 Nephi 18:18-21.)

However, I'm not sure that they understood the real power in prayer until they witnessed the Savior in prayer and experienced the reality of his oneness with God, the beauty of his tender expressions of love and concern.

That first prayer, as recorded in Third Nephi, is an experience of power and compassion even in the reading of it. On the first day, after the healings of sick and maimed, Christ asked that the Nephite children, his models for simplicity and purity, encircle him as he prayed. It was a prayer, like many other prayers, that began in sorrow for "the wickedness of the people of the house of Israel," and culminated in joy so profound for the faith of the Nephites that he wept. (3 Nephi 17:9-21.)

We do not know what he said as he poured out his heart to his Father. Those present could not record his words, although they did testify to the prayer's effects upon them: "And no tongue can speak, neither can there be written by any man, neither can the hearts of men conceive so great and marvelous things as we both saw and heard Jesus speak; and no one can conceive of the joy which filled our souls at the time we heard him pray for us unto the Father." (3 Nephi 17:17.)

The prayer ended, but the multitude was so overcome with joy that they remained on their knees until he bade them arise, testifying of his joy in them with tears. Then he took the Nephite children, one by one, and blessed them, inviting the parents, as he wept again, to "behold [their] little ones" encircled with fire and attended by angels. (3 Nephi 17:21-24.)

The second day, when they heard him pray again, the multitude had just been baptized and were "filled with the Holy Ghost and with fire." (3 Nephi 19:13.) As angels ministered to them, the Master came and commanded the multitude to kneel and the twelve disciples to pray. While they were praying—to him, interestingly, because he was in their midst (3 Nephi 19:18, 22)—the Master left the group three times and offered up his own feelings to the Father. For the disciples, their own experience was extraordinary; they prayed—"not multiply[ing] many words, for it was given unto them what they should pray, and they were filled with desire." (3 Nephi 19:24.) The Savior rejoiced in prayer that the Father had granted them the Holy Ghost, implored the same blessing for all who believe, and beseeched "that I may be in them as thou, Father, art in me, that we may be one." (3 Nephi 19:23.)

As Jesus smiled upon the Twelve in joy and blessing, they seem to have been transfigured, because they became "as white as the countenance and also the garments of Jesus; and behold the whiteness thereof did exceed all the whiteness, yea, even there could be nothing upon earth so white as the whiteness thereof." (3 Nephi 19:25.) Rejoicing, the Savior thanked the Father for purifying them because of their faith.

(3 Nephi 19:28.) When he prayed a third time, as the manifestation of glory continued, the multitude heard and testified, but "so great and marvelous were the words which he prayed that they cannot be written, neither can they be uttered by man." (3 Nephi 19:34.)

The Savior's prayers indicate that he was deeply moved by this spiritual feast. And when he returned to the disciples after his third prayer, he told them, rejoicing, that their great faith, faith such as he had never experienced in Palestine, had opened the gates to the miraculous: "There are none of them that have seen so great things as ye have seen; neither have they heard so great things as ye have heard." (3 Nephi 19:36.) Their faith is our blessing, too, as we share vicariously in an experience that was so deeply meaningful to the Savior that he wept for joy. In reading the account we seem also to sense the disciples' joy in pleasing their Redeemer.

We also see elements of the Savior's love and compassion manifested to the Nephites in ways not open to him in Palestine, because of the Israelites' relative lack of belief. The first day, after delivering his great sermon, he sensed the Nephites' struggle to understand what he had told them. (3 Nephi 17:2-3.) In particular, he seems to have been sensitive to the concern he had created by announcing the end of the law of Moses, a law that every Israelite was taught to cherish and defend with his own life from the time of his birth. (See 3 Nephi 15:2-10.)

Therefore, in compassionate clarity, Jesus explained that it was he who initially gave the law to Moses and that he was simply adding to the law. Jesus made a major point of this: Old things were simply becoming new; the law was being fulfilled, completed, brought to its rightful conclusion in him. "Behold," he summarized, "I am the law, and the light. Look unto me, and endure to the end, and ye shall live; for unto him that endureth to the end will I give eternal life." (3 Nephi 15:9.)

Then, after giving more information to the twelve disciples, he counseled the multitude to return to their homes, "ponder" his message, ask the Father to help them understand, and "prepare your minds for the morrow." (3 Nephi 17:3.)

However, as he looked into their eyes, he "beheld they were in tears, and did look steadfastly upon him as if they would ask him to tarry a little longer with them." (3 Nephi 17:5.) "Filled with compassion," he stayed.

The first thing he did was to call for their sick, their lame, their blind, their deaf, and those who had been afflicted in any manner. Healed, they bathed his feet with tears of gratitude. (3 Nephi 17:7-10.) (Apparently he performed healings the second day as well, probably for those who had not been present earlier, and also raised a man from the dead. [3 Nephi 26:15.])

His healings provide one of our insights into his compassion. He had healed many individuals in Palestine, but it is the multitude of healings and the unity of spirit—a complete absence of skepticism—that is unique here. When he next called the little children to him for blessing, he was again doing as he had previously done. But the ministering of angels and manifestations of fire made it unique. (3 Nephi 17:24.) Later, during the second or third day, Jesus again taught and ministered to the children, and it is recorded that "he did loose their tongues, and they did speak unto their fathers great and marvelous things, even greater than he had revealed unto the people." (3 Nephi 26:14.) In fact, the next day the entire multitude "gathered themselves together," and "even babes did open their mouths and utter marvelous things; and the things which they did utter were forbidden that there should not any man write them." (3 Nephi 26:16.)

No one, it seems, was too insignificant for the Master's compassion and genuine concern. Although he spent a certain amount of time instructing the leaders, he continued in service to all from the time he came until his departure. This fact in itself tells us much about him and his sensitivity and love.

However, his concern for those chosen twelve was particularly intense. He knew well the weight of their new responsibility and carefully worked with them to ensure their understanding. Finally, just before leaving, he offered them the desires of their hearts. (3 Nephi 28:1.)

Nine of the disciples desired a continuation of what they had known for the last three days—service in the presence of the Master. Their desire was to serve the Lord on earth throughout their normal lifespan and then to go speedily to serve the Lord in the next life. Three others, feeling that same joy in serving the Lord among mortal men, asked the Lord to let them stay on the earth until he came again. They did not love the Savior's presence less than the other nine, but rather recognized that Christ's love is always with those doing his work whenever it is needed. And he, rejoicing in their desire, promised them a fulness of joy and eternal life: "Ye shall sit down in the kingdom of my Father; yea, your joy shall be full, even as the Father hath given me fulness of joy; and ye shall be even as I am, and I am even as the Father; and the Father and I are one." (3 Nephi 28:10.)

Such a promise can be ours too as we, like those disciples, come to know the Master. In the sense of understanding him and becoming like him, knowing him is life eternal, and Christ's three-day experience with the Nephites can help us progress a little further in our quest for such knowledge and understanding.

Arthur R. Bassett is an associate professor of humanities at Brigham Young University.

Jesus' Sermon to the Nephites

Arthur R. Bassett

Often at clear mountain streams, fascinated by their abundant refreshment for soul and body, I have remembered the Master's statements to the Samaritan woman, calling himself the source of "living water." (John 4:10.) His teachings do indeed continue, in clarity and simplicity, to refresh and satisfy even the most unquenchable thirst for understanding.

Especially is this true of his first sermon to the Nephites, found in Third Nephi. It is obviously a retelling of many of his teachings to those in the old world, for he remarked: "Behold, ye have heard the things which I taught before I ascended to my Father." (3 Nephi 15:1.)

It also seems to have contained a pattern for a Christian life, and this, I assume, was why he gave the sermon before emphasizing to the Nephites the great priesthood ordinance of baptism. Many of the Nephites present had been baptized under the Mosaic covenant; now they were about to be baptized under a new covenant. President Joseph Fielding Smith has explained the Nephite condition at the time of the coming of the Savior: "The Church among the Nephites before the coming of Christ was not in its fulness and was under the law of Moses. The Savior restored the fulness and gave to them all the ordinances and blessings of the gospel. Therefore, it actually became a new organization, and through baptism they came into it." (*Answers to Gospel Questions* 3:205.)

Shortly after Jesus introduced himself to the Nephites, he selected twelve and gave them the authority to baptize. (3 Nephi 11:21-22.) Then he gave the sermon, extending from chapter 11 through chapter 14, that outlines the new covenant. Eventually all who desired to enter into the new covenant received baptism.

That sermon is rich with a multiplicity of thoughts, yet I also find great value in standing back, as it were, and examining the major contours of the sermon, just as I can enjoy the shape of the mountain stream as much as the individual rivulets, rapids, and eddies.

The idea of seeing the sermon's organic unity first came to me years ago. There is perhaps nothing definitive about the shape I perceive in the sermon. Comparisons shared by others have been fascinating to me because of their diversity. Indeed, every time I review the sermon myself, it takes on slightly new contours. Like other great creative pieces, the sermon continues to grow in grandeur and profundity as each student pushes his or her own spiritual dimensions wider or deeper.

I sense five major segments in the sermon's broadest outlines. First, after a brief introduction explaining baptism, the Savior invites all to come to him, to enter into discipleship under the new covenant, to partake of the ordinances, to come under the guidance of the Holy Ghost, and to receive a remission of their sins. (3 Nephi 12:1-3.)

The second section (3 Nephi 12:4-48) outlines the Master's pattern and suggests the character of his disciples. The third segment (chapter 13) focuses on how to gain the spiritual strength to become a disciple in actuality. The fourth (3 Nephi 14:1-12) suggests the manner in which his disciples should approach others, especially in attempting to share the gospel.

The fifth, and culminating, point (3 Nephi 14:13-27) issues another invitation to enter into Christian discipleship, to demonstrate outwardly the results of the inward change, to truly come to know the Master, and to build one's life upon foundations of stone.

Point One: The Invitation to Come to Christ

I feel a culmination of the first part of the sermon in the statement usually considered to be the first of the Beatitudes, "Yea, blessed are the poor in spirit who come unto me, for theirs is the kingdom of heaven." (3 Nephi 12:3.) The sense of summary is clearer in both the Book of Mormon and the Joseph Smith Translation of the Bible. It begins with "yea," implying an affirmation of something that has come before. The next verse begins with "And again," implying a reaffirmation of the thought.

Even more clearly, the contents are a good summary of the gospel message, an invitation to come to Christ. The first principle of the gospel is faith in Christ, in his saving power, in his life-style, in his love. This appears to have been the message of the prophets from the beginning. (See especially 2 Nephi 25:26.) That message is suggested in the very name of Jesus, the Greek equivalent of the Hebrew "Joshua," meaning "Jehovah saves."

When we believe—in the fullest sense of that word—in the Master, we seek to model our lives after his. This in turn leads us to repentance, with all of its ramifications. Not only do we forsake the errors of our past, but also we seek to incorporate into our lives those principles of the Christlike life that we may not yet have fully embraced—love, compassion, mercy, long-suffering. We enter into a covenant with the Lord through the designated ordinances. As we remain true to this covenant, acting under the direction of the Spirit of the Lord, we begin to pattern ourselves after the mold of the Master. Coming to Jesus implies total surrender and total dedication.

Ordinances, Church participation, and activity within the Kingdom all strengthen us in our drive to become more like the Master.

As Christ points out in his introduction, those who come to him with true humility, "poor in spirit," who enter into covenant with him through baptism, who receive the gift of the Holy Ghost and embrace the kingdom of God, will receive a remission of their sins.

Point Two: The Mold of the Master

This part of the sermon seems to culminate in the admonition "Therefore I would that ye should be perfect even as I, or your Father who is in heaven is perfect." (3 Nephi 12:48.) This portion of the sermon contains two approaches to a description of perfect character. First he seems to describe, in the Beatitudes, the general pattern of the Christian life, and then he underscores the point by contrasting the new law with practices that had developed under the Mosaic law.

The Savior begins the Beatitudes to the Nephites with the statement, "Blessed are all they that mourn." (3 Nephi 12:4.) Besides the comfort the Savior thus extends to those who face sorrow in this life, he may also be referring to those who come to him with broken hearts and contrite spirits—two terms that he uses often, and two terms that suggest mourning and true humility before the Master.

I have come to understand through watching myself and others that significant personality changes can be made only when there is genuine sorrow for the present situation. I, like others, have often made resolves to practice new virtues and to change bad habits, but only when my heart has been broken and when my spirit is truly contrite do I have the motivation and the power to change. Mourning for past sins and present weaknesses, then, seems to be the first step to conversion and repentance.

In turn, mourning leads one to surrender his present

situation ("meekness"); it leads him to seek a better one ("hungering and thirsting after righteousness"). The first step is toward greater humility, a greater desire to be instructed by those who can help give guidance and help with problems that caused the mourning. In short, one becomes open to other influences, willing to receive help. The Savior uses the phrase "Blessed are the meek." (3 Nephi 12:5.)

Second, the person seeks help with full intent. This aspect is active in nature. Nothing in life becomes more important than relief from his suffering; his behavior testifies of his true earnestness. The Lord states simply, "Blessed are all they who do hunger and thirst after righteousness, for they shall be filled with the Holy Ghost." (3 Nephi 12:6.)

His metaphor is powerful. Few things stimulate us to activity more forcibly than hunger and thirst. Waiting doesn't make them go away. They gnaw until they receive attention. How different our life-styles would be if our desire for righteousness were that strong.

The metaphor also brings us back to the Lord's statements in Palestine, when he referred to himself as the "bread of life," and the source of "living water," and promised: "He that cometh to me shall never hunger; and he that believeth on me shall never thirst." (John 6:35.)

When we acquire the Holy Ghost's companionship as a result of hungering and thirsting after righteousness, a change in the inner man results. According to the pattern outlined in the Beatitudes, we feel merciful toward others. In turn, we receive mercy. (3 Nephi 12:7.) Justice and mercy are important elements in the Master's character; they should also be important in the life of his disciples.

Further, as the next Beatitude suggests, the guidance of the Spirit leads those who hunger and thirst after righteousness to purity of heart (3 Nephi 12:8), toward the establishment of Zions throughout the world, places where the pure in heart dwell. In short, it leads one to attempt the work of a peacemaker (3 Nephi 12:9), following the pattern of the Prince of Peace. Eventually, this work will culminate in establishing the New Jerusalem, and it is not without significance that the core of the name itself—"salem"—denotes peace.

Ironically, the inevitable consequence of this process is persecution and opposition, the lot of the children of God from the beginning. And yet the Master exclaims, "Blessed are all they who are persecuted for my name's sake." (3 Nephi 12:10.) Suffering for his cause will be followed by eventual joy in his kingdom.

Finally, suffering for the gospel makes the righteous mourn for a third reason: not just for the sorrows of life, and not just for their own sins, but also for the sins of those who have rejected the Master's message. This mourning, in turn, seems likely to lead to greater meekness before the Lord, an even greater desire to understand, and a greater hunger for righteousness. In this context, perhaps, the metaphor of "one eternal round" used by the prophet Alma (Alma 37:12) may be applied. In a spiraling process one proceeds from grace to grace, from understanding to understanding. This great knowledge of Christ means that the disciple, like the Master, comes to be a light for the world in times of confusion, a seasoning influence in times of purposelessness. (3 Nephi 12:13-16.)

To underline the lesson he has just taught, the Master contrasts rigid and often Spiritless interpretations of the old covenant with the total dependence on the Spirit of the new. (3 Nephi 12:17-20.) Whereas the emphasis in the past had often been placed on performance alone—the letter of the law—the new emphasis places equal stress on motives, on the inner man. Almost two centuries earlier, Abinadi had described the old law as "a law of performances and of ordinances, a law which they were to observe strictly from day to day, to keep them in remembrance of God and their duty towards him." (Mosiah 13:30.) The new law went further, demanding more perfect obedience, while giving us an opportunity to know God, through Christ as he lived in the flesh, and through the Holy Ghost, who could come to us at any time.

Those who observed the old law to the letter were often good, righteous people: but it was (and is) possible to try to live the letter of the law while searching for seeming loopholes that allow one to wear a cloak of legality, or to become piously smug about one's obedience to law, losing the "broken heart and contrite spirit" necessary to salvation.

Accordingly, under the new covenant the Lord emphasizes that there are no loopholes. The Lord requires disciples to seek purity of heart, a kind of transparency of soul in which the heart is shown through the action. We are enjoined not only to control our actions, but also to reshape our very soul. In this sense the old law is fulfilled—not abolished or set aside, but given greater dimension. For example, anger arises far more often and more easily than the urge to kill, but the true Christian will rise above even anger. (3 Nephi 12:21-26.) He will strive toward perfection. (3 Nephi 12:48.) But how?

Point Three: The Source of Strength

Anyone who has tried to change a serious flaw in his personality knows the problem. Thus in the next segment of the sermon, after instructing his disciples to seek perfection, the Lord turns to the problem of how we can generate the strength to change character. His answer, contained in 3 Nephi 13, is intriguing. It contains some of the richest instruction we have on giving offerings, on meaningful prayer, and on acceptable fasting. Furthermore, it tells us that the Saint will do all of these in secret. (See, for example, verses 3-6, 16-18.) His actions concern him and his God, first and foremost. Jesus understood well that religious activity could also be prompted by unrighteous motives. Harsh, judgmental personalities sometimes gravitate to religious organizations. Even during his earthly ministry the Lord had moved constantly among those he called hypocrites (literally "actors"), those who were not pure in heart, those who entered into religious activity to be seen of men.

The Master is realistic. He points out that conspicuous piety can have its rewards, but that one should not expect double pay, to be rewarded by man *and* God. Each one needs to choose between receiving the praise of man or inner strength from God. The point is important. Christ seems to imply that the disciple must be prepared to be satisfied with treasures that are not necessarily of this world. We must, as disciples, "come out" of the world. (Verses 19-21.)

To the Twelve whom he had just chosen, the Lord further teaches how they must interpret this principle of turning from the world and placing total faith in him. In what still remains one of the most beautiful passages in all literature—"Consider the lilies of the field . . ." (verses 28-30)—the Lord explains the kind of single-heartedness with which they must fulfill the new covenant.

Point Four:
The Christian's Relationship to Others

The next segment of the sermon deals with how a peacemaker should treat others. Certain aspects of this segment become clearer perhaps with a careful reading of the Joseph Smith Translation of the Bible (Matthew 7:1-21), which specifies that these instructions concern what disciples should teach others. Significantly, in the Book of Mormon sermon, the instructions are applicable to the Saints as well, as they prepare to enter into the new covenant.

A good summation of this segment appears in what I consider to be its closing statement: "Therefore, all things whatsoever ye would that men should do to you, do ye even so to them, for this is the law and the prophets." (3 Nephi 14:12.)

Simple advice, yet how often it is overlooked, especially in the context of teaching others the gospel! If we could only keep in mind our own conversion experience and remember how we had to grow from precept to precept, we would be in a much better position to share the gospel with others. The Master instructs his followers not to be impatient with others, yet he also warns them not to "cast their pearls" before those who are spiritually incapable of understanding. I assume that he means for us to focus initially on the gospel basics. The advice he gives is to teach prayer first. We should encourage those investigating the gospel to ask of the Master, to seek him, and to knock at his door with their petitions. Only then will they understand the beauties and message of the gospel. Until this contact between man and God is made, the work of the missionaries is of small effect.

Point Five: A Final Invitation

Four points have been made thus far in the sermon by the Lord: (1) an invitation to come to him for help, (2) a description of the character demanded of the disciple, (3) the source of strength to aid in achieving this character, and (4) the work of the Christian in sharing the message of the gospel. It is probably no accident that these points parallel the major points of the Beatitudes, the form of the sermon itself reinforcing its message.

The final point made by the Master appears to be a summary statement of sorts, with special emphasis on the urgency of accepting the conditions of the covenant. He begins by inviting those assembled into the "strait gate." (3 Nephi 14:13.) Note that the word is *strait,* not *straight.* Besides the obvious reference to the strictness of the standards for exaltation, this can connote the idea of being bound together tightly. The idea of binding has, for me, overtones of covenant-making and is, at the same time, an invitation away from laxity and ease to the strenuous work of the true disciple.

The point is also made that the role of the disciple is more than just lip-service, more than simply identifying oneself superficially with the Master's cause. Even those who have succeeded in prophesying, casting out devils, and doing other marvelous works in his name will find themselves outside the kingdom if they have not come to know the Master.

(See 3 Nephi 14:21-23.) I assume that this means Church members as well as those outside the covenant.

Coming to know the Master, which Jesus equated with eternal life (John 17:3), seems to imply far more than just a superficial knowledge *about* him. It connotes an understanding of him, a union with him through the companionship of his Spirit, an awareness of his goals and his aspirations, and a kinship born of common experience. It implies a total commitment, action as well as understanding. Faith in the Master means doing the works that he would do if he were here, bearing the loads that he would bear, and seeking to shape oneself totally in his mold.

The Master explained all this to the Nephites before they entered into a covenant relationship with him through baptism at the hands of his ordained servants. Yet the sermon is as relevant today as it was for the Nephite disciples nearly two millennia ago. Like a river of living water, running perpetually, it is a source of comfort and instruction for people of all ages who earnestly desire the Christlike life.

Arthur R. Bassett is an associate professor of humanities at Brigham Young University.

Mormon: The Man and the Book

Jeffrey R. Holland

The Prophet Joseph Smith once wrote in his journal, "It was an awful responsibility to write in the name of the Lord." *(History of the Church* 1:226.) One who must have felt that "awful responsibility" as much as any other in this world was Mormon, who at the tender age of ten years was introduced to the weighty assignment that would be his.

After nearly a thousand years of Nephite history he was called of God to select and summarize the story of his people. That story tells in part of "peace in the land" and "all manner of miracles," including the appearance and sermons of the resurrected Son of God.

But the story also contains the terror and depravity of that civilization gone awry, a dispensation concluding "without order and without mercy" in which women were fed on the flesh of their husbands and children were offered as sacrifice to dumb idols. In the end, Mormon's was a painful and very lonely task.

Of the record Mormon helped to produce, the Prophet Joseph Smith said: "I told the brethren that the Book of Mormon was the most correct of any book on earth, and the keystone of our religion, and a man would get nearer to God by abiding by its precepts, than by any other book." *(History of the Church* 4:461.) After long decades of darkness, the appearance of Mormon's book would be one of the first contributions toward the "restitution of all things" (Acts 3:21) in preparation for the fullness of times. His task was as crucial in the eternal plan of salvation as it was unique.

One prevailing impression we have as we read of Mormon's life and times is that he has been almost too modest, too brief (scarcely twelve pages) with the inspiration and insight of a man so uniquely chosen and prepared to write. Indeed, we are grateful that his son, Moroni, shared with us both his memories of and his personal correspondence with his father, which reveal Mormon's great doctrinal strength, his humanity and hope, and his abiding devotion to his people. (See Moroni 7–9.)

While acknowledging our indebtedness to Moroni for including these wonderfully inspiring chapters, we nevertheless wonder what other great discourses we might have received from Mormon if the book he abridged or the times in which he lived had not restricted his hand and limited his opportunity to speak to us. What we do have from him—and thus what we come to know of him—is of the highest order and places him in the front ranks of ancient America's prophetic voices.

We know that "every man who has a calling to minister to the inhabitants of the world was ordained to that very purpose" in his premortal existence. *(Teachings of the Prophet Joseph Smith,* p. 365.) Perhaps that call has an effect on those men even in their earliest mortal years, for Mormon was recognized by his predecessor Ammaron as being "a sober child" and one "quick to observe." (Mormon 1:2.) As a lad only ten years of age, Mormon received a charge from Ammaron that some fourteen years later he should "go to the land Antum, unto a hill which shall be called Shim," and there obtain the ancient and faithfully recorded history of his people. (Mormon 1:3.) It was a charge he accepted and faithfully fulfilled.

Under the guidance of his father, for whom he was named (see Mormon 1:5-6), young Mormon moved to the land of Zarahemla when he was eleven years of age and prepared for his prophetic role. But these were difficult times. After more than two hundred years of peace and righteousness introduced on the western hemisphere by the Savior himself, the civilization had now declined to the point where "both the people of Nephi and the Lamanites had become exceedingly wicked one like unto another. . . . And there were none that were righteous save it were the disciples of Jesus." (4 Nephi 1:45-46.) Indeed, that wickedness continued unchecked upon the whole of the land until even the disciples of Jesus, that last remnant of Christ's ministry among the people, were taken away by the Lord: "And the work of miracles and of healing did cease because of the iniquity of the people. And there were no gifts from the Lord, and the Holy Ghost did not come upon any, because of their wickedness and unbelief." (Mormon 1:13-14.)

Maintaining his integrity and faithful independence amidst such evil practice, Mormon was, at approximately the same age as the young prophet Joseph Smith, "visited of the Lord." (Mormon 1:15.) Still in his teens, he tried valiantly to preach to his people, but because these people had willfully rebelled against their God and because their wickedness continued to run rampant, he was finally forbidden of God to speak. "My mouth was shut," he records, "and I was forbidden that I should preach unto them . . . because of the hardness of their hearts." (Mormon 1:16-17.)

Other, if less divine, opportunities for service were given to him. Like his ancestor Nephi, Mormon was also "large in stature" (Mormon 2:1), and with both a strong body and a resolute spirit he was chosen to lead the armies of the Nephite people—at the age of sixteen.

Even as Nephite blood flooded the battlefields, however, an army of domestic adversaries—thieves, robbers, murderers, and magicians—sheared the more private fabric of Nephite society. There was despair at home and abroad, and great sorrow among the people.

But as Mormon recorded, "Their sorrowing was not unto

repentance, because of the goodness of God; but it was rather the sorrowing of the damned, because the Lord would not always suffer them to take happiness in sin. And they did not come unto Jesus with broken hearts and contrite spirits, but they did curse God, and wish to die. . . . The day of grace was passed with them, both temporally and spiritually." (Mormon 2:13-15.)

The theft of personal property naturally grew into more conquest of home and lands until Mormon watched these, his brothers and sisters, stand in open conflict against each other and fall in open rebellion against their God. The bodies of the dead were "heaped up as dung upon the face of the land." (Mormon 2:15.)

In the midst of this kind of personal and public destruction, Mormon made his way to the hill Shim and obtained the plates of Nephi in fulfillment of Ammaron's commandment. There on these ancient metal plates he would, over the weeks and months ahead, give "a full account of all the wickedness and abominations" of his people, for there was little else to record. Indeed, these scenes of wickedness and abomination had been before his eyes "ever since I have been sufficient to behold the ways of man." (Mormon 2:18.) Nephite history in the fourth century A.D. was by every standard an unpleasant story to tell.

Striving to maintain what military defense he could, even as he recorded the inevitable demise of his people, Mormon urged that the Nephites "stand boldly" and defend "their wives, and their children, and their houses, and their homes." (Mormon 2:23.) Although there was an occasional temporary gain, Mormon faced the most hopeless of all military tasks—fighting when "the strength of the Lord was not with us." He wrote in his history, "Yea, we were left to ourselves, that the Spirit of the Lord did not abide in us; therefore we had become weak like unto our brethren." (Mormon 2:26.)

As he fought against the enemy with sword and shield, he also tried to pierce the heart of his own people with strong testimony. But his cry was in vain. These people would not make that one crucial admission that the Lord God of Israel held the keys to their success. (See Mormon 3:2-3.) The warring would go on.

Both armies fought on in the feeble strength of the arm of flesh; and after two surprisingly successful defenses against Lamanite attacks, the Nephites "began to boast in their own strength." (Mormon 3:9.) In utter despair Mormon threw down his weapons of war and vowed he would have no more to do with their cause. Though he "had loved them" (Mormon 3:12), he refused to lead their military forces and, by the Lord's command, waited "as an idle witness" for total destruction (Mormon 3:16).

Yet at such moments of disappointment and frustration we learn something special about the heart and hunger of this man. His faith, his hope, and his charity were irrepressible. He could not abandon his own people. Notwithstanding their wickedness, he agreed once more to lead them. But some critical threshold had been passed. These people had decisively chosen darkness over light, evil over goodness, blood over benevolence. Prayer unto God "all the day long" (Mormon 3:12) for that kind of soul was difficult indeed, but so Mormon prayed. Nevertheless, the judgments of God overtook his people, and the degree of Nephite wickedness was equaled only by their loss of life.

Mormon recorded: "It is impossible for the tongue to describe, or for man to write a perfect description of the horrible scene of the blood and carnage which was among the people, both of the Nephites and of the Lamanites; and every heart was hardened, so that they delighted in the shedding of blood continually. And there never had been so great wickedness among all the children of Lehi, nor even among all the house of Israel, according to the words of the Lord, as was among this people." (Mormon 4:11-12.)

Undoubtedly it was in one of these times that Mormon wrote the painful letter to his son that Moroni recorded in his own book.

"My beloved son," he wrote, "I am laboring with [the Nephites] continually; and when I speak the word of God with sharpness they tremble and anger against me; and when I use no sharpness they harden their hearts against it. . . . They have no fear of death; and they have lost their love, one towards another; and they thirst after blood and revenge continually." (Moroni 9:1, 4-5.)

But Mormon's remarkable and indomitable spirit prevailed. He held to faith, hope, and charity, and to the miraculous intervention of angels and heavenly priesthood powers, as a prophet always will. Indeed, he loved his people with a "perfect love" that "casteth out all fear." (Moroni 8:16.) He would simply try once again.

"And now, my beloved son," he wrote, "notwithstanding their hardness, let us labor diligently; . . . for we have a labor to perform." (Moroni 9:6.)

The Spirit of Christ could yet lead this people if they would permit it to do so, and by his light they could yet "lay hold on every good thing." (Moroni 7:21.) Even in the midst of these wicked days there was an opportunity to repent, a message delivered by the very angels of heaven. In the midst of his people's abject wickedness, Mormon reminded his son that, in the past, "by the ministering of angels, and by every word which proceeded forth out of the mouth of God, men began to exercise faith in Christ; and thus by faith, they did lay hold upon every good thing." (Moroni 7:25.)

And what God did in the past, he would do now: "Have angels ceased to appear unto the children of men? Or has he withheld the power of the Holy Ghost from them? Or will he, so long as time shall last, or the earth shall stand, or there shall be one man upon the face thereof to be saved? Behold I say unto you, Nay; for it is by faith that miracles are wrought; and it is by faith that angels appear and minister unto men." (Moroni 7:36-37.)

What a remarkable message to be delivered in what we know were frightful and unfaithful times! We wonder what miracles might have been wrought, even at that late hour, if congregations of Nephite saints had claimed the privileges that could have been theirs. But they did not choose to claim them and so, for them, the day of miracles did indeed cease.

Gradually, inevitably, inexorably the Nephites lost men, women, children, property, and possessions to the increasingly powerful Lamanites; they "began to be swept off by them even as a dew before the sun." (Mormon 4:18.) And as Nephite women and children were being sacrificed to Lamanite idols (Mormon 4:21), Mormon once again took command of the Nephite army, though he knew it was in vain and would be the last time.

"I was without hope," he said, "for I knew the judgments of the Lord which should come upon them; for they repented not of their iniquities, but did struggle for their lives without calling upon that Being who created them." (Mormon 5:2.)

Mormon achieved some temporary victories and maintained some temporary positions, but ultimately the Lamanites moved upon them in numbers so vast that "they did tread the people of the Nephites under their feet." (Mormon 5:6.)

In solitude and sorrow Mormon withdrew from the horde and wrote to an audience yet unborn but certain to receive his record. For Jew, Lamanite, and Gentile he described the destruction of what had once been "a delightsome people," a nation who once had "Christ for their shepherd." (Mormon 5:17.) Now he recorded that "they are led about by Satan, even as chaff is driven before the wind, or as a vessel is tossed about upon the waves, without sail or anchor, or without anything wherewith to steer her; and even as she is, so are they." (Mormon 5:18.)

At Mormon's request, the Lamanites let the Nephites gather in the land of Cumorah (Mormon 6:2-4) to wage "the last struggle" of these peoples (Mormon 6:6). Mormon, now old and hoping only to protect the record, hid in the Hill Cumorah all the plates with which he had been entrusted, save the brief abridged record that he gave to his son Moroni. (Mormon 6:6.) In fearful anticipation and finally horrible realization, Mormon and Moroni fought as the remaining Nephite men, women, and children fell before the oncoming armies of the Lamanites. Mormon himself fell wounded, but his life, for a time, was spared as the Lamanite armies swept on. Only he, Moroni, and 22 other Nephites remained; 230,000 of their nation had fallen.

The scope and significance of that horrible slaughter may be seen more readily when we realize that the great American Civil War of the 1860s, the costliest war, in terms of human life, that the United States has ever known, took the lives of 140,000 men in a five-year period. Here, 230,000 fell in a single day.

Looking out over that carnage, Mormon cried: "O ye fair ones, how could ye have departed from the ways of the Lord! O ye fair ones, how could ye have rejected that Jesus, who stood with open arms to receive you! . . . O ye fair sons and daughters, ye fathers and mothers, ye husbands and wives, ye fair ones, how is it that ye could have fallen! But behold, ye are gone, and my sorrows cannot bring your return." (Mormon 6:17, 19-20.)

As his own death approached, Mormon concluded his record with one great and final testimony.

To the mighty remnant of the house of Israel he testified that they must come to know that they are God's covenant people. They must come to know that repentance is the only course to salvation. They must come to know that war must cease and the peace of the gospel of Jesus Christ is the only victory over death and the grave. If indeed the great remnant of the house of Israel will lay hold upon his record and the gospel of Jesus Christ which it teaches, then, he promises, "it shall be well with you." (Mormon 7:10.)

Having seen a devastating day of judgment upon his own people, Mormon closed his weary eyes, seeking the rest of the valiant and the consolation of the saints. But to his eternal credit—and for our eternal good—he left behind a testament that would one day speak "out of the dust" and "hiss forth from generation to generation." (Moroni 10:27-28.) It would be in every way "a marvellous work and a wonder." (Isaiah 29:14.)

"I cannot write the hundredth part of the things of my

people," wrote Mormon. (Words of Mormon 1:5.) And as he repeats that statement again and again (see Helaman 3:14; 3 Nephi 5:8, 26:6), we sense something of the task he faced in abridging a thousand years of Nephite history in order to give us the Book of Mormon in our time.

Mormon was ten years old when Ammaron charged him to "remember the things that ye have observed concerning this people" and "engrave on the plates of Nephi" everything he would see. (Mormon 1:3-4.) If Mormon had merely obeyed that original instruction, it would have been challenge enough for any historian, for the story he had to write was the long, terrible tale of the destruction of his people. But Mormon went beyond Ammaron's admonition and prepared another record, abridging the entire history of his people. Why did he prepare this abridgment in which he wrote only "the hundredth part" of the original record that had been kept?

In the book of 3 Nephi, Mormon explains: "I have made my record of these things according to the record of Nephi, which was engraven on the plates which were called the plates of Nephi. And behold, I do make the record on plates which I have made with mine own hands. . . . And it hath become expedient that I, *according to the will of God,* that the prayers of those who have gone hence, who were the holy ones, should be fulfilled according to their faith, should make a record of these things which have been done—yea, *a small record* of that which hath taken place from the time that Lehi left Jerusalem, even down until the present time." (3 Nephi 5:10-11, 14-15; italics added.)

Mormon may not have known why he was to make the separate, shorter account. He was following the will of God, and he knew that the work of abridgment he was doing would answer the prayers of his faithful forefathers.

And when he found the small plates of Nephi, he joined them with his own abridgment, because "they are choice unto me; and I know they will be choice unto my brethren." (Words of Mormon 1:6.) He was once again acting out of faith, for he confessed, "I do this for a wise purpose; for thus it whispereth me, according to the workings of the Spirit of the Lord which is in me. And now, I do not know all things; but the Lord knoweth all things which are to come; wherefore, he worketh in me to do according to his will." (Words of Mormon 1:7.) These and other experiences like them tell us much about the faith of the man.

It should also be clear that Mormon does not claim his abridgment will give equal time or equal emphasis to all historical events. He was not working at a flat-rate, assessing every event to be the equivalent of every other. For example, an account of war and civil disorder covering just a little over a dozen years is given nearly sixty pages of documentation (Alma 43–62), while the most righteous period in all of Nephite history—the two hundred years of peace and purity that prevailed after Christ's appearance in the New World—receives less than two pages of review (4 Nephi).

Is Mormon, the Nephite soldier, preoccupied with these tragic warring cycles that began so early and were still recurring in his own day? Or is there perhaps something in the war accounts that our generation—or a later one—must learn, prompting Mormon to stress it?

Is it, on the other hand, impossible—for whatever reason—to write of perfect righteousness? Some events in the Nephite experience were indeed so sacred that "tongue cannot speak the words . . . neither can they be uttered by man." (3 Nephi 19:32, 34.)

In any case, the selection of material from so many years and so many records was a private and inspired one. Mormon, too, undoubtedly received "line upon line, precept upon precept" (2 Nephi 28:30) as he prepared material so important for us to receive.

The thoroughness of the records from which Mormon drew his material is impressively revealed in the long passages of direct quotation that he was able to extract, such as King Benjamin's address, Abinadi's pointed call to repentance, Alma's missionary messages and detailed counsel to his three sons, Ammon's conversations among the Lamanites, Amulek's doctrinal discourses, the later Nephi's prophecies and words of warning, Samuel the Lamanite's declaration, and of course the detailed instruction given by the Savior himself. These and many other passages, running into scores of pages, are quoted by Mormon in the language and expression of those who uttered them. Surely only the limitations of time and space and the priorities given him by the Spirit kept him from giving us more. (See, for example, Alma 11:46; 13:31.)

This attention to verbal detail simply confirms what we already know—that record keeping was a very serious matter to the Nephites. During Christ's visit to the Nephites he reminded them that every designated teaching and testimony had to be recorded: "And it came to pass that he said unto Nephi: Bring forth the record which ye have kept. And when Nephi had brought forth the records, and laid them before him, he cast his eyes upon them and said: Verily I say unto you, I commanded my servant Samuel, the Lamanite, that he should testify unto this people, that at the day that the Father should glorify his name in me that there were many saints who should arise from the dead, and should appear unto many, and should minister unto them. And he said unto them: Was it not so? And his disciples answered him and said: Yea, Lord, Samuel did prophesy according to thy words, and they were all fulfilled. And Jesus said unto them: How be it that ye have not written this thing, that many saints did arise and appear unto many and did minister unto them? And it came to pass that Nephi remembered that this thing had not been written. And it came to pass that Jesus commanded that it should be written; therefore it was written according as he commanded. And now it came to pass that when Jesus had expounded all the scriptures in one, which they had written, he commanded them that they should teach the things which he had expounded unto them." (3 Nephi 23:7-14.)

Such prophetic sermons and discourses were available

to generation after generation only because Mormon's predecessors had so faithfully recorded them in detail.

Of course it is possible that some of the passages Mormon gives us were not taken from any written record but were revealed directly to him. For example, we know we receive the major portion of Abinadi's preaching from Alma's account of it. (Mosiah 17:4.) But who recorded Abinadi's final testimony after Alma had fled from Noah's assassins? Perhaps some bystander preserved it (or even some court recorder taking minutes of the execution), but perhaps, too, it was revealed directly to Mormon or another historian.

In this same vein it would seem that the beautiful prayer of the Savior recorded in 3 Nephi 19 may or may not have been heard (or recorded) by those who were present. The scripture says that "Jesus departed out of the midst of them, and went a little way off from them" and there prayed to his Father. (3 Nephi 19:19.)

Someone might have heard that prayer and recorded it (compare 3 Nephi 19:33), or the Master may have repeated it a second time for the historical record. But another possibility for such private declarations running throughout the Book of Mormon is that the Spirit simply revealed in every necessary detail what Mormon—and we—needed to know. Obviously nothing was to be lost that would be essential to the latter-day message, no matter how privately it may have been uttered initially.

In the midst of this historical review, Mormon was not hesitant to interject an occasional editorial discourse of his own. Frequently the detailed recounting of earlier days that were, time and again, so much like his own brought out the flame in his own pen—or rather, his own stylus.

For example, after writing what must have been eleven frustrating chapters of the book of Helaman, Mormon boldly inserts his own feelings into the twelfth chapter and cries out against "the unsteadiness of the hearts of the children of men." (Helaman 12:1.) Indeed, he says that man is "less than the dust of the earth" (Helaman 12:7)—not at all in the sense that man is without value to God, but rather because "the dust of the earth moveth hither and thither, to the dividing asunder, at the command of our great and everlasting God." (Helaman 12:8.) Hills, mountains, seas, earth—all obey his voice. But man does not obey his voice; in willfulness and pride he tramples under foot the words of the Holy One.

In a great, painful lamentation Mormon mourns in earlier generations the sins that brought destruction to his own: men "do not desire that the Lord their God, who hath created them, should rule and reign over them; . . . they do set at naught his counsels, and they will not that he should be their guide." (Helaman 12:6.) And Mormon pleads with a future generation to change that pattern.

In perhaps no other chapter does Mormon more forcefully use what comes to be his most reliable editorial technique—the use of a phrase such as "and thus we can behold," or "and thus we see." (Compare, for example, Alma 24:30 and Helaman 3:27-29 for other samples of this practice.)

Besides the "and thus we see" device, it is not likely that many literary flourishes survived the intense condensation and editing Mormon employed in cutting 99 percent of the material he had been given. "And thus we see" and "it came to pass" were more necessary than literary in the edited passages, allowing Mormon to focus on important points while moving very rapidly over geographical terrain, years of elapsed time, and extensive prophetic discourse.

But some of the more traditional literary forms can be found in the unedited, uncondensed materials, such as the sermons Mormon quoted verbatim. The ancient Semitic device called chiasmus was often preserved by Mormon in his quotations of major doctrinal discourses. As John Welch first pointed out, the Book of Mormon follows the pattern of the Hebrew prophets wherein things are frequently said twice, except the second time they are said in reverse order.

For a single example from Mormon's work, note how effectively he preserves King Benjamin's use of the chiasm (see Mosiah 5:10-12):

a And now . . . whosoever shall not take upon him the name of Christ
  b must be called by some other name;
    c therefore, he findeth himself on the left hand of God.
      d And I would that ye should remember also, that this is the name . . .
        e that never should be blotted out,
          f except it be through transgression;
          f therefore, take heed that ye do not transgress,
        e that the name be not blotted out of your hearts. . . .
      d I would that ye should remember to retain the name . . .
    c that ye are not found on the left hand of God,
  b but that ye hear and know the voice by which ye shall be called,
a and also, the name by which he shall call you.

(See John Welch's discussions of chiasmus in *New Era,* February 1972, p. 6; and *Ensign,* September 1977, p. 46.)

Of course, in addition to the great service Mormon rendered to us, some benefit was returned directly to him, as with all service. The theological bread he cast upon the water returned to further open his own spiritual eyes and understanding. With a mixture of admiration and sympathy we see him wrestle, for example, with the records of Third Nephi, wherein he finds recorded the doctrine of translated beings.

He writes of the three disciples who could rend prisons in two, who could escape the deepest earthen pits, who could three times withstand the flames of an open furnace, and who then could play with wild beasts as one would play with a nursing lamb. But "whether they were mortal or immortal, from the day of their transfiguration, I know not," Mormon says. (3 Nephi 28:17.) Concerned about his lack of understanding, Mormon "inquired of the Lord," and recorded that "since I wrote . . . the Lord . . . hath made it manifest unto me that . . . there was a change wrought upon their bodies." (3 Nephi 28:37-38.) Indeed he comes, three hundred fifty years after their transfiguration, to the moment when he is visited by these three Nephite disciples whose nature he had so faithfully prayed to comprehend. "I was about to write the names of those who were never to taste of death, but the Lord forbade; therefore I write them not, for they are hid from the world. But behold, I have seen them, and they have ministered unto me." (3 Nephi 28:25-26.) Mormon was learning even while he taught.

In this latter-day dispensation we see, through Mormon's work, great prophets and great principles, mighty doctrines and disciples from an earlier and eternally important time. Mormon provided for us—if we include the 116 pages of his message that were lost—an introduction to every major Nephite prophet and message from Lehi to the end of the Nephite world.

It is a story of a people who soared to great celestial heights—"surely there could not be a happier people" (4 Nephi 1:16)—and dipped to dismal, satanic lows—"they have become strong in their perversion" (Moroni 9:19). But through it all beats the cadence of an insistent message: that God does speak to men, that he does minister to his children, and that his Beloved Son will bring all things—including our willful souls—under his gentle rule if we so desire it.

These great prophetic profiles, images, and doctrines of the Nephite faithful reach out to us and beckon as we read of them through Mormon's hand. The alternative to heeding that message is the grisly end that Mormon personally witnessed and passed on in ominous warning.

Because of his "most correct book," we, too, increase our faith, hope, and charity. We, too, increase our personal theological understanding as Mormon did. After pondering over these pages, we also feel spiritually ministered to by ancient Nephite disciples, by being touched with the same Spirit that guided them. For every human soul and for every mortal season, it is that book which will bring us "nearer to God by abiding its precepts, than by any other book." *(History of the Church* 4:461.)

Through Isaiah the Lord said, "I will proceed to do a marvellous work among this people, even a marvellous work and a wonder." (Isaiah 29:14.) Today we can read the book that helps fulfill that prophecy; and in its pages, we can meet the great prophet Mormon, whom the Lord chose to write that marvelous work.

Jeffrey R. Holland is president of Brigham Young University.

Moroni

W. Cole Durham, Jr.

Moroni was a prophet well prepared for the responsibility of bridging two worlds: from the beginning it seems that he was sensitized to the spiritual anguish and disintegration of modern society. He was born into a righteous home but was surrounded by a world that, like much of contemporary society, was pervaded by violence and degradation. All the external influences of society were at war with his parents' desire to raise a righteous son. His father, Mormon, described the tide of evil that was sweeping the land as a "complete revolution"—both social and spiritual—against the values that just two centuries earlier had created a civilization rivaling the City of Enoch in the perfection of its peace. (Mormon 2:8; compare 4 Nephi 1:16.)

In a profound sense, then, Moroni was born into two worlds: one of decadence, in which the people were "without principle, and past feeling" (Moroni 9:20), and another of faith, in which parental righteousness ensured continued exposure to the gifts of the Spirit. Like the children of Noah, Lot, Lehi, and, in fact, of every active Church member, Moroni grew up at the frontier of decision between these two worlds.

The scriptures provide only a limited account of Moroni's family relationships and focus solely on father and son, but the glimpses suggest a tie rich with natural affection, strengthened by mutual concern for the ministry. The very structure of Moroni's writings reflects a profound respect for his father. His initial writings (Mormon 8 and 9) were intended to do no more than complete his father's record.[1] Later, when Moroni added his own book, approximately two-thirds of its space was devoted to a presentation of his father's teachings and letters.

Mormon's gratitude and love for his son are equally apparent. At his son's birth, Mormon gave him the same name as that held by one of the mightiest generals in Nephite history—a general so significant that nearly a fifth of Mormon's abridgment focuses on his deeds. Perhaps implicit in the name is a father's dream that his son, like the general before him, would be, in the words Mormon had written, "a strong and a mighty man; . . . a man of a perfect understanding; . . . a man who [would] labor exceedingly for the welfare and safety of his people," and a man who above all would be "firm in the faith of Christ, . . . even to the loss of his blood." (See Alma 48:11-13.) If that was the father's hope, it was amply fulfilled. When Moroni was called to the ministry, Mormon wrote to his son indicating his happiness concerning the calling and the joy he felt in observing Christ's goodness to his son. "I am mindful of you always in my prayers," Mormon wrote, "continually praying unto God the Father . . . that he . . . will keep you through the endurance of faith on his name to the end." (Moroni 8:3.)

Moroni served under his father as a leader of ten thousand in the great battle that culminated in the destruction of the Nephites. (Mormon 6:12.) Father and son were also both witnesses to the spiritual decay that brought about this destruction, and they shared an unflagging concern for a people hardened against the strivings of the Lord. (Mormon 6:17-22; Moroni 9:3-6.) Their joint efforts were motivated not only by the immediate demands of the time, but also by faith in the Lord's covenants with his people. As Moroni stated, "These things which we have desired concerning our brethren, yea, even their restoration to the knowledge of Christ, are according to the prayers of all the saints who have dwelt in the land." (Mormon 9:36.) Both Mormon and Moroni understood their stewardship over the sacred records as part of a grand plan through which the Lord's covenants to restore the gospel to their brethren would be fulfilled. (See Words of Mormon 1:2, 8; Mormon 8:15; Moroni 1:4, 10:1.) It is in this connection that the Doctrine and Covenants refers to Moroni as the holder of the keys of the stick of Ephraim. (D&C 27:5.)

With the loss of his father and his people, Moroni inherited a burden of loneliness virtually unparalleled in human history. By the time of his first entry on the plates, Moroni had already wandered alone for some sixteen years, and another twenty years were still to pass before he finally sealed up the records. (See Mormon 6:5; 8:6; and Moroni 10:1.) Perhaps only Ether before him had shared the experience of being left alone to record in scripture the total destruction of a people. (See Ether 15:33-34.)

Moroni's opening words are suffused with an infinite sorrow: "*I am alone.* My father hath been slain in battle, and all my kinsfolk, and I have not friends nor whither to go; and how long the Lord will suffer that I may live I know not. . . . The Lamanites have hunted my people . . . from place to place, even until they are no more. . . . and I even remain alone to write the sad tale of the destruction of my people. But behold, they are gone." (Mormon 8:5, 7, 3; italics added.)

Moroni's isolation connects him in significant ways with modern life. Our century, perhaps more than any other, has been experienced by people outside the Church as a century of loneliness. The increasing disintegration of families, the anonymity and isolation of modern urban life, the problems of old age—these and related phenomena have created broad undercurrents of loneliness throughout much of our society. Moroni was forced to confront these problems in their starkest form. Because of his allegiance to Christ, he was condemned to live out his days as a fugitive from human society. "I make not myself known to the Lamanites," he wrote, "lest they should destroy me. For behold, . . . they put to death every Nephite that will not deny the Christ. And I, Moroni, will not deny the Christ; wherefore, I wander whithersoever I can for the safety of mine own life." (Moroni 1:1-3.)

Moroni chose to suffer isolation from the world rather than alienation from God. But Moroni knew that men become truly isolated only to the degree that they harden themselves against the promptings of the Spirit. (See Moroni 10:21-34.) The gifts of the Spirit obliterate the sense of loneliness, because "all these gifts come by the Spirit of Christ" (Moroni 10:17), and he who walks with Christ is not alone. As one contrasts the condition of Moroni with the fierce society of his Lamanite brethren, one begins to wonder which is the true victim of separation. What greater loneliness can there be than isolation from God? And what greater consolation can there be than that expressed by Moroni when he said, "I have seen Jesus, and . . . he hath talked with me face to face"? (Ether 12:39.)

The years alone brought with them not only a profound understanding of the problem of loneliness, but also a deepened perception of the meaning, significance, and destiny of family bonds. Part of the little we know of his travels derives from an account of an incident that occurred on April 25, 1877, the day the Manti Temple site was dedicated. Early that morning, President Brigham Young is reported to have gone to the site and said, "Here is the spot where the Prophet Moroni stood and dedicated this piece of land for a temple site, and that is the reason why the location is made here, and we can't move it from this spot."[2] As is apparent when one considers Moroni's work in the current dispensation, his years of isolation from the family of men must have deepened his appreciation for the eternal family and his awareness of the significance of temple work. Much of what Moroni told the young Joseph Smith during their first encounter takes on added meaning in this context. After describing the nature and location of the plates, Moroni, with slight variations, quoted the passages from Malachi that the Savior had expounded and caused to be written when he appeared to the Nephites (see 3 Nephi 24–25): "For behold, the day cometh that shall burn as an oven, and all the proud, yea, and all that do wickedly shall burn as stubble; for they that come shall burn them, saith the Lord of Hosts, that it shall leave them neither root nor branch." (Joseph Smith—History 1:37; compare Malachi 4:1; 3 Nephi 25:1.)

Only someone in Moroni's position, cut off in time from both ancestors and descendants, could begin to appreciate the unspeakable loneliness of being left eternally with "neither root nor branch." And he could understand the hope implicit in the words that followed: "Behold, I will reveal unto you the Priesthood, by the hand of Elijah the prophet, before the coming of the great and dreadful day of the Lord. . . . And he shall plant in the hearts of the children the promises made to the fathers, and the hearts of the children shall turn to their fathers. If it were not so, the whole earth would be utterly wasted at his coming." (Joseph Smith—History 1:38-39 and D&C 2; compare Malachi 4:5-6; 3 Nephi 25:5-6.)

The Manti Temple incident and the references to the prophecies of Malachi suggest Moroni's concern for the day when the Lord would remember "the promises made to the fathers." Moroni knew the content of those promises and the magnitude of the faith that had elicited them. He knew the prophecies of Isaiah, and repeated the insistent Book of Mormon admonition to our generation to search them. (Mormon 8:23.) And he testified that "as the Lord liveth he will remember the covenant which he hath made" with the saints who had gone before him. (Mormon 8:23.)

As a prophet without a people, Moroni's audience was the future. "Behold," he wrote, "I speak unto you as if ye were present, and yet ye are not. But behold, Jesus Christ hath shown you unto me, and I know your doing." (Mormon 8:35.) From the wealth of his own spiritual life and the history of Jaredite civilization, he assembled a collage of insights designed to have particular relevance to our time. Having witnessed the collapse of one civilization and having abridged an account of the demise of another, Moroni was particularly conscious of the causes of social disintegration and of the need to record the principles necessary to reverse it. He knew from personal experience that the decadence that ultimately pervaded the Nephite and Jaredite societies could prove fatal.

It is particularly poignant that it was Moroni who translated and abridged Ether's record. Indeed, with the combined insight of both prophets, there is good reason to assume that the passages Moroni preserved for us are those of greatest significance in averting the calamities that befell their societies. (See D&C 1:17.)

What Moroni discerned in the events he reported was a process. Nephite society, like the Jaredite society before it, had suffered the sickness of decadence; and Moroni, like his counterpart Ether, had witnessed the fatal stage of the disease.[3] The letters from Mormon to his son reported that the people "in this part of the land . . . are also seeking to put down all . . . authority which cometh from God; and they are denying the Holy Ghost." (Moroni 8:28.) "They are without order and without mercy . . . and I cannot any longer enforce my commands. And they have become strong in their perversion; and they are alike brutal, sparing none, neither old nor young; and they delight in everything save that which is good." (Moroni 9:18-19.) By the end of the process, society degenerates into total anarchy and savagery.

The process of increasing corruption is the antithesis of the process of faith depicted in Alma 32: it is the ripening of the seeds of unbelief into a tree of death. As Moroni records, men in this vicious cycle do not merely cease to believe; "they *dwindle* in unbelief, and depart from the right way, and know not the God in whom they should trust." (Mormon 9:20; italics added.) As belief wanes, men are no longer susceptible to the gifts and revelations and guidance of God.

They forget the Lord's abundance and come to love money and costly apparel more than their fellowmen. Speaking of precisely this type of self-centered pride in the last days, Moroni asks: "Why are ye ashamed to take upon you the name of Christ? Why do ye not think that . . . endless happiness [is of greater value] than that misery which never dies—because of the praise of the world? Why do ye adorn yourselves with that which hath no life, and yet suffer the hungry, and the needy, and the naked, and the sick and the afflicted to pass by you, and notice them not?" (Mormon 8:38-39.)

In a world guilty of such vices may arise secret combinations for power and gain which are "most abominable and wicked above all, in the sight of God." (Ether 8:18.) As society at large becomes increasingly apathetic about principles of righteousness, incentives of status, power, and wealth become more enticing, and secret combinations arise and proliferate. At first merely festering sores, these combinations ultimately destroy all authority and order. "When ye shall see these things come among you," Moroni warned, "ye shall awake to a sense of your awful situation," for "they have caused the destruction of [the Jaredites], and also the destruction of the people of Nephi." (Ether 8:24, 21.)

Contrasting with this process of decadence and death are the affirmative teachings of Moroni, which characterize the process of sanctification and life. The six brief chapters with which the book of Moroni begins are a repository of some of the most sacred practices in the ecclesiastical life of the Nephites. But these chapters are not merely appendices on ancient church procedure; they also constitute a skeletal picture of the only type of community (other than a family such as Mormon's) capable of withstanding the buffetings of a disintegrating world. Surely Moroni must have longed for the church community of these chapters, which was "nourished by the good word of God," and whose members met "together oft, to fast and to pray, and to speak one with another concerning the welfare of their souls." (Moroni 6:4-5.)

Although significant, the teachings about the Church are

overshadowed by the deeper and more central themes of faith, hope, charity, and the humble quest for Christ. These themes are prevalent both in the writings of Mormon that Moroni quotes and also throughout Moroni's portion of the Book of Mormon. (See Mormon 9:27-29; Ether 4:7, 11-19; 12:23-41; Moroni 7; 10:4-23.) Their centrality in Moroni's writings reflects two dimensions of his own experience. First, having witnessed the destruction of his people, Moroni was vitally interested in identifying the personal attributes that must be nurtured to avoid the onset of social decay. Where individual faith flourishes, society is less likely to enter into the pathway of unbelief and wickedness that ultimately destroyed Jaredite and Nephite civilization. One of the great passages Moroni included in the book of Ether proclaims: "Whoso believeth in God might with surety hope for a better world, yea, even a place at the right hand of God, which hope cometh of faith, maketh an anchor to the souls of men, which would make them sure and steadfast, always abounding in good works, being led to glorify God." (Ether 12:4.)

Faith and hope for a better world are mutually supportive, and whether directed at improved conditions in this life or in the next, both inhibit the process of decadence. Both allay the despair and self-abandonment that lead to disintegration; both engender in their stead the abundance of good works that is the outer manifestation of charity. Moreover, men cannot possess faith, hope, and charity unless they are "meek, and lowly of heart" (Moroni 7:43); and accordingly, where these traits are found, the pride and envy and self-seeking that undermine social order cannot take root (see Moroni 7:45). Finally, to the extent that men are engaged in the humble quest for Christ, they are involved in a process whereby they may "lay hold on every good thing" (Moroni 7:21), which is quite the reverse of courting tragedy through decadence.

Moroni was anxious not only to prevent the seeds of decay from taking root in the individual and society, but also to see that the seeds of faith come to fruition, both in his own life and in the lives of others. Undoubtedly, no dimension of Moroni's experience was more moving and profoundly personal than the process of coming to Christ. Like the brother of Jared, through whose experiences Moroni depicts the glory of an encounter with the Lord, Moroni himself had seen Jesus and been comforted by him. (Ether 12:39.) His concern for faith, hope, and charity was a yearning to help others partake in full measure of that which is "white, to exceed all . . . whiteness" and sweet above all that has ever been tasted. (1 Nephi 8:11; see Mormon 1:15.) "Were it possible," Moroni wrote, "I would make all things known unto you." (Mormon 8:12.) But since that was not possible, Moroni did all in his power to point the way. He pleaded: "When ye shall receive these things, I would exhort you that ye would ask God, the Eternal Father, in the name of Christ, if these things are not true; and if ye shall ask with a sincere heart, with real intent, having faith in Christ, he will manifest the truth of it unto you, by the power of the Holy Ghost. And by the power of the Holy Ghost ye may know the truth of all things." (Moroni 10:4-5.)

We hear this scripture so often in the Church that we generally forget it was written by an individual who had experienced its meaning in ways that few mortals ever do. Not only did Moroni have unique insight into the power of faith; he also understood the significance of hope, both in sustaining faith and charity and in comforting the individual sincerely engaged in the struggle to endure and to attain perfection. Responding to Moroni's fears about weakness in writing, the Lord told him that "because thou hast seen thy weakness thou shalt be made strong, even unto the sitting down in the place which I have prepared in the mansions of my Father." (Ether 12:37.)

Above all, Moroni understood charity—the pure love of Christ. (Moroni 7:47.) He understood it because he had felt it emanating from Christ and within himself. He had felt it radiating toward not only the future generations he addressed, but also toward the very individuals who had destroyed his people. No wonder that he added his father's sermon on charity to his writings. The words are Mormon's, but the concern—as evidenced by its inclusion in Moroni's book—was shared by Moroni:

"Wherefore, my beloved brethren, pray unto the Father with all the energy of heart, that ye may be filled with this love, which he hath bestowed upon all who are true followers of his Son, Jesus Christ; that ye may become the sons of God; that when he shall appear we shall be like him, for we shall see him as he is; that we may have this hope; that we may be purified even as he is pure." (Moroni 7:48.)

Moroni's significance for our time is not limited to the molding influence he exerted on the final fifty pages of the Book of Mormon. He has likely had more contacts with our dispensation than any other ancient prophet.[4] As President Heber J. Grant has noted, the Lord allowed Moroni to meet the Prophet Joseph Smith at Cumorah for four long years, to "instruct him regarding the principles of the gospel, and fit and prepare him to stand at the head of [the] Church, again established upon the earth, the Church of [the] Son, Jesus Christ."[5] Moroni was often in the shadows during the formative years of Joseph's youth. The Prophet's mother recorded, for example, that at the time Joseph first beheld the plates, "the angel showed him, by contrast, the difference between good and evil, and likewise the consequences of both obedience and disobedience to the commandments of God, in such a striking manner, that the impression was always vivid in his memory until the very end of his days."[6]

But however great Moroni's role in preparing Joseph Smith, it is clear that his mission was in accord with his fundamental concerns and experiences while still in mortality. "Having the everlasting gospel to preach unto them that dwell on the earth" (Revelation 14:6), and being filled with its spirit and power, Moroni's central aim to the end was instilling in others the desire to follow the path he had taken:

"And now, I would commend you to seek this Jesus of

whom the prophets and apostles have written, that the grace of God the Father, and also the Lord Jesus Christ, and the Holy Ghost, which beareth record of them, may be and abide in you forever." (Ether 12:41.)

"Yea, come unto Christ, and be perfected in him, and deny yourselves of all ungodliness; and if ye shall . . . love God with all your might, mind and strength, then is his grace sufficient for you, that by his grace ye may be perfect in Christ." (Moroni 10:32.)

Infused into these lines is all the depth of Moroni's earthly experience and all the vibrancy of his soul; they reflect the testimony of one who truly saw Christ, and suggest the promise and the glory awaiting all those who accept his challenge.

W. Cole Durham, Jr. is a professor of law at the J. Reuben Clark Law School, Brigham Young University.

Notes

1. Mormon 8:1; Sidney B. Sperry, *Book of Mormon Compendium* (Salt Lake City: Bookcraft, 1968), pp. 18-24.
2. Orson F. Whitney, *Life of Heber C. Kimball* (Salt Lake City: Bookcraft, 1967), p. 436, as quoted in the *Ensign*, January 1972, p. 33.
3. See Hugh Nibley, *Since Cumorah: The Book of Mormon in the Modern World* (Salt Lake City: Deseret Book Co., 1970), pp. 390-409.
4. For accounts of several such contacts, see Lucy Mack Smith, *History of Joseph Smith* (Salt Lake City: Bookcraft, 1958), pp. 83-85, 99-101; B. H. Roberts, *A Comprehensive History of the Church* 1:112-13, 124-27.
5. Heber J. Grant, Prayer Dedicating Statue of Moroni on the Hill Cumorah, July 21, 1935, quoted in LaPreal Wight, "I Am Brought Forth to Meet You," *Improvement Era* 53:781.
6. Lucy Mack Smith, *History of Joseph Smith*, p. 81.

The Brother of Jared

Henry B. Eyring

Everyone carries painful memories of being scolded by a parent or a teacher for not trying to learn. I can still hear in my mind a German teacher, short enough to look me in the eye as she stood at my desk, saying, "Du bist ein ______," which translated means that she thought I was a donkey for not learning and that some day I would be sorry. Indeed, I am sorry. And I'm sorry for a hundred other times and places I was slow or unable to learn. But more than the regret I feel for choosing not to learn from a German teacher and a piano teacher and so many others, my heart aches for the days—even months and years—when the Master would have taught me how to use faith and repentance and the Holy Ghost and charity, and could not get my attention.

If you share those regrets with me—and surely you have a few—and if you long to be a better learner, you will find both solace and suggestion in the life of the brother of Jared. Bow with him, as the book of Ether describes a rebuke that changed his life and can help change yours: "And it came to pass at the end of four years that the Lord came again unto the brother of Jared, and stood in a cloud and talked with him. And for the space of three hours did the Lord talk with the brother of Jared, and chastened him because he remembered not to call upon the name of the Lord." (Ether 2:14.)

The numbers in that sad account are keys to the brother of Jared's problem and to the Master's solution: four years and three hours. The brother of Jared and his caravan of people and animals had been stopped four years in a journey they knew was to take them over many waters to a promised land. And the Master took not a minute, not five minutes, but *three hours* of His time to rebuke inattention. What do those four years and three hours show us about barriers and gateways to learning?

To me, the importance of the four years stems from the fact that the Jaredites were in a time of inaction during a journey that began with the chaos of the tower of Babel, then swept across the uncharted wastes of Asia and would, following the Lord's rebuke, take them through the depths of hurricane-tossed oceans to a land choice above all others—all under the Lord's direction. President Spencer W. Kimball captured that drama in a general conference talk: "This unparalleled book should intrigue navigators: unprecedented land treks near-unbelievable in length, scope, and hazard are chronicled and ocean crossings, and the circling of the world centuries before the Vikings—crossings fraught with all the dangers imaginable, including storms, hidden reefs, hurricanes, and even mutiny. This first recorded ocean crossing was about forty centuries ago, of seaworthy, ocean-going vessels without known sails, engines, oars, or rudders—eight barges like and near contemporary with Noah's ark, long as a tree, tight as a dish, peaked at the end like a gravy boat (see Ether 2:17), corked at top and bottom, illuminated by molten stones (see Ether 2:20; 3:1 ff.), perhaps with radium or some other substance not yet rediscovered by our scientists. Light and like a [fowl] upon the water, this fleet of barges was driven by winds and ocean currents, landing at a common point in North America probably on the west shores." *(Conference Report,* April 1963, pp. 63-64.)

The leader of this perilous journey was the brother of

Jared (from other sources we know his name is Mahonri Moriancumer [see *Messenger and Advocate* 1:112]). Except for those four years, his recorded life exemplifies the fusing of a capacity for bold action with teachability. That unlikely combination is revealed early in the story, when both his personal power and unresisting relationship with his brother Jared appear as background in the narrative while the Lord confounds the tower builders: "And the brother of Jared being a large and mighty man, and a man highly favored of the Lord, Jared, his brother, said unto him: Cry unto the Lord, that he will not confound us that we may not understand our words. And it came to pass that the brother of Jared did cry unto the Lord, and the Lord had compassion upon Jared; therefore he did not confound the language of Jared; and Jared and his brother were not confounded." (Ether 1:34-35.)

Once Mahonri Moriancumer had obtained that blessing for himself and his brother, he accepted counsel from Jared again to pray that their friends not be confounded, and that blessing, too, was granted. Again he accepted counsel to ask if God would lead them to a promised land, and he got that blessing. In fact, he got more than the blessing; he got the call to leadership: "And it came to pass that the Lord did hear the brother of Jared, and had compassion upon him, and said unto him: Go to and gather together thy flocks, both male and female, of every kind; and also of the seed of the earth of every kind; and thy families; and also Jared thy brother and his family; and also thy friends and their families, and the friends of Jared and their families. And when thou hast done this thou shalt go at the head of them down into the valley which is northward. And there will I meet thee, and I will go before thee into a land which is choice above all the lands of the earth." (Ether 1:40-42.)

The man who could take counsel from his brother, as well as from God, was told the reason for his blessings: "And thus I will do unto thee because this long time ye have cried unto me." (Ether 1:43.) Mighty and large as Moriancumer was, his leadership position came only partly because of his capacity for action; he also relied on the Master, who taught him constantly in the practical details of the journey: "And it came to pass that the Lord commanded them that they should go forth into the wilderness, yea, into that quarter where there never had man been. And it came to pass that the Lord did go before them, and did talk with them as he stood in a cloud, and gave directions whither they should travel. And it came to pass that they did travel in the wilderness, and did build barges, in which they did cross many waters, being directed continually by the hand of the Lord." (Ether 2:5-6.)

How could Moriancumer—a man able to accept his brother's counsel, a man blessed by the Master's personal attention for his mighty prayer, a man strong enough to lead people and flocks of every kind across trackless wastes and seas and finally reach the edge of the great ocean—how could he pitch his tent and, four years later, be chastened for forgetting the Lord?

The very brevity of the description of those four years tells much: "And now I proceed with my record; for behold, it came to pass that the Lord did bring Jared and his brethren forth even to that great sea which divideth the lands. And as they came to the sea they pitched their tents; and they called the name of the place Moriancumer; and they dwelt in tents, and dwelt in tents upon the seashore for the space of four years." (Ether 2:13.)

Can't you almost hear the sighs of relief as the burdens are set down, the flocks are let to feed in the coastal plain, the tents are pitched, and the place is named for the great leader who brought them safely through? The scriptures don't tell us why the people "remembered not to call upon the name of the Lord" (Ether 2:14) during those years, but our own experience may give us a clue. When we face an unknown wilderness or a strange sea, which may for us be a move to a new place or mortal sickness in a loved one, our hearts soften and we beg for blessings and weep when they're given. But when it's harder to see the needs or the blessings—when our tents are pitched—it's easy to forget the Master and think more of the part our own courage and exertions may have contributed. Sometimes those around us make that forgetfulness more likely by praising us and attributing the victory to us. Most of us spend a good part of our lives in perils so nearly invisible that self-reliance comes easily, and accepting counsel from brothers, or from God, comes hard.

No rebuke could have a happier ending than this one did for Moriancumer; nor can we hope for a much more helpful example. He repented.

"And the brother of Jared repented of the evil which he had done, and did call upon the name of the Lord for his brethren who were with him. And the Lord said unto him: I will forgive thee and thy brethren of their sins; but thou shalt not sin any more, for ye shall remember that my Spirit will not always strive with man; wherefore, if ye will sin until ye are fully ripe ye shall be cut off from the presence of the Lord." (Ether 2:15.)

Repentance brought back teachability: Moriancumer again followed the directions he had received previously for building barges and also solved the problem of lack of air in the ships as directed by the Lord in detail. He then presented the problem of light to the Master. The way the Lord answered that question illuminates another aspect of teachability: a willingness on the part of the student to do his homework.

The Lord knew uncounted ways to light the ships, but he took time to define the problem and then offered help only after Moriancumer had designed the solution. The brother of Jared did all he could to bring it into being and defined precisely what remained for the Master to do: "And the Lord said unto the brother of Jared: What will ye that I should do that ye may have light in your vessels? For behold, ye cannot have windows, for they will be dashed in pieces; neither shall ye take fire with you, for ye shall not go by the light of fire. For behold, ye shall be as a whale in the midst of the sea; for the mountain waves shall dash upon you. Nevertheless, I will bring you up again out of the depths of the sea; for the winds have gone forth out of my mouth, and also the rains and the floods have I sent forth. And behold, I prepare you against these things; for ye cannot cross this great deep save I prepare you against the waves of the sea, and the winds which have gone forth, and the floods which shall come. Therefore what will ye that I should prepare for you that ye may have light when ye are swallowed up in the depths of the sea?" (Ether 2:23-25.)

The brother of Jared heated rock to make sixteen transparent stones, and then on Mount Shelem he asked the Lord for the part of the solution he could not provide: to make the stones emit light. But he didn't simply ask as a child might ask a hurried parent or a student might ask a teacher flitting from pupil to pupil. He took time to plead for forgiveness. He acknowledged blessings. He proclaimed faith in God's power.

The Lord honored the brother of Jared's solution by touching the stones, and as he did so, the veil was removed from Moriancumer's eyes and he saw the Lord's finger. Astonished, he asked the Lord to show himself unto him. The Lord not only granted that request but also showed him a vision of the full panorama of the world's history. So marvelous were the things shown to the brother of Jared that the record of it is hidden from us until we are prepared to receive it. Joseph Fielding Smith, in a conference address, told us how to qualify as a people for that blessing: "Now the Lord has placed us on probation as members of the Church. He has given us the Book of Mormon, which is the lesser part, to building up our faith through our obedience to the counsels which it contains, and when we ourselves, members of the Church, are willing to keep the commandments as they have been given to us and show our faith as the Nephites did for a short period of time, then the Lord is ready to bring forth the other record and give it to us, but we are not ready now to receive it. Why? Because we have not lived up to the requirements in this probationary state in the reading of the record which had been given to us and in following its counsels." (*Conference Report,* October 1961, p. 20.)

That sober assessment seems to say that we need to be learners like Moriancumer after his repentance. Our negligence or lack of diligence in studying and keeping the commandments may be akin to the laxness of the Jaredites during the four years.

If we will open ourselves to learning as the brother of Jared did, we can some day share the record of his spiritual blessings. The story seems to suggest that the main barrier to such blessings is our inability to feel the danger we are in if we do not receive spiritual counsel—if we forget to call on the Lord. The story also aptly illustrates the main gateway to these blessings, which is faith. Clearly shown in the time and care that the Master lavished on rebuking and teaching Moriancumer is the lesson that mighty prayer is heard and answered.

President Brigham Young directs our attention away from the sensational visions in the book of Ether and toward the lessons that must come first: "But if you had faith to go out to the graveyard and raise up scores of the dead, that alone would not make you Latter-day Saints, neither if the visions of your minds were opened so as to see the finger of God. What will? Keeping the commandments of the Lord, to walk humbly before your God, and before one another, to cease to do evil and learn to do well, and to live by every word that proceeds from the mouth of God; then you are a Latter-day Saint, whether you have visions or not." (*Journal of Discourses* 3:211.)

This statement seems to suggest that, since few of us will have spectacular manifestations as the brother of Jared did, we might well add to that frequent picture of Moriancumer that pops into our minds (the blinding light from the stones on a mountaintop) the quiet scene of four years by a lovely seaside and the image of a three-hour interview. The tents by the sea could remind us that our dependence and gratitude must be unending, not just when we are in the "trackless wastes" or buried in some raging spiritual ocean. And a three-hour interview, longer than we may ever give our child or brother or husband or wife, could remind us of the availability, the patience, and the love of our Teacher. And with that sense of need and with that faith in God's availability, we will have learned a crucial lesson from the brother of Jared, a master learner.

He remained teachable throughout his life, as shown by his last act: he accepted the counsel of his brother to give the people a king, despite his conviction that it would lead to captivity. Humble trust in a brother's judgment also marked the last decisions of the Prophet Joseph Smith, who said to Hyrum, as they weighed the choice to cross the river to Nauvoo, to Carthage, and to martyrdom: "Brother Hyrum, you are the oldest, what shall we do?" *(History of the Church* 6:549.) Despite personal power and visions of the future from heaven, both Joseph and Moriancumer still sought trusted counsel. Apparently we can never know so much of heaven that we can't learn from each other.

Henry B. Eyring is commissioner of education for the Church Educational System.

Our Book of Mormon Sisters

Marjorie Meads Spencer

A long-standing curiosity about women in the scriptures has recently prompted me to study the standard works. I have hungered to learn more about my ancient female counterparts—what they were like, how they coped with their pressures, how they nurtured their spirituality.

Admittedly, there have been times, during my sporadic adventures into the standard works, when I have been disappointed in my search for scriptural women. Women characters seemed to be so few and far between among the overwhelming numbers of men that it was easy to conclude that women had been slighted.

But a year ago, in conjunction with a religion class, I began a project that challenged my former impressions. As I worked my way from cover to cover in the Book of Mormon, I undertook a thorough and exacting examination of all verses that explicitly referred to women. As my list grew longer than I had ever expected, I was nicely surprised—perhaps thrilled—to discover so much that was not noticed in my previous casual reading. I found that the Book of Mormon has more than one hundred fifty passages of explicit references to women, offering an exciting bundle of information about our foresisters in the gospel.

Outwardly, the Book of Mormon fails to create a strong impression of women. There are reasons for this: individual women in the record are few, rarely spotlighted, and usually anonymous; women in groups often become obscure; the concise index in the current edition includes few entries dealing with women, and so on. In recent conversations with Latter-day Saint friends, I have asked how many women characters they can remember from the book. My friends have been hard pressed to list as many as half a dozen. Lehi's wife, Ishmael's family, and the mothers of the two thousand young warriors were the most familiar; other women were more elusive to the memory.

While the number of women is in no way a comparison to the number of men mentioned in the Book of Mormon, there are actually twelve or so individual women who are noted. Only six (Eve, Sariah, Mary, Sarah, Abish, and Isabel) are identified by their names, which may be part of the reason why the women are not remembered easily. Nevertheless, there *are* a dozen women presented in enough depth to reveal interesting personalities and provide role models for individual study.

Individual Women

Three Book of Mormon women are familiar to us from the Bible. Eve is named in the brass plates account of our first parents (see 1 Nephi 5:10-11) and again when Lehi instructed Jacob about partaking of the forbidden fruit, banishment from Eden, and the beginning of the "family of all the earth" (see 2 Nephi 2:18-25). This information was probably extracted from a more complete account of Adam and Eve on the brass plates. The very fact that this story was recorded in both the brass plates and the Book of Mormon underscores the importance of Eve's role in the inception of humanity.

Consistent with the Book of Mormon's stated purpose, that of serving as another witness of Christ (see title page), new testimonies regarding Mary, the mother of Christ, are included. (Mosiah 3:8, Alma 7:10.) Nephi beheld the mother of the Son of God, "most beautiful and fair above all other virgins," cradling the Lamb of God in her arms. (See 1 Nephi 11:14-21.) The Lamanite king Lamoni also bore testimony that his Redeemer was to be "born of a woman." (Alma 19:13.)

Sarah, wife of Abraham, is mentioned only in passing as "she that bare you." (2 Nephi 8:2.)

Two women were wives of prophets. Both were closely tied to Nephi, yet one is a comparatively major Book of Mormon character while the other remains anonymous. The first, Sariah, was the helpmate of the visionary Lehi and mother of the eight or so sons and daughters who were the roots of the extensive Nephite and Lamanite civilizations. But more meaningful to me than her role as a progenitress is the model she presents of a woman growing in testimony of the Lord's purposes through a worrisome trial that strengthened her faith. (See 1 Nephi 5:1-9.) Not uncomplaining (how human!) and grieving for unreturned sons, Sariah was comforted by Lehi's language expressing his faith. After her family was reunited, she testified of her newfound surety that the Lord had told Lehi to flee into the wilderness, had protected her sons, and had given them power to accomplish his commands.

The unnamed wife of the great leader Nephi comes across with a less clear profile. However, she does present a good example of a distraught woman turning to prayer when her husband's life was endangered. "With her tears and prayers" and in spite of threatenings, she tried to persuade the rebellious brethren to release her bound husband. (See 1 Nephi 18:19.) Perhaps she was the same daughter of Ishmael who, with her mother, pleaded for Nephi's life on an earlier occasion. (See 1 Nephi 7:19.)

Another Nephite woman who appears briefly was one of the maidservants of Morianton, "a man of much passion." (Alma 50:30.) She became the victim of beating at the hands of her angered master. In response to this abuse, she fled to Moroni's camp with information that thwarted the intended plans of Morianton's people to occupy the land northward. (See Alma 50:31-36.)

The first of the Lamanite women discussed is Isabel, who led away the hearts of many—including Alma's youngest son Corianton—through her wicked harlotry. He abandoned his missionary work for conduct with Isabel that caused his father's and others' continuing missionary efforts among the Zoramites to suffer lost credibility. (See Alma 39:3-4, 11.) In this example, readers learn from a negative representation of womanhood. The lesson is powerful because it notes the consequences of immorality to innocent others and also the degree of seriousness to its participants. In God's eyes, Isabel's harlotry in Siron was an abomination, "yea, most abominable above all sins save it be the shedding of innocent blood or denying the Holy Ghost." (Alma 39:5.)

The first of three Lamanite queens, the vigil-keeping wife of King Lamoni, and Abish, who was her servant, illustrate for us excellent ideals of faith. By summoning Ammon and then believing his words that her husband would rise on the morrow, Lamoni's wife demonstrated greater faith than that among all the people of the Nephites, according to the lofty compliment paid her. (See Alma 19:1-13.) Later, Abish, who had been a convert in secret for many years because of a "remarkable vision of her father," ran to gather a crowd of Lamanites to witness their royal court prostrated by the power of God. Having maintained her faith over a long period, she saw this as a missionary opportunity, a chance to show her people the power of God. (See Alma 19:16-18.) Sorrowed at the crowd's contention, she tearfully took her mistress, the queen, by the hand to raise her from the ground. The queen, as she arose, uttered a joyful testimony of Jesus Christ and in turn raised her husband. (See Alma 19:28-30.)

In contrast to this queen's response to her husband's "sleep," another queen, the wife of Lamoni's father, angrily commanded that Aaron and his missionaries be slain when her husband was overcome. In spite of her anger and determination, she and the entire household were later converted as a result of the restored king's ministrations. (See Alma 22:19-23.)

The third Lamanite queen was widowed when her husband was stabbed at the order of Amalickiah, a conspiring Nephite who wished to be king over the Lamanites. She initiated an investigation of the murder but was appeased by Amalickiah's lying witnesses. Amalickiah later "sought the favor of the queen, and took her unto him to wife," thereby fraudulently becoming the Lamanite king. (See Alma 47:32-35.) She was again widowed when the sleeping Amalickiah was slain by Teancum. (Alma 51:34.)

Finally, the sole Jaredite woman we learn of is the wicked daughter of the wicked Jared. Wily and "exceedingly expert," she devised a sinful plan to help her father regain his lost throne. It included her dancing to entice Akish to behead her reigning grandfather in exchange for marriage to her. (See Ether 8:3-12.) Credit goes to her for planting the desire in Jared's heart to search for the secret plans of old for obtaining glory, kingdoms, and power. (Ether 8:16-17.) Her suggestion led to Akish's establishment of a secret combination like those of old, "most abominable and wicked above all, in the sight of God." (Ether 8:18.) She reaped her reward later, however, when Akish in turn had her father murdered and jealously starved their young son in prison. (See Ether 9:4-7.)

Groups of Women

With only a dozen individual women to study, references to women in general are the next basic source of additional insights. These references usually concern women in various groupings—familial, small, or general in nature—with varying degrees of specific involvement in important Book of Mormon occurrences. For example, Nephi had sisters (see 2 Nephi 5:6) who are mentioned only once compared to the more substantially presented brothers. This is in contrast to the daughters of Ishmael, about whom there is a lot of information—how they went into the wilderness and became wives for Lehi's sons and Zoram, suffered and were blessed with childbearing, mourned at their father's death, followed righteousness or shared the Lamanite mark. Another small group of women was the twenty-four Lamanite daughters who were kidnapped by the wicked priests of King Noah and later became their wives. (See Mosiah 20:1-5; 23:33-34.)

In much larger groups, the northward migration from Zarahemla of fifty-four hundred men included their wives and children; and Hagoth's vessels also sailed forth with women and children abroad. (See Alma 63:4-7.) In an endearing passage from Third Nephi, it is told that Jesus blessed the little children and that the multitude who heard and bore record of angels ministering to the children included women. (See 3 Nephi 17:21-25.) Although these common terms *wives* and *women and children* can be easily skimmed past, the underlying information that women took part helps create a more complete understanding of the whole scene.

Most often women are referred to in terms of their relationships to other people, by the use of words such as wife, mother, widow, daughter, queen, or servant. It appears that the use of these terms instead of names reflects the cultural norms rather than any attempt on the writers' part to lessen the worth of women. For example, the Ammonite mothers of Helaman's two thousand young warriors do not seem to lack importance because they are labeled "mothers" and "daughters." They instilled incredible obedience and faith in their sons. "Yea, they had been taught by their mothers, that if they did not doubt, God would deliver them." The young warriors rehearsed their mothers' words and added, "We do not doubt our mothers knew it." (Alma 56:47-48.) What an unusual illustration of success for modern Latter-day Saint mothers to emulate! At the other extreme, a failure model that Mormon daughters of all ages should choose to avoid may be found in several verses. Third Nephi 8:25 and 9:2, Mormon 6:19, and Ether 13:17 all deal with the anguishing and lamenting for destroyed daughters that could have been avoided by repentance.

Descriptions

Beyond the ways in which Book of Mormon women are grouped or identified, I was curious about the adjectives used to describe their personalities. Fairness, beauty, strength, and tenderness are some of the traits specifically noted.

"Fairness" is a frequently used term, yet perhaps our modern language fails to give it the complete meaning it had then. Beyond the distinction of whiteness of skin, the word *fairness* perhaps indicated a quality of character or beauty. The virgin of Nazareth was described as "exceedingly fair and white." (1 Nephi 11:13.) Mormon mourned over the nonrepentant "fair ones" that had fallen. (See, for example, Mormon 6:17-22.) The "fair sons and daughters" of the Jaredites also did not repent. (See Ether 13:17.) Jared's cunning daughter is described as "exceedingly fair." (Ether 8:9.) The "fair daughters" of the Nephites were sent to plead with the enemy, and Nephite lives were spared because of these Nephite women. (See Mosiah 19:13-15.)

As part of Lehi's group struggling in the wilderness, the women were "strong, yea, even like unto the men; and they began to bear their journeyings without murmurings." (1 Nephi 17:2.) In a different vein, however, the Lord of Hosts referred to the "tenderness" of the daughters of his people. (Jacob 2:33.) Two verses later, there is another reference to "tender" wives whose hearts had been broken and "died, pierced with deep wounds" from their husbands' iniquities.

Women are described not only through adjectives but also through their many actions and behaviors. They plead, mourn, suffer, praise, show faith, pray, complain, bear children, fear, cry, convert, summon, make merry, are comforted, murmur, sin, run, are overcome, love, mother, hide, flee, are slain, believe, have broken hearts, toil, spin cloth, sing, dance, charm, are rude, escape, fight, are captured, and so forth.

It would be difficult to create a "composite" Nephite, Lamanite, or Jaredite woman from these ideas, but these bits of information help to develop our mental pictures of them.

Occasionally, representations of women supply analogies in which the feminine imagery is not especially flattering, but useful. With considerable emphasis between 1 Nephi 13 and 14, for example, the great and abominable church is repeatedly likened unto a harlot and is dubbed the "whore of all the earth." (1 Nephi 14:10.) And in the latter part of 2 Nephi 13, Isaiah uses vivid description of erring women rulers and haughty daughters of Zion in outlandish extremes of dress who "shall be desolate." (2 Nephi 13:26.)

Tribulations

Affliction and suffering seem to have come in mighty doses to Book of Mormon women throughout the text in both the religious and the more secular parts of the record.

Ishmael's daughters mourned because of afflictions of "hunger, thirst, and fatigue." (1 Nephi 16:35.) Their husbands stated emphatically: "It would have been better that they had died before they came out of Jerusalem than to have suffered these afflictions," for they had suffered "all things, save it were death." (1 Nephi 17:20.) Alma and Amulek witnessed women and children being painfully consumed by fire because of their beliefs and what they had been taught. (See Alma 14:8-11.) And Mormon, in his final epistle to Moroni, told of the depravity of the people: "The suffering of our women and our children upon all the face of this land doth exceed everything; yea, tongue cannot tell, neither can it be written." (Moroni 9:19.)

In addition to physical suffering, there was much mourning because of the great losses of loved ones. Many times hundreds became widowed or fatherless and terrible mourning cries were heard for lost kindred, even to the point of howling. (See Ether 15:17; also Alma 28:5.) Most of this grief was due to the almost commonplace battling among these societies.

In cultural conditions shadowed by numerous battles

and wars, the need for women and children to be protected must have been a wearing constant. Nor could women always take a passive role in battle. On occasion, the situation appeared so desperate that persons of both sexes and of all ages were expected to take up weapons. In one instance, Moroni had threatened Ammoron that if certain conditions of prisoner exchange (one Nephite family for one Lamanite warrior) were not met, Moroni would come against him: "Yea, even I will arm my women and my children, and I will come against you." (Alma 54:12.) Later, Moroni's men smuggled arms in to his people held prisoner in the city of Gid. Although the drunken Lamanite captors were outwitted without actual fighting, weapons had been given to all the Nephite prisoners, "yea, even to their women, and all those of their children, as many as were able to use a weapon of war." (Alma 55:17.)

In the final Jaredite battle, women and children actually did fight along with the men to the literal end of their civilization. Four years were spent gathering all the people together, that they might have "all the strength which it was possible that they could receive." Sides chosen, a lamentable scene unfolded: "Both men, women and children being armed with weapons of war, having shields, and breastplates, and head-plates, and being clothed after the manner of war—they did march forth one against another to battle." (Ether 15:14-15.) Women were not immune to death by the sword, unfortunately, and slaughter claimed untold numbers of female lives. Even before this great and final battle, Coriantumr sorrowed that "two millions of mighty men, and also their wives and their children," had been slain (Ether 15:2), to the extent that the bodies of men, women, and children covered the face of the land (see Ether 14:21-22.)

Also unfortunate were the women who "survived" battles to be taken as prisoners of war. Imprisoned women sometimes experienced gruesome fates up to and including death. The Lamanite daughters captured by the people of Moriantum were deprived of "that which was most dear and precious above all things, which is chastity and virtue," and were then murdered by torture and their flesh eaten by the Nephites as proof of bravery. (Moroni 9:9-10.) On the other hand, Nephite women and children captured from the tower at Sherrizah were made to eat the flesh of their slain husbands and fathers. (Moroni 9:8.) The distressing reports of all the atrocities suffered in the Book of Mormon because of fighting seem to indicate that much of the high price of war was dearly paid by women.

Doctrines

Leaving the heinous deeds of war behind, I have been particularly gladdened in my research by several specific scriptures presenting doctrinal principles. In these instances, the inspired writers were careful to address their messages to women as well as others. This approach seems to lend the ideas more impact than if they had been trusted to the assumption that a general presentation reaches all.

The process of being born of Christ and becoming his spiritually begotten children, correctly "his sons and his *daughters,*" is presented more than one time in this manner. The hearts of King Benjamin's people were changed, for example, when they made a covenant with God that earned them the right to become "children of Christ, his sons, and his daughters." (Mosiah 5:7.) Also, the reformed younger Alma reported that the Lord told him that "all mankind, yea, men and women . . . must be born again" to be "redeemed of God, becoming his sons and daughters." (Mosiah 27:25.) And when he appeared to the brother of Jared, the Savior stated that those who believe on his name shall become "my sons and my daughters." (Ether 3:14.)

In a similar vein, Nephi gave an invitation to both sexes to "come unto [the Lord] and partake of his goodness; and he denieth none that come unto him, . . . male *and* female," for "all are alike unto God." (2 Nephi 26:33; italics added.) This equality with respect to blessings also holds true with respect to condemnation. According to Jacob, those who fight "against Zion, . . . both male *and* female, shall perish," for those of either sex who are against God are labeled "the whore of all the earth." (2 Nephi 10:16; italics added.)

Additional gospel teachings are presented in this male-and-female frame of reference. For example, the promise of restoration from temporal death as Amulek explained it to Zeezrom "shall come to all, . . . both male *and* female." (Alma 11:44; italics added.) Both will be restored to their perfect frames to be arraigned and judged at the bar of Christ according to their works. Another instance is the instruction that the receiving of heavenly messages is not limited to men. As Alma preached to the poor class of Zoramites, he told them that God "imparteth his word by angels unto men, yea, not only men but *women also.*" (Alma 32:23; italics added.) Finally, on a rare occasion when Nephi's brothers wished to worship him, Nephi told them that they should worship the Lord and "honor thy father *and* thy mother" (1 Nephi 17:55; italics added), making the same distinction as the third of the Ten Commandments, that honor is due *each* parent.

Elsewhere there are other fundamental gospel principles—charity and chastity—that reflect evident concern for women. For example, an admirable standard of charity was set by the church in the second year of Alma's reign: "They did not send away any . . . ; therefore they were liberal to all, . . . both male and female, whether out of the church or in the church, having no respect to persons as to those who stood in need." (Alma 1:30.) In an earlier era when the women of King Limhi's people outnumbered the men because many were slain, Limhi "commanded that every man should impart to the support of the widows and their children, that they might not perish with hunger." (Mosiah 21:17.) Christ also, in repeating the words of Malachi to the Nephites, said, "I will be a swift witness against . . . those that oppress . . . the widow and the fatherless." (3 Nephi 24:5.)

In final summary, I have come a long way from my earlier impressions that women were next to nonexistent in the Book of Mormon. I think I was originally motivated to study that premise by a disturbing feeling that the apparent dearth of women implied they were insignificant or unimportant. I am glad I was bothered enough to look closer. By watching closely and carefully for the passages that explicitly noted women, I truly surprised myself in uncovering far more about womanhood than I had anticipated. This experience has altered my former thinking: women are not so absent as I once believed!

Still, questions remain for me: Why aren't the records more complete when it comes to the lives of our foresisters in the gospel? Why does so much between-the-lines reading still seem to be necessary to fill in the gaps? In spite of these questions, as I look over the bulk of my newly discovered evidence of women in the Book of Mormon and consider the enlightenment that has come from pondering why women appear as they do (or don't), I feel there is a great deal that can be useful to us in positive ways. Examples of our ancient Book of Mormon sisters *are* there; and if we use what we have and become personally acquainted with them, this can aid us all—male and female—in our growth in the gospel.

Marjorie Meads Spencer, an Ogden, Utah, homemaker, has been on the staffs of *Exponent II, Sunstone,* and *Dialogue.*

Index